Library of
Davidson College

AMERICAN LEGAL AND CONSTITUTIONAL HISTORY ★ A Garland Series of Outstanding Dissertations

Edited by
HAROLD HYMAN
William P. Hobby Professor of History,
Rice University

STUART BRUCHEY
Allan Nevins Professor of American
Economic History, Columbia University

THE AMERICAN LEGAL PROFESSION AND THE ORGANIZATIONAL SOCIETY 1890–1930

Wayne K. Hobson

Garland Publishing, Inc.
New York & London ★ 1986

Copyright © 1986 Wayne K. Hobson

All rights reserved

Library of Congress Cataloging-in-Publication Data

Hobson, Wayne K.
  The American legal profession and the organizational society, 1890–1930.

  (American legal and constitutional history)
(A Garland series of outstanding dissertations)
  Bibliography: p.
  1. Lawyers—United States—History. 2. Bar associations—United States—History. I. Title.
II. Series. III. Series: Garland series of outstanding dissertations.
KF298.H58 1986   340'.06'073   86-22941
ISBN 0-8240-8270-2

All volumes in this series are printed on acid-free, 250-year-life paper.

Printed in the United States of America

THE AMERICAN LEGAL PROFESSION AND THE
ORGANIZATIONAL SOCIETY, 1890-1930

Wayne K. Hobson
California State University, Fullerton

PREFACE

The legal profession, like much of the rest of American society, was transformed between 1890 and 1930. This study examines the shifting professional ideology of the American bar elite as it reacted to and shaped the new professional environment. It focuses on the leadership of three institutions central in the bar's transformation: the large law firm, the law school, and the bar association. It also evaluates the adequacy of the "organizational synthesis," the reigning paradigm in studies of turn-of-the-century professionalization movements. The legal profession fits that paradigm less well than do such professions as medicine or engineering. Most professions experienced heightened power and influence in these years. Many leading lawyers, however, believed that the political programs and ideological currents of the progressive era, including the ideology of professional modernization, directly challenged their historic cultural and political influence. Therefore, professional modernizers in the legal profession, especially bar association activists and many leading law professors, had to contend with those who were suspicious of the ideology of professional modernization.

In the years since 1977, when this Garland edition was originally written, legal historians have greatly added to our understanding of both legal history proper and the history of the legal profession. In addition, there have been a number of excellent and pathbreaking studies on the history of other professions, especially medicine and higher education. However, there is as yet no new synthesis reinterpreting the history of the legal profession. I believe the data and analysis provided in this book remain a reliable guide to understanding the professional ideology and self-image of leading lawyers in the crucial turn-of-the century years.

Were I to completely revise this text, I would shift my focus to reflect the contributions of this new research. I would now interpret the bar elite's professional ideology as a response to a crisis of cultural authority the bar faced in these years rather than as a response to structural changes in the profession. Both contexts are important, and both are considered in the book as written, but I now think the cultural context needs more emphasis than the structural context. The legal profession suffered a crisis of cultural authority because law was not able to benefit from the professions' general rise to cultural authority in the late 19th and early 20th centuries. Leading lawyers certainly experienced great power and social authority in these years, but the cultural authority of the profession suffered (to use Paul Starr's useful distinction between social and cultural authority).

This crisis of authority stimulated major divisions among leading lawyers. I now see a competition among at least five major groups of leading lawyers to define or redefine the bar's professional ideology in the 1890-1930 period: (1) advocates of a liberal culture professional ideal; (2) conservative constitutionalists; (3) professional modernizers; (4) liberal modernizers; (5) pragmatic modernizers. As the perspective of each of these groups was shaped, debated, accepted, rejected, or modified, a new ideology of legalism was in the making, which, by the 1930s, would help the profession regain a significant measure of cultural authority, but on an altered basis.

I have not yet completed my analysis of these divisions within the bar elite. I have published a revised version of this book's chapter five in a book of essays on the history of the legal profession edited by Gerard W. Gawalt, The New High Priests: Lawyers in Post Civil War America. (Westport: Greenwood Press, 1984). That revision does not alter the basic argument of chapter five, but does incorporate new research and provides data on large firm growth at five year intervals rather than the ten year intervals presented here.

I want to thank my dissertation adviser, Barton J. Bernstein of Stanford University, for helping me formulate the original topic, for retaining faith in it and me, and for providing shrewd and sound strategic and tactical advice on a wide range of matters throughout the period of research and writing. His colleague David Tyack provided great encouragement and very helpful advice on conceptualization and writing style. Stanford University's Weter Fellowship funded my first year of research, and a Faculty Research Grant from the California State University, Fullerton, Foundation provided travel funds at a crucial stage.

Finally, it is a pleasure to acknowledge the contributions provided by my wife, Nancy Hobson. She not only believed in the value of my work throughout, but also lent her editorial skill to improve my sometimes crude efforts when taking pen to paper. If any infelicities remain, I am sure it is because I have indulged a stubborn streak and occasionally failed to take her advice.

Laguna Beach, California
October 1986

TABLE OF CONTENTS

PREFACE iv

LIST OF TABLES ix

PART I THE MODERN LEGAL PROFESSION: AN INTERPRETATION

Chapter
1. SOCIAL CHANGE AND THE ORGANIZATIONAL SOCIETY 2

2. SOCIAL CHANGE AND THE LEGAL PROFESSION 25

PART II MODERNIZATION AND THE LEGAL COMMUNITY: AN OVERVIEW OF STRUCTURAL CHANGES

3. OLD PROFESSIONS MODERNIZE: LAW, ENGINEERING, MEDICINE 76

4. CHANGES IN LEGAL TRAINING: FROM THE LAW OFFICE TO THE LAW SCHOOL 104

5. RISE OF LARGE LAW FIRMS 141

PART III IDEOLOGY AND ORGANIZATIONAL STRUCTURE OF PROFESSIONALISM

6. THE BAR ASSOCIATION MOVEMENT, 1870-1900 210

7. THE BAR ASSOCIATION MOVEMENT, 1900-1920 262

8. "A BAR WITHIN THE BAR:" THE LAW PROFESSORS' IDEOLOGY, 1870-1900 314

9	"A BAR WITHIN THE BAR:" THE LAW PROFESSORS' IDEOLOGY, 1900-1920	359
10	SURVEYS, SYSTEMATIZATION, AND CONSERVATIVE REFORM, 1920-1930	402

BIBLIOGRAPHY 443

LIST OF TABLES

1. Law Schools and Law Students 108
2. Law Schools by Categories 109
3. Proportion of Lawyers and Other Professionals to Total Population 112
4. Percentage of Those in Professional Service Who Were Lawyers 112
5. Growth Rate of Professions 113
6. Number of Future Major Firms of At Least Large Firm Size, by Year, for Top Ten Cities 165
7. Number of Major Firms, by Year, for Top Ten Cities 166
8. Total Number of Large Firms, by Year, for Top Ten Cities 168
9. Total Number of New Large Firms, by Year, for Top Ten Cities 169
10. Development of Large Firms Outside Top Ten Cities 171

PART I

THE MODERN LEGAL PROFESSION:

AN INTERPRETATION

CHAPTER 1

SOCIAL CHANGE AND THE ORGANIZATIONAL SOCIETY

Historians have long recognized the period between 1890 and 1920 as one of transition, as the beginning of our own time, the modern era. The exact nature of the transition has been the subject of considerable disagreement. Until recently, and to a certain extent still, the focus of attention has been on the emergence of the positive state liberal tradition, which was thought to be the most distinctive feature of the period. Hence, the years 1900-1920 have been denominated the "progressive era," and a seemingly endless search for the essence of the era and for the archetypal progressive has dominated historical writing about the period.

Recently, with the revival of social history and a growing skepticism about the liberal tradition, a new conception of the transition period has emerged. As yet, this new conception is understood only in general terms and it has not completely dissociated itself from the study of progressivism, as perhaps it could not. One historian has named the new conception the "organizational synthesis," noting thereby the main theme, which is the emergence of an "organizational society."[1] According to this conception, the period between the 1890s and 1920s was the time when American society shifted from a predominantly localistic, individualistic, moralistic, or community orientation to a more universalistic or bureaucratic orientation. The period was characterized by a "search for order," a search whose direction was regulated primarily by the dynamic introduced into American society by industrialization. Island communities were broken up. New social environments, such as large cities, and new linking institutions, such as large corporations, professional associations, and trade unions, were created. The dominant American ideology and social forms changed from emphasizing laissez faire and individualism to emphasizing bureaucratic structures and groups. Specialization of function came to characterize public roles.

The leading sector in these changes was the new middle class, composed of professionals, elite businessmen, agriculturalists, and labor leaders. Systematization and rationalization were at the heart of their occupations. They came to identify with their occupational

---

[1] Louis Galambos, "The Emerging Organizational Synthesis in Modern American History," Business History Review 44 (Autumn 1970), 279-290.

role rather than with status, ethnic, political party, or other non-occupational affiliations, and they behaved accordingly. That is, they acted as the agents of new scientific knowledge and technology. They sought to institutionalize that knowledge and technology by creating more universalistic and bureaucratic organizations and forms of social, political, and economic life.[2]

As one of the leading proponents of this new conception emphasizes,

> This view of social change between the late 1890s and the Depression of 1929 differs from traditional accounts. While older views focus on the differences between private and public impulses, this stresses the similarities between them; while older views stress the difference between profit-making and non-profit-making

---

[2] Robert Wiebe and Samuel P. Hays have produced the most influential work constructing the organizational synthesis. See Wiebe, *The Search for Order 1877-1920* (New York, 1967), 111-223; Hays, "The Politics of Reform in Municipal Government in the Progressive Era." *Pacific Northwest Quarterly* 55 (October 1964), 157-169; Hays, "Political Parties and the Community-Society Continuum," in Walter D. Burnham and William N. Chambers, *The American Party Systems* (New York, 1967), pp. 152-181; Hays, "The Social Analysis of American Political History, 1880-1920," *Political Science Quarterly* 80 (September 1965), 373-394; Hays, "The 'Shame of the Cities' Revisited: The Case of Pittsburgh," in Herbert Shapiro, ed., *The Muckrakers and American Society* (Boston, 1968), pp. 75-81; Hays, "A Systematic Social History," in George A. Billias and Gerald N. Grob, *American History; Retrospect and Prospect* (New York, 1971), pp. 315-366; Hays, "Introduction--The New Organizational Society," in Jerry Israel, ed., *Building the Organizational Society, Essays on Associational Activities in Modern America* (New York, 1972), pp. 1-16.

activities, this emphasizes their similarities.
New forms of social organization were all-pervasive,
affecting business and government and profit-making
enterprise and non-profit-making service institutions in medicine, education, and welfare. More
important, while older views are based upon the
orderly arrangement of evidence about ideologies
into opposing categories and forms of political
conflict, the view presented here is concerned
with evidence about people in context, their
environment, their relationships with others, their
perceptions of their world, their values.[3]

That is, traditional accounts have over-emphasized ideological and partisan political conflicts and divisions. The task of the organizational synthesis is to point out the major dimensions of social structural change, which have been neglected in traditional accounts, and to show how such structural change has shaped cultural change.

An interpretation of the transition period which has many affinities with the organizational synthesis is the "corporate liberal interpretation" constructed by New Left historians.[4] Like the organizational

---

[3]Hays, "The New Organizational Society," p. 13.

[4]Gabriel Kolko, The Triumph of Conservatism (New York, 1963); James Weinstein, The Corporate Ideal in the Liberal State: 1900-1918 (Boston, 1968) are two variants of the standard corporate liberal interpretation. One of the few attempts to deal explicitly with professionals in terms of this interpretation is David W. Eakins, "The Origins of Corporate Liberal Policy Research, 1916-1922: The Political-Economic Expert and the Decline of Public Debate," in Israel, ed., Building the Organizational Society, pp. 163-180.

synthesis, the corporate liberal interpretation argues that the essential thrust of twentieth-century liberalism has been to construct and legitimize an elitist bureaucratic society and polity. But in contrast to the organizational synthesis, the corporate liberal interpretation relies on explicit concepts of power and ideology. It argues that an amalgam of leading businessmen, professionals, and trade unionists came to think of the social order in terms of "a kind of syndicalism based on organizing, balancing, and co-ordinating different functional groups."[5] This syndicalism, or corporate liberalism, served the needs of industrial capitalism; it did so by creating bureaucratic structures which rationalized social and economic relations, thereby eliminating ruinous competition, and by creating an illusion of the progressive amelioration of social ills, which co-opted radical dissent. According to this interpretation, the main actors knew what they were doing and fully intended the results, although they might have used different terms to describe their intentions and behavior.

---

[5]William Appleman Williams, The Contours of American History (Cleveland, 1961), p. 358.

A wide variety of historians are coming to agree that the <u>effect</u> of bureaucratic and other liberal reforms may have been as the corporate liberal interpretation asserts.[6] However, the evidence that the reformers were class-conscious in their <u>intentions</u>, at least during the transition period, is more dubious, at least in the sweeping sense that those presenting the corporate liberal interpretation usually argue. In addition to the problem of interpreting liberal intentions, there is the problem of accommodating the rhetoric and behavior of powerful conservatives, like leading lawyers and many leading businessmen, to the corporate liberal thesis.

It is not clear that those writing from the perspective of the corporate liberal interpretation have succeeded in going beyond one of the major points established by the organizational synthesis: In structural

---

[6] Stanley P. Caine, <u>The Myth of a Progressive Reform;</u> <u>Railroad Regulation in Wisconsin 1903-1910</u> (Madison, 1970); Elinor M. Gersman, "Progressive Reform of the St. Louis School Board, 1897," <u>History of Education Quarterly</u> 10 (Spring 1970), 3-21; William H. Issel, "Modernization in Philadelphia School Reform, 1882-1905," <u>Pennsylvania Magazine of History and Biography</u> 94 (July 1970), 358-383; Roy Lubove, "Workmen's Compensation and the Prerogatives of Voluntarism," <u>Labor History</u> 8 (Fall 1967), 254-279; Grant McConnell, <u>Private Power and American Democracy</u> (New York, 1966) make this point for a variety of reforms. So, too, do most of the essays in Israel, ed., <u>Building the Organizational Society</u>.

terms, there is a close fit between changes instituted
by progressive reforms and those brought about in the
private sphere by the growth of large corporations.
It is true that by introducing questions about power and
ideology, the corporate liberal interpretation adds
important dimensions missing or not systematically
developed in most versions of the organizational
synthesis. In this respect, the corporate liberal
interpretation contains a compelling critique of one
major tendency within modern liberalism. Liberalism
has enabled capitalist society to modernize social
control in an efficient way, under the guise of
democratic and humanitarian reform. But this generalization does not encompass all liberal intentions or all
effects of liberal measures. Thus, the corporate
liberal interpretation provides a set of questions to ask
about events and historical actors but does not provide
an adequate synthesis.

Unfortunately, evaluations of the organizational
synthesis have tended to focus on Robert Wiebe's statement
that "the heart of progressivism was the ambition of the
new middle class to fulfill its destiny through bureaucratic means."[7] That is, the organizational synthesis
has been evaluated in terms of how well it explains

---

[7] Wiebe, Search, p. 166.

progressivism, either as a political phenomenon or as a sociocultural mood. These evaluations have concluded that technocratic themes were important, and that prior to Wiebe and Hays, they were largely neglected factors in twentieth-century liberalism; but liberalism cannot be reduced to technocratic themes. Historians have reminded themselves of how moralistic, evangelistic, humanitarian, and democratic progressives could be.[8]

> The distinctive feature of the period from 1898 to 1918 is not the preeminence of democratic ideals or of bureaucratic techniques, but rather a fertile amalgamation of the two. An extraordinary quickening of ideology occurred in the very midst of a dazzling elaboration of technical systems. Instead of continuing to retreat as technical systems expanded, the old ideological framework was temporarily revitalized. For a time it seemed that a modernized Americanism and a social gospel could be the moving spirit of a technical society.[9]

---

[8] Otis L. Graham, The Great Campaigns: Reform and War in America, 1900-1928 (Englewood Cliffs, 1971), pp. 135-159; David P. Thelen, The New Citizenship; Origins of Progressivism in Wisconsin, 1885-1900 (Columbia, Mo., 1972), pp. 55-129; Clyde Griffen, "The Progressive Ethos," in Stanley Coben and Lorman Ratner, eds., Development of an American Culture (Englewood Cliffs, 1970), pp. 120-149; Otis Pease, "Urban Reformers in the Progressive Era: A Reassessment," Pacific Northwest Quarterly 62 (April 1971), 49-58; David M. Kennedy, "Overview: The Progressive Era," The Historian 37 (May 1975), 453-468.

[9] John Higham, "Hanging Together: Divergent Unities in American History," Journal of American History 61 (June 1974), 24.

In addition, some historians have shown it was incorrect to assume that when the professional impulse found political expression, it would always be on the side of progressives or liberals. Professionals played fully as important a role in the Taft Republican Party as in the Progressive Party, for example.[10]

Important as these critiques are, they miss the point that the organizational synthesis can potentially help us understand more than merely progressivism. The organizational synthesis is intended, at least by some of its exponents, to serve as the building block for "a systematic social history," a comprehensive model of social change. The major cleavage in American life, according to this version of the organizational synthesis, was not between liberals and businessmen, or even between the professional-minded and the business-minded. Nor was the major issue of the period property rights. The major cleavage was between those at either end of what Hays has called the "community-society continuum": At one end of the continuum stood those who were becoming cosmopolitan and organizational-minded and who were creating bureaucratic structures to serve their interests. At the other end stood those who remained localistic,

---

[10] Norman Wilensky, Conservatives in the Progressive Era; The Taft Republicans of 1912 (Gainesville, Fla., 1965), pp. 32-39.

and parochial, preferring to retain small-scale, community-based institutions.

Hays has contrasted this theory of social change to earlier views:

> American historians have long argued . . . that business generally is conservative, resistant to change, and that forces making for change come from the lower levels of the economic order. Yet it seems more accurate to argue that private corporate business has been a powerful force for change in modern America, sweeping away old institutions and creating new, and that innovation generally has come distinctively from the upper levels of the social structure, where psychological mobility, science, technology, education and administrative systems have found distinctive support. On the other hand, conservatism--resistance to change--more frequently has been located in the lower reaches of the social order where familiar primary group relationships provided protection against innovation from the outside, cosmopolitan world.[11]

---

[11] Hays, "Systematic Social History," p. 343. But note that Hays does recognize that there were differences in perspectives between businessmen reformers and professional reformers. He describes business motives in terms of the substantive ends which they expected the reforms to achieve: A change in the class composition of municipal decision-makers and a more rationalized and economical political environment in which their businesses could function. Hays assumes that professionals did not have the same economic concerns as businessmen. In addition, he has determined that, with a few exceptions, most reform professionals were not included in the upper class directories. Therefore, "for the most part [the professionals'] interest in reform stemmed from the inherent dynamics of their professions rather than from their class connections." (Hays, "Politics of Reform," p. 160). Professionals, in Hays' view, were more interested in the means municipal reforms were going to use than in the ends those means would serve. Thus, it would seem to be Hays' position that although the viewpoint of big businessmen and elite professionals did not entirely converge, there was not much likelihood of conflict between them. Hays places elite lawyers in the

In assessing the organizational synthesis as a theory of social change, it is useful to note the similarity between the concept of community-society continuum and the structure-functionalist conception of modernization that sociologists and political scientists have developed to explain large-scale social change, especially in the Third World. The resemblance is hardly accidental, since modernization theory draws on the history of Western industrialization as the model. Both modernization theory and the organizational synthesis assume that societies are equilibrium-seeking and that there is a systemic character to social change. Change in one segment of the social structure is assumed to produce change in other segments and to produce cultural and even personality changes which somehow fit the "logic" of the structural changes. In addition, significant change is uni-directional; increasing social differentiation is its main characteristic.[12]

---

camp of the upper class rather than of the professionals among his urban elite. However, he does not spell out what he thinks the precise relationship was between these two groups.

[12] Robert Wiebe, "The Progressive Years, 1900-1917," in William H. Cartwright and Richard L. Watson, eds., The Reinterpretation of American History and Culture (Washington, 1973), pp. 425-442 makes explicit the connection between the organizational synthesis and the modernization concept. Louis Galambos, "Parsonian Sociology and Post-Progressive History," Social Science Quarterly 50 (June 1969), 25-45 is testimony of the direct influence of Talcott Parsons' structure-functionalism on one exponent of the organizational synthesis.

This modernization theory has come under an imposing barrage of criticism in recent years, attacking its ideological bias, its conflict with empirical data, and its conceptual and methodological weaknesses.[13] The empirical critique has great relevance to American social historians. That critique, based on accumulated empirical evidence on the "modernization" process, mainly in the Third World, challenges the "systemic" character of modernization. S. N. Eisenstadt concludes his extensive review of the empirical evidence bearing on modernization by noting that the key point to be made is the variability of institutional development attendant on modernization:

> Partial "modernization" or development--i.e., development of some institutional or organizational frameworks sharing many characteristics of modern organization, for example a modern factory--might take place in segregated parts of a still "traditional" social structure without necessarily giving rise to an overall change in the direction of modernity.[14]

---

[13] Dean C. Tipps, "Modernization Theory and the Comparative Study of Societies: A Critical Perspective," *Comparative Studies in Society and History* 15 (March 1973), 199-225; S. N. Eisenstadt, "Studies of Modernization and Sociological Theory," *History and Theory* 13 (1974), 225-252 provide good guides to recent critiques of structure-functionalist modernization theory. Ironically, these criticisms have begun to appear just at the time when modernization theory is being explicitly adopted by social historians as a new model.

[14] Eisenstadt, "Modernization and Sociological Theory," p. 239.

Not only is institutional development not uniform within societies, but the observed persistence of historical cultural traditions suggests to Eisenstadt that students of modernization need to be sensitive to "the relative autonomy of the symbolic sphere in its relation to structural aspects of social life."[15] In other words, a pervasive bureaucratization of social relations might not necessarily imply an equally pervasive shift of social thought in the direction of bureaucratic-mindedness.

Eisenstadt is unwilling to concede, however, that modernization theory requires an even greater modification so that the causal rather than merely the autonomous or reactive role of culture can be considered. Such a modification, as British sociologist J. D. Y. Peel has pointed out, requires that we conceptualize culture more in terms of "cognitive ideas, beliefs about 'reality' or how the world *is*" than in terms of values. In modernization theory, culture tends to be discussed in terms of values, which are treated as "a symptom, indicator or characteristic of behavior" rather than as a cause of behavior.[16]

---

[15]Ibid., p. 241.

[16]J. D. Y. Peel, "Cultural Factors in the Contemporary Theory of Development," Archives europeenes de sociologie 14 (1973), 283-303.

Closely related to the empirical critique of modernization theory is the methodological critique, which tries to account for the failure of the data to fit the concept. The clearest formulation of the methodological critique has been presented by L. E. Shiner. He argues persuasively that "tradition" and "modernity" (or "community" and "society") are ideal types, not empirical types, and thus their proper use is as heuristic devices in the formulation of hypotheses. They should not be used, as they too often are, as if they were empirically-derived concepts to be tested against other empirical data. "Tradition" and "modernity" refer to polar constellations of characteristics which each seem to be _logically_ interrelated; they are not terms which were constructed by empirically observing clusters of characteristics in two different types of societies.[17]

As Dean Tipps has pointed out, several social scientists have demonstrated that many "traditional" values and institutions have persisted in supposedly modern industrial societies and "that in both 'modern'

---

[17] L. E. Shiner, "Tradition/Modernity: An Ideal Type Gone Astray," Comparative Studies in Society and History 17 (April 1975), 245-252. The same point was made by Reinhard Bendix, "Tradition and Modernity Reconsidered," ibid. 9 (April 1967), 313-315.

and 'modernizing' societies the dynamics of modernization have consisted not in the substitution of one set of attributes for another, i.e., of 'modernity' for 'tradition,' but rather in their mutual interpenetration and transformation."[18] Philip Abrams has shown that although social scientists from the classical writers of the nineteenth century to the structure-functionalists and neo-evolutionists of the twentieth century have, explicitly or implicitly, relied heavily on the modern-traditional dichotomy for their theoretical frameworks, they have betrayed a remarkable complacency by relying on an ahistorical conception of "traditional society," one whose reality they have not been concerned to confirm or deny by empirical research.[19]

To summarize the critiques of modernization theory most applicable to the organizational synthesis: "community" and "society" are ideal types and hence should be used for heuristic purposes, not reified into

---

[18] Tipps, "Modernization Theory," p. 214. Another excellent essay making the same point and assessing its implications for the revival of historical sociology and social history is Charles Tilly, "Clio and Minerva," in John C. McKinney and Edward A. Tiryakian, eds., Theoretical Sociology; Perspectives and Developments. (New York, 1970), pp. 433-466.

[19] Philip Abrams, "The Sense of the Past and the Origins of Sociology," Past and Present 55 (May 1972), 18-32.

explanatory concepts as if they were empirically derived. When the concepts are used as heuristic devices, they can help us identify tendencies but cannot provide us with a ready-made causal explanation. We should not expect to find "pure" and systematically integrated examples of change from one orientation to the other. Instead, we should expect any given sector of society to be a mixture of "community" and "society" orientations, and we should expect that the ideas and beliefs of the historical actors will provide important clues about the reasons for deviations from the historical progression predicted by the ideal types. We need to develop richer and more subtle interpretations of social change, interpretations which go beyond the logical neatness that the macrosociological conception of the stages of modernization predicts. As sociologist Louis Schneider has remarked,

> It is a hazardous enterprise to set out evolutionary schemes in the social science field. . . . the individualizing skepticism of the historian is extremely valuable as a disturber of the peace of the stage-maker. In many areas of inquiry, we are still far from knowing securely what is comparable and what is not, what can be subsumed under usefully generic categories and what cannot. The materials of the stage-maker obviously need the closest scrutiny of the historian intimately familiar with the historical and structural particulars, say, of various societies that are considered by the

stage-maker as legitimately classifiable in certain ways.[20]

The point is not to abandon the search for a "systematic social history," but to refine the one we have by reconceptualizing and rethinking it. The tools for part of that process are at hand, both in the work of historians who are reconsidering the strength of institutional structures and thought in the antebellum period and in the work of historians who are turning their attention to the significance of work and occupations in the twentieth century.

---

[20] Louis Schneider, "On Frontiers of Sociology and History: Observations on Evolutionary Development and Unanticipated Consequences," *Social Science Quarterly* 50 (June 1969), 10-11. The situation is actually more complex than Schneider makes it out to be. The new social history, while relishing the details of historical particularism, has also sought to imbed these details in macrohistorical explanations of social change. Many social historians, not just those writing in the context of the organizational synthesis, have relied on the developmentalist perspective for such explanations. Thus, a cumulative reading of such social history makes it appear that "community" declined virtually every decade from the seventeenth century on, only to rear its head again for the next period of decline. Examples of works for earlier periods which rely on the "community-society" developmental perspective include Kenneth Lockridge, *A New England Town, The First Hundred Years: Dedham, Massachusetts, 1636-1736* (New York, 1970); Richard L. Bushman, *From Puritan to Yankee: Character and the Social Order in Connecticut, 1690-1765* (Cambridge, Mass., 1967); Richard D. Brown, "The Emergence of Urban Society in Rural Massachusetts, 1760-1820," *Journal of American History* 61 (June 1974), 29-51.

As John Higham has pointed out, there was a gradual development of a technical order during at least the last fifty years of the nineteenth century.[21] The idea developed by Stanley Elkins that ante-bellum society was essentially anti-institutional has been effectively criticized by a number of students of nineteenth-century institutional history.[22] Many Americans had a cosmopolitan, or "society," perspective throughout the nineteenth century, and primitive forms of bureaucracy also existed. This is not to deny that a significant reorientation of American life did not occur between 1880 and 1920, but only to suggest that its dimensions may not be fully capsulized in the community-society distinction.[23]

---

[21] Higham, "Hanging Together," p. 24n.

[22] Stanley Elkins, Slavery (New York, 1963). Major works effectively criticizing the anti-institutional perspective include David J. Rothman, Discovery of the Asylum (Boston, 1971); Michael B. Katz, The Irony of Early School Reform (Boston, 1968); Aileen S. Kraditor, Means and Ends in American Abolitionism: Garrison and His Critics on Strategy and Tactics, 1834-1850 (New York, 1969).

[23] For example, David B. Tyack argues that the distinction between mid-nineteenth-century and early twentieth-century urban school systems was not between bureaucratic and nonbureaucratic, but between two different models of bureaucracy. The One Best System: A History of American Urban Education (Cambridge, Mass., 1974), pp. 28-77, 126-176.

Students of the history and sociology of work and occupations are also demonstrating in their careful empirical studies that more complex and subtle analyses are required than the broad strokes the organizational synthesis permits, although that synthesis provides an essential starting point for assessing the historical significance of evidence on work and occupations. The professions are beginning to be well studied in this regard.

The organizational synthesis' conception of "professionalism," which depicts professional leaders in the progressive period as elitist technocrats seeking to systematize, modernize, and discipline their professions and to extend the influence of their professions and of technocratic principles, is best seen as an ideal type rather than as an empirically constructed concept. It is based on the supposed inherent logic of the new scientific and technical knowledge and skills developed by professionals in the late nineteenth and early twentieth centuries. For empirical support, it could rest on the unmistakable fascination with techniques and knowledge for their own sakes in the writings of many professionals in the 1890-1930 period.

However, historians and sociologists studying the professionalization process as it has unfolded from the late nineteenth to the latter half of the twentieth century have detected other themes and motives. Such professionalization activities as strengthening professional associations, rationalizing, raising, and enforcing entrance rules for the profession, establishing codes of ethics, discrediting non-scientific or quasi-scientific competitors, shrouding the special knowledge and skills of the profession in mystery, unifying training for the profession and locating it in universities---all can be seen as responses to particular historical and situational problems faced by an occupation or by a stratum within the occupation. These problems often have as much to do with matters of the wealth, status, power, and cultural orientation of the profession and its practitioners as they do with the "natural" consequences of increased specialization or with a fixation on technical knowledge.[24]

---

[24]Monte A. Calvert, The Mechanical Engineer in America, 1830-1910: Professional Cultures in Conflict (Baltimore, 1967); Eliot Friedson, ed., "Professions in Contemporary Society," American Behavioral Scientist 14 (March-April 1971), entire issue; Corinne Lathrop Gilb, Hidden Hierarchies: The Professions and Government (New York, 1966); F. H. Goldner and R. R. Ritti, "Professionalization as Career Immobility," American Journal of Sociology 72 (March 1967), 489-502;

In addition, the pattern of professionalization activities differed in important respects from profession to profession. Admittedly, there was a general "culture of professionalism" shared by most professions or aspiring professions, which defined many of the goals and much of the organizational strategy of the professions. But by focusing too exclusively on this "culture of professionalism," we ignore important differences in the

---

Alvin W. Gouldner, "Cosmopolitans and Locals: Toward an Analysis of Latent Social Roles," Administrative Science Quarterly 2 (December 1957, March 1958), 281-306, 444-480; Richard H. Hall, "Professionalization and Bureaucratization," American Sociological Review 33 (February 1968), 92-104; Barry Dean Karl, "The Power of Intellect and the Politics of Ideas," Daedalus 97 (Summer 1968), 1002-1035; Edwin T. Layton, The Revolt of the Engineers; Social Responsibility and the American Engineering Profession (Cleveland, 1971); Gerald E. Markowitz and David Karl Rosner, "Doctors in Crisis: A Study of the Use of Medical Education Reform to Establish Modern Professional Elitism in Medicine," American Quarterly 25 (May 1973), 82-107; Paul D. Montagna, "Professionalization and Bureaucratization in Large Professional Organizations," American Journal of Sociology 74 (September 1968), 138-145; Dietrich Rueschmeyer, "Doctors and Lawyers: A Comment on the Theory of the Professions," Canadian Review of Sociology and Anthropology 50 (February 1964), 17-30; Rosemary Stevens, American Medicine and the Public Interest (New Haven, 1971); Ronald C. Tobey, The American Ideology of National Science, 1919-1930 (Pittsburgh, 1971); Harold L. Wilensky, "The Professionalization of Everyone?" American Journal of Sociology 70 (September 1964), 137-158.

way professions defined their social role, viewed their relationship to clients, evaluated whether their profession was ascending or descending in power and prestige, conceptualized their relationship to emerging patterns of big business and big government, and the like.

It is the task of empirical research to sort out the relative importance of the various possible motives for the professionalization efforts and to explain the different degrees of success of the various professions in those efforts. It will certainly be the case that each profession, and very likely each stratum and specialty within each profession, will have its own unique constellation of motives. The point is that each profession has experienced a different history and that the history of professionalization breaks down into the particularistic history of each profession, depending upon the characteristics of recruitment, training, ideology, and work situation within each profession. As medical historian Rosemary Stevens has remarked, "Professional development, as with other political processes, moves in a series of conflicts and compromises suited to the crises of particular times, rather than to any long-term and global rationalization."[25]

---

[25]Stevens, <u>American Medicine</u>, p. 32.

CHAPTER 2

SOCIAL CHANGE AND THE LEGAL PROFESSION

The new, more theoretically-oriented, approaches to the social history of the 1890-1930 period are very important to the history of the legal profession, the study of which is only beginning to move beyond the progressive interpretation. According to that interpretation, the bar and bench, with a few individual exceptions, played the villain of "the interests," blindly defending property rights against the "human rights" supported by "the people." This image of the modern legal profession owes much to the fact that the only contact most historians have with the history of lawyers *qua* lawyers is via constitutional history.

Most students of constitutional history or of legal thought and jurisprudence in the late nineteenth and early twentieth centuries draw a sharp contrast between two modes of social thought: on the one hand, the mechanical jurisprudence and laissez faire constitutional thought which seem to have dominated

Supreme Court decisions between the 1890s and 1930s, striking down liberal and social welfare legislation, and, on the other hand, the pragmatic, instrumentalist, environmentalist, and anti-formalist modes of thought coming to dominate in the social sciences, informing and directing the energies of reformers seeking to make urban industrial life more humane.[1] This interpretation recognizes that there were some men on the bench and in the bar and the law schools who opposed mechanical jurisprudence and laissez faire. These were men of a scientific and often liberal temperament, such as Roscoe Pound, Louis D. Brandeis, Oliver Wendell Holmes, and Benjamin Cardozo. But this interpretation emphasizes that the main trend until at least some time in the late 1930s was a conservatism serving the interests of wealth and property.[2]

---

[1] Henry Steele Commager, The American Mind; An Interpretation of American Thought and Character Since the 1880's (New Haven, 1950), pp. 359-373 makes the contrast vividly; see also the corpus of work by Edward S. Corwin, for example, American Constitutional History, ed. Alpheus T. Mason and Gerald Garvey (New York, 1964), pp. 67-133; see also the work by Corwin's student, Benjamin R. Twiss, Lawyers and the Constitution (Princeton, 1942).

[2] As mentioned, this is the interpretation probably subscribed to by most historians. Lawyers have their own guild history, probably best codified by Roscoe Pound, The Lawyer from Antiquity to Modern Times (St. Paul, 1953). Pound emphasizes the increasing professionalization of the bar in the twentieth century. James Willard Hurst,

This interpretation contains an important critique of the legal profession. Law certainly has been one of the most elitist of the professions, as witness its extreme reluctance in comparison to other professions to welcome ethnic and racial minorities and women into its ranks, much less on a basis of equality. It has consistently opposed social welfare legislation and been unwilling to embrace fully the social science world view, as witness the trend of Supreme Court decisions from the 1890s to the 1930s. It has countenanced a severe bias in the distribution of legal services and in the development of the law itself. Areas of the law which touch on matters vital to large corporations or the wealthy have been well developed, whereas consumer, landlord-tenant, welfare, and domestic relations law, for example, have been relatively underdeveloped and

---

The Growth of American Law: The Law Makers (Boston, 1950) falls somewhere in between the two perspectives, somewhat closer to the historians' than to the lawyers' views. Hurst's book is the single most important work on the profession in print, an essential starting point for all future students. Jerold S. Auerbach, Unequal Justice; Lawyers and Social Change in Modern America (New York, 1976) is an important new departure. Auerbach draws on the traditional historical approach but extends it beyond the confines of constitutional history and social thought to an analysis of the profession's failure to meet liberal conceptions of social responsibility.

treated as routine by the lawyers who deal with them. The legal profession has been unimaginative in meeting the needs of the poor, the working class, and even the middle class, both in terms of legal doctrines and in organizing the delivery of legal services. The organized bar, which has taken its cue from the leaders of the profession, has done little to alleviate this situation.[3]

Despite the validity of this critique, interpretations which stress the contrast between formalistic constitutional thought and the revolt against formalism in sociological jurisprudence draw our attention away from an important point of similarity between the two views. It is a similarity which the organizational synthesis and corporate liberal interpretations sensitize us to see. In the twentieth century, both

---

[3] A number of sources make these points, among which the following are representative: Hurst, Growth of American Law, pp. 366-375; Jerome Carlin, Lawyers' Ethics: A Survey of the New York City Bar (New York, 1966), pp. 177-178; Joseph C. Goulden, The Superlawyers; The Small and Powerful World of the Great Washington Law Firms (New York, 1972), passim; C. Wright Mills, White Collar (New York, 1951), pp. 121-122; Harold J. Laski, The American Democracy; A Commentary and An Interpretation (New York, 1948), pp. 574-576; Murray L. Schwartz, "Changing Patterns of Legal Services," in Geoffrey C. Hazard, ed., Law in a Changing America (Englewood Cliffs, 1968), pp. 112-115; S. M. Miller and Pamela Roby, The Future of Inequality (New York, 1970), pp. 106-107.

conservative and liberal constitutional thought have implicitly accepted, with some reservations, the assumption that the economy, if not the entire society, is composed of competing functional units and that constitutional doctrines can and ought to be framed with their effect on these functional units in mind.

William Appleman Williams, while being overly cryptic and conflating too much, nevertheless captures an important point when he observes that during the Gilded Age leaders in the private sector reaffirmed and reinforced the ideology of laissez faire while at the same time creating institutions which would ultimately make laissez faire irrelevant. Leading lawyers exemplified this process very well.

> In the narrow sense, the lawyers staunchly upheld individualism, private property, and laissez faire. "The great curse of the world," they declared, "is too much government." But they also accepted the individual's shift to corporate organization and the concurrent restriction of the market place. Defending monopoly as "often a necessity and an advantage," they justified trusts as a "defensive weapon of property interests against the communistic trend."[4]

---

[4] William Appleman Williams, *The Contours of American History* (Cleveland, 1961), p. 304.

The evidence compiled by Arnold M. Paul, one of the few historians who have made an attempt to link constitutional history to the changing attitudes of the bench and bar, shows that the shift in the 1890s in the bar elite's ideology from what he refers to as "traditional conservatism" to "laissez faire conservatism" involved an implicit acceptance of a kind of corporatist thinking.[5]

Paul defines "traditional legal conservatism" as

> that branch of legal thought not too much aroused to the necessity for social reform and not too much interested in the protection of property values, but concerned primarily, in the strictly professional sense, with the due observance of the precedents and procedures of law, and, in the larger political sense, with the maintenance of a proper balance between the democratic and the restrictive elements of American constitutionalism.[6]

Of course, such traditional conservatism as found in legal thought was not so purely divorced from the

---

[5] Arnold M. Paul, <u>Conservative Crisis and the Rule of Law</u> (Ithaca, 1960). Although Paul's evidence and even his interpretation of that evidence point in the direction of the corporate liberal interpretation, his book is basically written within the assumptions of the progressive tradition of historiography, a point which will be developed later.

[6] Ibid., p. 88.

protection of property values in practice or in the consciousness of the bar elite.[7] However, Paul's main point is clearly valid; the political dimension predominated over the economic dimension in this thought.[8] Paul draws from this what may be a dubious generalization: that traditional conservatism conceived of the role of lawyers and the judicial branch as one of independence and neutrality. In any case,

---

[7] Throughout the nineteenth century, most law business and certainly the largest incomes came from matters dealing with property rights rather than with personal rights. For a discussion of the romanticized picture of the nineteenth-century bar, see Robert T. Swaine, "Impact of Big Business on the Profession: An Answer to Critics of the Modern Bar," <u>American Bar Association Journal</u> 35 (February 1949), 90-91.

[8] Paul's evidence for the centrality of such thought is its predominance in bar association speeches during the 1880s. Paul found traditional conservatism expressed in the speeches and writings of such leading lawyers and jurists as U. S. Senator Waitman T. Willey, New York corporation lawyer John F. Dillon, Connecticut Governor, state supreme court justice, and Yale Law School professor Simeon E. Baldwin, U. S. Supreme Court justice Henry B. Brown, Philadelphia lawyer Richard C. McMurtie, University of Pennsylvania Law School professor William Draper Lewis, Boston railroad lawyer J. H. Benton, Jr., and Chicago corporation lawyer Edgar A. Bancroft. See especially ibid., pp. 28-29, 35-38, 102-103 for the analysis of the speeches of several of these men.

it would appear to be Paul's view that such lawyers were highly professional-minded but not yet corporatist-minded.[9]

During the 1890s, Paul argues, traditional legal conservatives lost their confidence that social order could be maintained by traditional means. They were frightened by such labor unrest as Coxey's army and the strikes at Homestead, Coeur d'Alene, Pullman, and elsewhere. They were also alarmed at an apparent radicalism in legislative majorities, which was the context within which they saw the income tax law and which they feared would be expanded upon by the Populist movement and Bryan's candidacy. Leading lawyers, Paul contends, came to see public affairs as a conflict between those who would protect and those who would tear down the institution and rightful enjoyment of private property. They saw themselves confronted with the problem of "how to restrain discontented majorities from riding roughshod over the

---

[9] This is an inference. Paul does not use these terms. However, the contrast he draws between the pre- and post-1890s bar is very similar to that of those who see the nineteenth-century bar as professional-minded ("independent and neutral") and the twentieth-century bar as commercialized and deprofessionalized.

rights and property of the individual and threatening in the process the foundations of the ordered society."[10] A "tumultous ocean of democracy"[11] threatened to upset the constitutional balance struck by the founding fathers and in the process "to deprive the owners--usually corporation owners--of their property by unjust or discriminating legislation in the exercise of the power of taxation, or of eminent domain, or of that elastic power known as the police power."[12]

Lawyers--meaning leading lawyers, since they were the only ones organized--were exhorted to sign up for the duration, to play an active public role. Thomas M. Cooley made the plea very explicitly in his 1894 presidential address to the American Bar Association. He called upon lawyers to become public leaders and teachers, defending the Constitution, legal system, and social order generally from both open and potential challenges. Significantly, Cooley identified the threat as stemming as much from "ignorance or unreasonable passion" among the public as from "revolutionary

---

[10] Paul, Conservative Crisis, p. 159.

[11] The phrase was John F. Dillon's in his presidential address to the ABA. ABA, Reports 15 (1892), 211.

[12] Ibid., p. 206.

purpose."[13] The legal elite never gave up its underlying belief in the consensual character of American politics and values. Irrational passion and ignorance might sweep through the majority, but if those committed to the rule of law could only prevail, social order could be reasserted through peaceful and institutional means.

In the 1890s lawyers looked to the courts to act for the party of reason, order, and property and to restrain the parties of passion, ignorance, democracy, and socialism. Apparently, leading lawyers no longer believed that the conservative influence of lawyers in legislatures or that traditional constitutional doctrines were sufficient. Instead, they turned to a body of "new constitutionalism," or laissez faire thought. These doctrines had been formulated in the previous twenty years, but had generally not been accepted by the courts.[14]

---

[13] Ibid. 17 (1894), 218-219.

[14] Paul, Conservative Crisis, pp. 12-18, 39-42. Laissez faire conservatism was applied to the labor movement in 1893 and 1894 as the federal courts perfected the use of the injunction and extended the Interstate Commerce and Sherman Anti-Trust Acts as anti-labor weapons. The most significant case, the one which firmly committed traditional legal conservatives to some laissez faire principles, and which brought to a head the conflict between majority rule and judicial interposition, was the Pollack case, challenging the constitutionality of the federal

One effect of the conservative crisis was to enshrine laissez faire and judicial supremacy doctrines in constitutional interpretations. Paul implies, although he does not explicitly argue, that another long-term effect was to alter the perspective of the legal profession by persuading it to drop the pose of neutrality and to side openly with the defense of private property. In this sense, the conservative crisis could be seen as setting the legal elite on the road toward adopting a corporatist world view.[15]

---

income tax law. The Supreme Court's decision in that case represented a clear acceptance of judicial supremacy by two formerly traditional conservative justices, George Shiras and Horace Gray. Ibid., pp. 107-124, 185-200.

[15] Paul does not carry his study of the attitudes of the bench and bar past the Pollack decision. A follow-up study to Paul's, applying his interpretive framework and methodology to the 1905-1912 period, is Barbara C. Steidle, "Conservative Progressives: A Study of the Attitudes and Role of Bar and Bench, 1905-1912" (Ph.D. dissertation, Rutgers University, 1969). This study is summarized in part in Steidle, "'Reasonable' Reform: The Attitude of the Bar and Bench Toward Liability Law and Workmen's Compensation," in Jerry Israel, ed., Building the Organizational Society, Essays on Associational Activities in Modern America (New York, 1972), pp. 21-41. She concludes that the bench and bar retained its commitment to judicial supremacy but dropped its slavish devotion to laissez faire and attempted to accommodate itself to the reform temper of the progressive years. The legal elite recognized that progressive reformers were not a majoritarian threat to private property or its prerogatives. Steidle's evidence suggests that the bar

In order to evaluate whether the conservative crisis did set the bar elite on such a road, it would be necessary to examine carefully the stance the bar adopted toward the increasing scale of organizational activity in the polity and the economy. This examination should include both the behavior of leading lawyers and their ideological orientation. Paul does not examine such activities. However, he writes within the context of an historical interpretation, the progressive view, which has, to a limited extent, examined such activities. The progressive view holds that the key to understanding the modern bar lies in the close association that has developed between the bar elite and the large corporation. This interpretation is usually phrased in terms of the increasing "commercialization" of the bar, by which is meant that because of their thralldom to large corporations, lawyers have shifted from professional-mindedness to business- or property-mindedness.

Samuel Untermeyer, a liberal New York corporation lawyer, stated the commercialization interpretation in 1933: "Fifty years ago skill and eloquence in advocacy

---

elite's commitment to a corporatist world-view was limited, at best, by 1912. Steidle mentions, but does not analyze, the bar's professionalization activities, which do seem more corporatist-minded.

were the prime requisites of the leaders of our bar.
Their reputations were made and had to be maintained
in the courts." But then large corporations began
"to draw away from advocacy the best minds of the bar
and by money temptations convert them into highly
paid clerks to teach financiers to keep 'prayerfully
within the law.'" When that happened, leading lawyers
found that in addition to knowing the law, they had to
develop business sense and expertise. As a consequence,
Untermeyer complained, the corporation lawyer's "legal
knowledge must not be thrust forward if he is to be of
aid to his clients."[16] The point is that not only
did some lawyers become counselors to large corporations,
but also these men were recognized both inside and outside
the profession as the leaders of the bar. They were the
best legal minds of their generation and they set the
standards of professional conduct.

Law school professors in elite universities have
historically been among the severest critics of
"commercialization" trends within the profession. They
contrast commercialization to their scientific ideal.

---

[16] Samuel Untermeyer, "What Every Present-Day Lawyer Should Know," American Academy of Political and Social Science, Annals 167 (May 1933), 173-174.

Harvard's Zechariah Chafee, for example, expressed confidence that "the lawyer who practices his profession in a spirit of scientific curiosity would seek primarily to know as much as he could about the social results of his and other lawyers' professional work" and would therefore "cease to be the highly specialized agent of particular interests."[17]

With this contrast between the commercial and scientific approaches to the practice of law in mind, Harlan Fiske Stone, dean of Columbia Law School from 1910 to 1924 before his elevation to U.S. Attorney General and then to the Supreme Court, lamented that the higher strata of the bar had become so commercialized that "they have little interest in raising [the bar's] standards, in improving its membership, or in improving the administration of the law in any substantial way." In addition, "you rarely find their services enlisted in any case which does not involve substantial remuneration, and almost never on the unpopular side of a case involving human rights and personal liberty."[18] Given these attitudes at the top,

---

[17] Zechariah Chafee, Jr., "Socializing Legal Education," *The New Republic*, April 14, 1926, pp. 211-213.

[18] Stone to Frederick Lewis Allen, n.d., copy enclosed in Allen to Zechariah Chafee, Jr., December 11, 1928, Chafee MSS, Box 1, Harvard Law School Library. The

Stone thought it was not surprising that the bar as a whole "has so little professional and public spirit throughout that it is lagging behind the other professions."[19]

Felix Frankfurter, who had one foot in the law school camp and one foot in the liberal camp, believed the bar elite's commercialization poisoned the very atmosphere of the law schools. His students were dominated by a "crass materialism," a desire to become "big money-making lawyers in New York and Chicago." "They hear from time to time noble talks. . . . But when all is said and done, these 'idealistic' influences, except in a negligibly few cases, are as nothing compared to the forces of example by 'leaders of the bar,' the career, the pursuits, the aims of those who are deemed the 'leaders.'"[20]

Stone letter is also printed in full in Alpheus T. Mason, Harlan Fiske Stone: Pillar of the Law (New York, 1957), pp. 376-377n. Mason dates the letter as October 5, 1926.

[19] Stone to Nicholas Murray Butler, December 3, 1926, reprinted in Mason, Harlan Fiske Stone, p. 210. Stone expressed these views privately in the 1920s and publicly in the 1930s. See ibid., pp. 376-378; Stone, "The Public Influence of the Bar," Harvard Law Review 47 (November 1934), 1-14.

[20] Frankfurter to Learned Hand, October 3, 1924, Frankfurter MSS, Box 63, Library of Congress.

Implicit in the criticisms of the modern bar is the view that prior to the rise of big business, the bar was a public-spirited profession whose leaders were regularly tested in the public forum of the courtroom and who therefore had to be attuned to the needs and demands of the public at large. According to this view, the fatal flaw in the modern development of the legal profession is that it has not trod the path of other professions, grounding itself in scientific principles and keeping its eye on the human values and service ideals which are thought to be the heart of modern professional-mindedness.

The impact of the large corporation on all professions is a very important topic, and the commercialization interpretation renders an important moral judgment on the bar's demonstrated lack of a meaningful sense of social responsibility. But the commercialization interpretation romanticizes the pre-1890 bar's professionalism and disinterestedness, and it assumes a greater humanitarianism and scientific detachment among other twentieth-century professionals than the historical record supports. In addition, the commercialization interpretation relies too heavily on an economic deterministic conception of the sources of the bar elite's ideology, to the neglect of the broader, more complex environment in which that ideology functioned and changed. The point made by nearly all post-progressive historiography--that liberal reform has done more to defend property rights than it has to erode them--suggests, if nothing else does, that we need a better explanation than narrow economic self-interest to explain the bar elite's ideology. They were defending property rights; but they understood those rights in the context of a broader class-conscious ideology, which they were both clinging to and subtly modifying.

The commercialization interpretation is unable to account for evidence that, despite its commercialization, the bar elite remained professional-minded in some sense after the 1890s. Even the concept of judicial supremacy and its defense can be seen as very professional-minded. In addition to defense of the judiciary, the bar elite engaged in other professional-minded activities after 1900. Bar associations were strengthened and the range of their activities was extended. By the 1920s, efforts were made in a number of states to make bar association membership compulsory for all lawyers. Bar associations established codes of ethics and promoted procedural reform and other innovations in the administration of justice, generally applying principles of efficiency. This movement led in the 1920s to bar sponsorship of the formation of judicial councils, as an attempt to rationalize court organization. Efforts were made to systematize the substantive law and to rationalize it by reducing discrepancies as between the states. The Commissioners on Uniform State Laws, first established in the 1890s, and the American Law Institute, which was founded in the 1920s, were major indications of these efforts. Both were founded at the instigation of the bar elite.[21]

It should not be surprising that leading lawyers could be both business-minded and professional-minded, given the elitism of other professionals and the structural similarity of the positions of professionals and businessmen in a bureaucratizing society. That is one of the main findings of the organizational

---

[21] All of these activities will be covered in detail in later chapters. For the basic data see Corrine L. Gilb, Hidden Hierarchies: The Professions and Government (New York, 1966); Gilb, "Self-Governing Professions and the Public Welfare; A Case Study of the California State Bar" (Ph.D. dissertation, Radcliffe College, 1956); Hurst, Growth of American Law, pp. 249-375; Pound, The Lawyer, pp. 251-349; Edson R. Sunderland, History of the American Bar Association and Its Work (n.p., 1953).

synthesis. As John Higham has remarked, summarizing this interpretation:

> Not equal rights but the hierarchical articulation of differentiated functions is [technical organization's] working principle. The more complex the knowledge required for maintaining a system, the further the professional expert is detached from public view.[22]

That is, specialization, division of labor, and the making of decisions according to the technical canons of authority, all of which are central to modern organizations and modern scientific knowledge, have produced behavior with elitist implications and have often encouraged an elitist cast of mind among twentieth-century professionals. Insofar as a concern for social justice can be found among such professionals, as it undoubtedly can be found in Frankfurter and Chafee, for example, it probably reflects the persistence of a cultural tradition extrinsic to the strict definition of the professional role. This tradition, it is true, was given freer rein for professionals working within a university setting than for those working for large

---

[22] John Higham, "Hanging Together: Divergent Unities in American History," *Journal of American History* 61 (June 1974), 26.

corporations. But it cannot be interpreted as a simple reflex of a commitment to the scientific ideal.

However, as pointed out above in the discussion of the organizational synthesis, there were important differences between the histories of the professions. What is striking about the history of the bar is that despite the energy and effort expended on professionalization activities, none of those activities had a <u>decisive</u> impact on the composition of the bar or on the administration of justice. Professionalism, in the form of associational activity, never became as fully developed in the legal profession as it did, for example, in the medical profession. To a very important extent, this was because bar leaders were motivated more by a desire to defend a fading image of the profession and its public role than by a positive conception of needed changes.

In this sense, the commercialization thesis is correct. The bar never developed as clear-cut a sense of professionalism as doctors did. In part, this was because elite lawyers were very involved in the circumscribed world of their corporate law practices. But, it was also because they, and many other members of the bar, were clinging to a definition of professionalism which had been forged in the nineteenth century, one which saw a transcendent role for the bar and bench in maintaining social stability and social control, but which did not envisage the bar acting as a corporate body.

In sum, the evidence of bar professionalism lends some support to the organizational synthesis and calls into question the adequacy of earlier formulations based on the belief that the bar became deprofessionalized in the twentieth century. On the other hand, the organizational synthesis predicts a more forcefully pursued and a more consequential level of professional and associational activity than occurred. In order to understand what was happening in the legal profession in the late nineteenth and early twentieth centuries, a new interpretation of its relationship to the organizational society is needed, an interpretation which draws on existing progressive and organizational interpretations, but which breaks free of their categories.

****

The starting point for such an interpretation must be an understanding of the social function and ideology of the legal profession during the nineteenth century.

The social changes between 1890 and 1930 that strongly affected the bar did not occur in a vacuum. Lawyers interpreted those changes in terms of their historic conception of their role.

All observers agree that the nineteenth-century bar was conservative in ideology and social function: conservative in the sense that lawyers saw themselves and were seen by others as restraining democratic impulses. Alex de Tocqueville, in his search for the source of stability in America, for the conservative force (the "aristocracy") he believed was necessary to restrain the expected excesses of the democratic element, believed he found it in the legal profession.

> Lawyers belong to the people by birth and interest, and to the aristocracy by habit and taste; they may be looked upon as the connecting link between the two great classes of society. . . . If I were asked where I place the American aristocracy, I should reply without hesitation that it is not among the rich, who are united by no common tie, but that it occupies the judicial bench and bar.[23]

The bar's conservatism was a professional-minded conservatism in that it emphasized, and almost sanctified, legal procedures and precedents. In so doing, nineteenth-century lawyers carved out a distinction between politics and the law. Politics was based on popular emotion and

---

[23] Alexis de Tocqueville, <u>Democracy in America</u>, ed. Phillips Bradley, 2 vols. (New York: Vintage Books, 1945), 1:286, 288.

the clash of self-interests. Law was based on reason and disinterestedness. Lawyers, because of their special training and knowledge of the law, were uniquely equipped, so the argument went, to be the guardians of the limits beyond which politics could not go.[24] In Willard Hurst's perceptive phrase, law was a primary factor in defining "the conditions of freedom" in the nineteenth century. Also, as Hurst and other legal history scholars have emphasized, "contract" was the ruling legal concept, just as the closely related concept of the market was the ruling metaphor in the society, polity, and economy.[25]

---

[24] Morton J. Horwitz, "The Conservative Tradition in the Writing of American Legal History," American Journal of Legal History 18 (July 1973), 275-294.

[25] James Willard Hurst, Law and the Conditions of Freedom in the Nineteenth-Century United States (Madison, Wis., 1956). See also Lawrence M. Friedman, Contract Law in America (Madison, 1965), pp. 21-26. Daniel H. Calhoun, Professional Lives in America: Structure and Aspirations, 1750-1850 (Cambridge, Mass., 1965), pp. 59-87 explicitly ties changes in the legal profession from the eighteenth to the nineteenth centuries to the general societal shift from an emphasis on communal values to a market orientation. A useful corrective to Hurst's almost exclusive focus on the law of contract and on the ties between the law and material progress is Harry N. Scheiber, "At the Borderlands of Law and Economic History: The Contributions of Willard Hurst," American Historical Review 85 (February 1970), 744-756. Scheiber points out that Hurst focuses on distributive economic policy--mainly resource allocation--and that the legal process concerned itself with many other issues in the nineteenth century.

Elite lawyers correctly saw the law and legal institutions as central to the maintenance of social control. Indeed, they saw them as central to any definition of what the great American mission, the great American experiment in republicanism, was all about. Their veneration for the Constitution and the Founding Fathers was not mere pious cant, although it could become that at times. Seeing the law and legal institutions as central to the American mission and to social order meant that lawyers believed that legal principles were somehow immutable and given. Any attack on them could be interpreted as an attack on social control and stability itself. "Social control" and "stability," in the hands of the legal elite, were concepts expressing class interests in neutral-sounding language. Insofar as there was a social consensus on these concepts, that consensus set the terms for a hegemonic relationship which perpetuated the inequalities of the existing class system.[26] With some exceptions,

---

[26] This is not to argue that the only function of the legal system is to perpetuate the existing class system. The legal system can be, and has been, used by a wide variety of groups and interests in American history, occasionally in ways subversive of the existing class system. The relationship between law and society is complex and requires the subtle analysis the new legal history, in the hands of such scholars as Willard Hurst

such a consensus did exist in nineteenth-century America. Law defined the limits of legitimate social and political action; lawyers and judges, for the most part, determined the law.

But lawyers understood that the law and the legal system could not be abstracted from the rest of society. They assumed that respect for the legal profession and for legal institutions was but one aspect of a broader set of values and attitudes which meshed to form the nineteenth-century social consensus. The market metaphor and the image of a society of atomistic individuals dominated social thought and pervaded basic institutions in the nineteenth century.[27] The success ethic, with its

---

and Lawrence M. Friedman, is applying to it. However, there would seem to be no serious challenge to the broad generalization that a primary function of the legal system and of legal precepts has been to legitimize the existing social order, contributing significantly thereby to a hegemonic relationship among the classes. Certainly, the legal elite saw matters this way.

[27]In light of the references that were cited above in chap. 1, fn. 22, this statement may need some qualification. Perhaps it will suffice to say that no society's institutions, values, beliefs, or norms are entirely internally consistent. American history from the beginning has been characterized by the dual, but not necessarily contradictory, values of individualism and collective enterprise. In the nineteenth century, individualism usually was understood to mean self-reliance; institutional innovations were often justified on the grounds that they would either free or regenerate individuals so they could function more effectively as self-reliant men or women. In the twentieth century individualism has been redefined so that it refers to the

insistence that upward and downward social mobility were based on individual strength of character, brought together this set of beliefs, values, and attitudes in the social psychological dimension of life just as legal doctrines brought them together in the realm of political economy.

Hence, it would be wrong to assume that leading lawyers[28] in the nineteenth century were exclusively professional-minded. They had a conception of social

---

rights individuals can claim against institutions whose legitimacy depends very little if at all on their powers of regeneration. These generalizations are suggested by James M. Banner, "Review of David Rothman, Discovery of the Asylum," Journal of Interdisciplinary History 5 (Summer 1974), 167-174; David M. Potter, "American Individualism in the Twentieth Century," in Potter, History and American Society, ed. Don E. Fehrenbacher (New York, 1973), pp. 256-276.

[28] The terms "leading lawyers" and "bar elite" are used in this study to refer to: (1) lawyers who held office in the American Bar Association or in state bar associations in the major industrial states; (2) members of the larger law firms in the major industrial states; (3) lawyers who gained a reputation as spokesmen for the profession. Evidence about their views was obtained from their writings in legal periodicals and their addresses to local, state, and national bar associations. Some evidence was also found in manuscript collections. For the most part, leading lawyers will be treated as a cohesive group. The evidence supports that view. They shared a consensus on the historic role and function of the legal profession and they tended to respond similarly to the challenges to that historic role and function. On some issues the bar elite was divided; when pertinent, these divisions will be discussed. Most differences were of style and tone, although occasionally there were ideological differences. For example, there were out

order and stability which went beyond a simple reification of their profession's expertise. They wished to defend an entire social order and understood that this defense involved preserving a set of social values, which in turn depended on the disciplining influence of the family, the community, and other vital institutions. On the other hand, not all aspects of nineteenth-century popular ideology were congenial to leading lawyers. In particular, there was a strong strain of egalitarianism and latent populism which lawyers wished to keep in check, which task was one of the central duties of the legal profession and legal institutions.

The change in bar elite ideology that Arnold M. Paul discovered in the 1890s was not so much a retreat from professionalism as it was a response to the growing recognition among leading lawyers that society was coming

---

and out reactionaries such as the brilliant New York corporation lawyer William D. Guthrie. There were formalists, such as William Howard Taft, who never had a corporate practice and whose chief reference points were the law and government, which he tended to think of as essentially one. There were those who were willing to use formalistic conventions when the occasion demanded, but who never fully internalized them as dogma and as ends in themselves. Most corporation lawyers probably fit into this latter category, although they divided between those like Charles Evans Hughes and Samuel Untermeyer, who had a more liberal cast of mind, and those like Elihu Root or John W. Davis, who had a strong conservative cast of mind.

to be composed of functioning groups rather than of
atomistic individuals and that the social control function of old values and of the law itself was losing some
of its efficacy. For a number of reasons, the bar elite
did not fully embrace a corporatist ideology, which would
have fully rationalized the changes they were beginning
to perceive. One reason was that nineteenth-century
social values, especially the success ethic, did continue
to serve a social-control function, even as their correspondence with reality declined (a fact which too many
liberal and radical historians, in their focus on
institutions rather than on values, have ignored).[29]
Another reason the bar elite did not embrace a full-scale corporatist ideology was that they were unwilling
to surrender the special position they had won for their
profession during the nineteenth century. It was a position which was based on the popular belief that lawyers
possessed a socially necessary expertise and which
enabled lawyers to keep egalitarianism and latent
populism in check. As de Tocqueville explained, lawyers in a democracy fell heir to the political power

---

[29] Lawrence Chenoweth, The American Dream of Success;
The Search for the Self in the Twentieth Century (North
Scituate, Mass., 1974); Aileen S. Kraditor, "American
Radical Historians on Their Heritage," Past and Present,
no. 56 (August 1972), 136-153.

exercised elsewhere by "the wealthy, the noble, and
the prince." Lawyers, as "masters of a science which is
necessary, but which is not very generally known"
obtained power both "as arbiters between the citizens"
and as political office holders. Armed with this
power, "the lawyers do not, indeed, wish to overthrow the
institutions of democracy, but they constantly endeavor
to turn it away from its real direction by means that
are foreign to its nature."[30]

Nineteenth-century lawyers exercised their
conservative influence not by acting together as a
corporate body, but rather by playing out the advocate's
role within the context of an organized institutional
setting, the court system. The advocate was the
embodiment of a number of nineteenth-century virtues.
He was learned but pragmatic, self-reliant and individualistic though serving a community function, bound
by the principles of law but shrewd and calculating in
their use, and possessed of the skills of rhetoric and
display, which the public could judge but not successfully match.

There were, however, a number of tensions in the
bar's idealized role and function, as Boston lawyer

---

[30] de Tocqueville, <u>Democracy in America</u>, 1:286, 288.

Joseph B. Warner reminded the American Bar Association in 1896:

> The truth is that there is something paradoxical in the advocate's position. He stands at the bar in theory, demanding justice--that is, asking to have strict principles of right strictly applied. This is simple to the point of severity. And yet he is holding himself out, at least in popular estimation (which is not wholly wrong), as ready to take any case of any man who will pay him for it, and to do his best to make that case prevail.[31]

That is, there was a widespread popular impression that lawyers best served the interests of those best able to pay, that the legal profession served particular interests rather than the general interest.

Although historical study of the nineteenth-century bar is in its infancy, it is clear that this popular impression was accurate. Daniel Calhoun found, for example, that advertising by lawyers in newspapers began to decline in Nashville, Tennessee, during the 1840s and 1850s, revealing that at least the leading lawyers were obtaining a large part of their practice through retainers, connections, and recommendations. Advertising aimed at the farmers or planters who rode into town on a court day and picked up the newspaper was now confined to the debt-collecting lawyers.[32]

---

[31] Joseph B. Warner, "The Responsibilities of the Lawyer," ABA, Reports 19 (1896), 319-320.

[32] Calhoun, Professional Lives, p. 83.

The image of the advocate served as a mask, albeit an imperfect mask, for the informal but hierarchically structured nature of the profession and for its distribution of services.

Another tension in the idealized conservative role of the nineteenth-century bar was that judges and lawyer-legislators were as fully under the influence of political parties as they were under the influence of their professional identity. Judges, whether elected or appointed, usually owed their position to political parties and were at least potentially open to legislative influence. Although lawyers have long been the dominant occupational group in state legislatures and the federal Congress, they seem to have come from a different stratum of the profession than the bar elite. There is a paucity of solid evidence on this for the nineteenth century, although the generalization is well substantiated for the twentieth century.[33] The usual assumption is

---

[33] Heinz Eulau and John D. Sprague, *Lawyers and Politics* (Indianapolis, 1964); Joseph A. Schlesinger, *Ambition and Politics: Political Careers in the United States* (Chicago, 1967); Schlesinger, "Lawyers and American Politics: A Clarified View," *Midwestern Journal of Political Science* 1 (May 1957), 26-39 are all solid studies and also good leads into the extensive literature by political scientists on lawyers in public office. David J. Rothman, *Politics and Power; The United States Senate 1869-1901* (Cambridge, Mass., 1966), pp. 111-136 presents data on the social background of senators which seems to support this view.

that there was more overlap between the legal elite and the political lawyers in the nineteenth century, but that the distinction did exist. Certainly by the last three decades of the nineteenth century, leading lawyers thought the distinction was very real, as will be shown below.

In addition to popular distrust of the bar and competition with political parties for the allegiance of lawmakers and law interpreters, the legal elite had to contend with a tendency toward lawlessness and a distrust of authority that had been deeply imbedded in American culture and society by the conditions of slavery and the frontier and by the myths and traditions of economic expansion and conquest of a new land. For the most part, this lawlessness did not threaten the stability or survival of the basic social, economic, or political institutions. It was as often as not conservative in its effect. But it was a threat to the hegemonic function of the profession and was perceived as such by leading lawyers, at the same time that it confirmed in lawyers' minds the irresponsibility of the popular will and the indispensibility of the lawyer's stabilizing influence.

Thus, throughout the nineteenth century, the legal elite had fought two battles: to keep the law in the hands of the profession and to keep law within the profession in the hands of the legal elite. To maintain the principles and doctrines of the Constitution and common law, the legal elite relied very heavily on the social prestige of the bar as one of the few learned professions, on popular veneration for the Constitution and the common law tradition, and on popular respect for the principle of judicial review.

From about 1870 on, social, economic, and political changes began to erode this traditional hegemonic role of the law and the legal profession. As a result, lawyers took measures to protect the traditional role. They also began to forge new conceptions of the relationship between law and society, in order to make legitimate a new but equally central and equally strong role for the law and the bench and bar. As legal historian Willard Hurst has pointed out, there was a basic change in the law itself. Until the late nineteenth century, most law was judge-made and stemmed from the common law. Beginning in the Gilded Age, law has been increasingly made by the legislature and, from about 1910 on, increasingly by the executive and administrative arms of government.[34]

Bar association speakers throughout the last two decades of the nineteenth century and for a period into the new century complained about the growing bacillus of "over-legislation" and urged leading lawyers to assert their professional unity against this trend. The increase in the sheer volume of legislation was a frequent object of complaint. From the beginning, the American Bar Association had mandated that the annual presidential address be largely devoted to a survey of major legislative enactments in each of the states. This exercise provided an excellent forum for the expression of the bar elite's uneasiness about trends in the state legislatures. In addition to the volume of legislation, leading lawyers decried corruption and the role of lobbyists in the legislative hall. Closely associated with this evil in the bar elite's mind was the steady influx of mediocrities into the legislatures. All of these factors, according to the bar elite, made the legislators very susceptible to the whims of the

---

[34]Willard Hurst, "The Legal Profession," Wisconsin Law Review, Fall 1966, pp. 969-978; Hurst, Growth of American Law, pp. 71-74.

public mood and led them to enact carelessly worded and often dangerous and pernicious laws.[35] University of Chicago Law School professor Ernst Freund expressed the view of many leading lawyers, noting that "the character of the legislature leaves room for much improvement," and that "statutory legislation leaves much to be desired." He hoped "that legislatures will deal with private law as little as possible."[36]

A number of specific remedies for the evil of "over-legislation" were proposed. Moorfield Storey suggested that the courts draw district boundaries to prevent gerry-mandering, that courts rather than legislatures decide contested elections, that the powers of the Speaker be reduced, that the power of the legislature to grant privileges be restricted, and that laws be enacted against improper expenditures in political campaigns. By these reforms, he hoped to reduce the influence of those seeking special privileges,

---

[35] For examples of these complaints see the following addresses to the ABA: Simone Sterne, "Defective and Slipshod Legislation," ABA, Reports 7 (1884); Moorfield Storey, "The American Legislature" 17 (1894); Charles F. Manderson, "Presidential Address" 23 (1900); Edmund Wetmore, "Presidential Address" 24 (1901); Alton B. Parker, "The Congestion of Law" 29 (1906).

[36] Ernst Freund, "Government and Law in America," American Law Review 34 (January-February 1900), 18, 26.

which in his Mugwumpish view was the root of the evil.[37] The Chicago Bar Association's Special Committee on Corrupt Political Practices urged the adoption in Illinois of an act similar to Great Britain's Corrupt Practices Act of 1883, which required careful reporting on campaign expenditures.[38]

Other remedies were suggested to the ABA by Charles Manderson and Alton Parker. Manderson wanted to see lobbyists, promoters, and (significantly) strikers kept away from legislative halls. He proposed certain procedural reforms, such as a restriction on special laws, an insistence on general laws, and the replacement of annual sessions with biennial ones. In addition, he called for constitutional amendments restricting even further the power of legislatures.[39] Alton Parker also called for less frequent meetings of legislatures. He invoked a newer, more bureaucratic-minded, theme when he called for the employment of trained official draftsmen to give laws the necessary legal and literary form, a project which the ABA

---

[37] Storey, "The American Legislature."

[38] Chicago Bar Association, Reports 27 (1900), 54-56.

[39] Manderson, "Presidential Address."

actively supported between 1911 and 1921, when it promoted legislative drafting bureaus and prepared a drafting model.[40]

Popular as all these technical and procedural remedies were in the minds of the "over-legislation" critics, they always came back to what were in fact the two strongest themes. One was that no sweeping changes in the behavior of legislatures could be expected so long as public opinion remained under "the influence of a wave of so-called socialism. . . . created and fostered as much, or more, from above as from below."[41] Edmund Wetmore, a New York City lawyer, believed the spirit of socialism,

> springs, primarily, from the enlargement of the sympathies, the increased desire to relieve suffering and want, the benevolence, the altruistic spirit that evolution and modern conditions have developed among the ever increasing class of the well-to-do in an age of increasing wealth and prosperity.[42]

---

[40] Parker, "The Congestion of Law," p. 392; M. Louise Rutherford, The Influence of the American Bar Association on Public Opinion and Legislation (Philadelphia, 1937), p. 260. It is not surprising that Parker, who served as president of the National Civic Federation in the early 1920s, should be thinking in terms of bureaucratic solutions.

[41] Wetmore, "Presidential Address," p. 236.

[42] Ibid.; for similar expressions of the belief that public opinion was what had to be changed, see Storey, "The American Legislature," and Manderson, "Presidential Address."

Wetmore recognized that broad cultural changes, somehow connected with the emergence of a new middle class, were at the root of the malaise which troubled his fellow leading lawyers. He counseled them that no short-term political remedies could be expected.

> We must look only to the gradual change which continued discussion and experience, that great silent teacher, will bring about, to correct its course and avoid the evils of which we are now conscious and against which we sound a warning.[43]

What Wetmore was really telling his fellow leading lawyers was that they had lost their role as molders of public opinion and that although they were right and time would eventually prove them right, they could not expect merely by rhetoric to sway public opinion to their viewpoint, especially when the altruistic and liberal segments of the new middle class seemed to be in the process of creating a cultural tradition very different from the one the bar elite felt comfortable with.

Not only could the bar elite not expect to mold public opinion any longer, it also seemed that their influence over their fellow lawyers in legislatures was very minimal. This was the second major theme in

---

[43]Wetmore, "Presidential Address," p. 237.

the bar elite's response to "over-legislation." In
the minds of some leading lawyers, the problem was that
the wrong sort of lawyers were serving in state
legislatures. Others understood that the increasing
specialization within the profession was the primary
explanation.

There was a widespread recognition that leading
lawyers were less attracted to service in state legislatures than they had been in previous decades. John
Randolph Tucker called it "a deadly radical change in
our habits and policy." He believed that in the past
the "thoughtful statesman-lawyer" had been eager not
only to help shape the statute law of his own state,
but to contribute thereby to "building up . . . the
historical jurisprudence of which we are the proud
inheritors."[44] As Tucker recognized, there was a general
retreat among the bar elite from political activity.
The money to be made in private practice simply could
not be even remotely matched by the pittance paid state
legislators. In addition, the bar elite was developing
a national consciousness which made Albany, Harrisburg,
and other state capitals seem provincial places indeed.

---

[44] ABA, Reports 16 (1893), 203.

Those leading lawyers who were attracted away from their lucrative practices into politics typically went into positions at the national level--in the Cabinet, in Congress, or in the diplomatic service. These sojourns were generally undertaken at the request of others and did not reflect an ambition to leave private practice. Elihu Root, for example, reported to his biographer that he was perfectly content with his law practice in New York and only entered federal work because President McKinley was so insistent, and then only when McKinley assured him he would be doing essentially lawyerly work. However, Root's career reveals the attractions that the political limelight could have for those who entered it. As he remarked,

> I was fifty-four when I went to Washington. Otherwise I would have stayed in New York in law practice and made a great deal of money which I should not have known what to do with, and which might have been of very doubtful benefit to the children. What did happen was that I went to Washington and a thousand new interests have come into my life.[45]

But, considering the close affinity between law and politics, a significant number of leading lawyers

---

[45] Philip C. Jessup, Notes on a conversation with Elihu Root, n.d. [1932], P. C. Jessup MSS, Box 243, Library of Congress.

avoided politics. For example, of the first thirty presidents of the ABA, eighteen never held political office.[46]

One purpose behind the re-emergence of bar associations from the 1870s on was to find some means to control the quality of lawyers in the lower ranks of the profession. In the eyes of leading lawyers, the behavior of these lawyers in the lower courts eroded popular respect for the profession as a whole, and their service in legislatures often led to "over-legislation." Bar association activity was a tacit recognition that the bar elite could not, or would not, change trends by individual private action. The bar associations did not succeed very well in these aims. Judicial review proved to be a more potent weapon against "over-legislation" although even its efficacy was limited.

After about 1905, complaints about "over-legislation" diminished in bar association proceedings, to be replaced by complaints about the alleged corrupting effects on the administration of justice of the growing influx of first- and second-generation immigrants into

---

[46] Maxwell Bloomfield, "Lawyers and Public Criticism: Challenge and Response in Nineteenth-Century America," American Journal of Legal History 15 (October 1971), 269-277.

the lower levels of the legal profession. The bar elite imagined that this influx threatened to debase the bar because the cultural traditions of immigrants had not prepared them to understand the unique role and position of the bar in Anglo-Saxon culture and society. In short, first- and second-generation immigrant lawyers became the symbolic focus for elite lawyers' growing uneasiness about both the increasing stratification within the bar and the modernistic trends in American culture generally, although the ethnic lawyers were not themselves in the vanguard of such modernistic trends. These trends were undermining not only the position of the legal profession, but also the old values associated with that position.

What was happening, of course, was that occupational specialization, the hallmark of the so-called organizational society, was appearing both within the legal profession and within the world of the professions generally. "Over-legislation," or the shift in the growing point of the law from the judiciary to the legislature, was but a symptom of this pervasive social change, albeit a symptom which signalled the demise of the <u>traditional</u> hegemonic function of the law and the legal profession.

Within the legal profession, specialization was especially noticeable at the higher levels, in corporate law practice where large firms emerged. The corporation lawyer came to replace the advocate as the leader and symbol of the profession. In fact, by the late nineteenth century, a paradox in the lawyer's role is apparent. At the same time that leading lawyers were extolling and protecting individualism in culture, politics, and social relations, they were developing the necessary legal instruments and were helping to organize the major organizational innovation in American society, the large corporation. In short, lawyers were at the center of the organizational revolution in American society, but at the same time they failed to develop a consistently bureaucratic-minded orientation.

One reason for this failure was that, although they recognized American society was increasingly composed of functional groups rather than atomistic individuals, lawyers were unwilling to admit the possibility that the law itself and the bench and bar were themselves simply another competing functional group or set of groups. Lawyers insisted on continuing to see the law as somehow transcendent. In addition, they understood that the older individualistic and moralistic social values, which they had always seen as functionally related to the rule of law, had not suddenly lost all of their hegemonic power.

But it would be misleading to portray leading lawyers as pure Machiavellians. They were also men who needed to make sense out of their own experience and whose ideologies therefore reflected the world as they came to know it through daily living. The professional lives of the bar elite increasingly isolated them from other classes to the extent that they were able to create unreal images of the dangerous tendencies lurking outside their select social circle. They therefore found it difficult to surrender their belief that the "best men" should rule and to think of social and governmental institutions in other than moralistic and individualistic terms. This moralism and individualism was buttressed by the fact that they saw themselves as individual successes, the products either of good genes or of strength of character, not as the products of a particular political economy. Another contribution to the continuing vitality of an individualistic orientation was that the law, like such other historic professions as medicine and the ministry, continued to be a "person" profession: that is, a profession which deals with its clients on an individual and often very personal basis, literally "getting inside the client" and becoming privy to his personal world.[47] This was true to some extent even when their clients were large corporations. In addition, because leading lawyers remained formally independent of the corporations whom they served, working out of large law firms rather than out of the corporation's legal department, they were able to maintain in their own minds the belief that they acted as individuals and as officers of the court rather than as appendages of the corporate system.

Because of the continuing individualist bias in their professional practice and because the bases of their expertise continued to be generally non-technical, elite lawyers were not strongly attracted to the progressive period marriage of technology and progress. This new style of progressive social thought, which was characterized by environmentalism and a revolt against formalism, assumed that the law should be seen as the product of social forces, as a dependent variable, so to speak, rather than as the independent variable

---

[47]William J. Goode, "The Theoretical Limits of Professionalization," in Goode, Explorations in Social Theory (New York, 1973), pp. 341-382.

and essential balance wheel that leading lawyers had
long believed it to be.[48] The bar elite was disposed
to be suspicious of these environmentalist and anti-
formalist views. The shift in middle class social
thought reflected the rise of new, more technically
based professions with interests in specific public
policies requiring greater state activism. Throughout
most of the nineteenth century, the lawyer had stood
out, with the physician, as a man of specialized
knowledge.[49] By the early years of the twentieth
century, the legal profession had to begin sharing this
special position with new professions. The roles of

---

[48] Richard Hofstadter, The Progressive Historians: Turner, Beard, Parrington (New York, 1968), pp. 181-206 contains a good discussion of these trends in social thought, as they affected conceptions of the law. He depicts these trends as the intellectual background against which Beard's book on the economic interpretation of the Constitution was written. Hofstadter refers to this revolt against formalism and this turn to a kind of realism as the emergence of a "modern critical intelligentsia." This was precisely the threat the bar elite saw.

[49] An important distinction needs to be made between the formalistic and traditional specialized knowledge of lawyers and doctors in the nineteenth century and the technically-based specialized knowledge of newer professions, including, by the end of the nineteenth century, the new generation of doctors.

these new professions were symbolized and implicit in the wider range of statutory and administrative law that was supplanting the historic conception of the rule of law the bar had constructed during the nineteenth century.[50] The bar elite's suspicion of such views turned into alarm and hostile defensiveness around 1910. At the time, some of the advocates of modernism in social thought and their political supporters openly attacked the bar and bench and proposed such measures as the popular recall of judges and of judicial decisions.[51]

At the same time, there were trends flowing in the other direction. The bar elite was surrendering its commitment to individualism in matters touching directly on the interests of its corporate clients. Leading lawyers, as a part of this general trend, were increasingly organizing their own practice in large quasi-bureaucratic law firms. To a lesser extent, the profession itself, under the guidance of the legal elite, was becoming organized and subject to bureaucratic rather than personal instruments of control. The courts, with the

---

[50] Hurst, "The Legal Profession," pp. 969-978.

[51] Steidle, "Conservative Progressives," pp. 313-374.

active support of local, state, and national bar associations, were becoming rationalized along the same lines, although here again, the trend was muted.

Perhaps most important, the locus of training for lawyers, including elite lawyers, was shifting from the personal supervision characteristic of the law office to the more bureaucratic setting of the law school. In those law schools, especially the elite ones, a new view of the law was emerging, one which insisted that legal knowledge could be systematized and made scientific and which at times suggested that perhaps the law was best seen as a dependent variable rather than as transcendent and immutable.

The legal elite, in its search for new means of achieving social stability, was open to considering such ideas. But during the progressive period, those ideas sounded too much like the themes expressed more crudely by the hostile and "fuzzy-minded" critics of the profession and by the advocates of judicial recall. However, by the 1920s, with the end of the progressive movement, several years of experience with economic regulatory agencies, the experience of "voluntarism" during World War I, and the increasing numbers of case-method-trained lawyers, the bar elite was willing to move in the direction of some of the new ideas--although never very far.

The crime survey movement and the establishment of the American Law Institute are prime examples of the rapprochment between leading lawyers and law school professors in the 1920s. Both were new departures, though in a very limited sense. Both involved the explicit recognition that organization and academic knowledge could simultaneously make the law and legal institutions more efficient and keep potential political issues concerning the law and legal institutions out of the public forum. The American Law Institute took as its mandate the clarifying and codifying of existing law, not the reconstruction or reform of the law. The crime survey movement was similar in many respects to civic reform efforts in which lawyers had been participating since at least the 1870s. The essential difference was that for the first time leading lawyers agreed that a legal topic should be the subject of a civic reform group involving more than lawyers. To be sure, local lawyers would be experts within that body, although even this principle was breached when outside academic experts were called in. In these instances and others during the 1920s, the bar elite was giving oblique recognition to the fact that they now had to accept a more circumscribed role within the local and national elite and that the legal system itself had become interdependent with the rest of society in a way it had not been in the nineteenth century. At the same time, the legal elite did not surrender its devotion to the market metaphor or to the belief that upward and downward social mobility were based on individual strength of character, two concepts which it continued to believe were the bulwarks of the rule of law and of social order in America.

These complex relationships between the social structure and ideology of the leading segments of the legal profession will be explored by examining in detail three crucial institutions, and the ideologies of the individuals who controlled these institutions, between 1890 and 1930: bar associations (local, state, and national), large law firms, and elite law schools.

PART II

MODERNIZATION AND THE LEGAL COMMUNITY:
AN OVERVIEW OF STRUCTURAL CHANGE

CHAPTER 3

OLD PROFESSIONS MODERNIZE:
LAW, ENGINEERING, MEDICINE

The three major structural changes in the legal profession during the 1890-1930 period were the development of large law firms, the growth in the number and importance of law schools, and the growth in the number and size of local, state, and national bar associations. These three structural changes were interrelated. Taken together, the three structural changes were both cause and consequence of a significant reorientation in the image and reality of bar professionalism.

Ideological and structural changes interacted in a complex way. That interaction can best be examined in the histories of those who were the most self-conscious and the most concerned to shape the course of events: the law professoriate and the leaders of the organized bar. Their histories will be examined in part three. But the ideas and activities of the law professoriate and the organized bar were not spontaneously generated. They developed in response to and were constrained by the growth of large law firms among the bar elite and by the emergence of law schools as the primary locus of legal training. These two structural changes, in turn, were shaped by larger forces outside the profession. Part two will examine the dynamics of these two structural changes prefatory to the more detailed examination of the relationship between ideology and structure in part three.

The pattern of structural changes in the legal profession was broadly similar to the pattern in other professions. However, when the structural changes of several professions are examined in detail, important contrasts are revealed. These contrasts provide a useful context within which to understand the significance of changes occurring in any one profession. Comparing changing elite career patterns and work situations in the legal profession to those in two other older professions, medicine and engineering, is especially instructive. Engineers became subordinate employees identifying as much or more with the interests of their corporate employers as with the ideals of an independent profession. Doctors managed to retain control of their employing organizations. Paradoxically, while reaping the benefits of organization, science, and technology, they were able to retain the traditional image of themselves as free professionals. Elite lawyers followed a pattern intermediate between these two extremes. They retained control of their own firms, but their interests and identities became attached to a narrower and more powerful set of clients than in the past.

****

During the ante-bellum period, medicine was practiced by a bewildering variety of sectarians. There were a few well-trained orthodox medical men in the largest cities. This elite group, often trained abroad, attempted during the early years of the century to create a well-educated profession in their own image. They scored some initial successes. But during the 1830s and 1840s, their efforts to create state licensing laws were defeated or repealed in several states, while in others they were emasculated by the granting of automatic licensing to all who graduated from a medical school. As a consequence, several diverse sectarian approaches to medical treatment were able to maintain a competitive position with orthodox medicine. The two most successful variants were Thomsonianism, which involved the use of steam baths and emetic herbs, and homeopathy, the vague belief that disease was a derangement of the immaterial vital principle pervading and animating the body by one of three chronic miasmas.[1]

As Joseph Kett has shown, the success of these sectarian variants was due to something more than the anti-institutional bias of the Jacksonian period. That was important, and it affected all professions. For example, bar admission standards were lowered in many states during these years. However, as minimal as they might have been, at least _some_ standards, some licensing requirements, were maintained for attorneys.

The public reluctance to define strictly who could practice medicine was due to the fact that the homeopaths, at least, served a real social need. (The Thomsonians did not and faded in the 1840s.) There simply were not enough trained orthodox medical men to serve the population. Orthodox medical men failed in their attempts to establish medical societies on the local, state, and national levels (the American Medical Association was not created until 1847) so as to distinguish the orthodox from the "quacks" and to exhort higher education standards. From about 1845 on, there

---

[1] Joseph Kett, The Formation of the Medical Profession: The Role of Institutions, 1780-1860 (New Haven, 1968).

was a general expectation that practitioners would have some medical training, but the specific content of that education was not mandated. The difference in the treatment provided by non-elite orthodox medical men and by homeopaths was not sufficiently great to warrant any other public attitude at a time when the supply of orthodox doctors was not great enough to serve the population adequately.[2]

The knowledge base, professional organization, and public reputation of the medical profession changed dramatically in the late nineteenth and early twentieth centuries. As the medical historian Rosemary Stevens has remarked,

> By World War I there was a standardized educational system geared to produce a highly trained medical journeyman and a standardized professional structure (the American Medical Association) geared to exert influence over the colleges and licensing bodies as well as over the practice of medicine. There was in short one unified medical profession, poised to become a politically active force.[3]

No other profession could make such claims by World War I, although others tried, including the legal profession. Medicine had become the model for other professions to

---

[2] Ibid.

[3] Rosemary Stevens, *American Medicine and the Public Interest* (New Haven, 1971), p. 73.

follow. Its claims to expertise were now based on solid scientific and technical accomplishments. Its internal self-discipline was almost complete, enlisting a majority of doctors in its national organization. The AMA extended its control over vital matters of training, admission, and ethics, and it exercised considerable influence over doctors and laymen who sought to introduce such changes as compulsory health insurance and group practice.

Paradoxically, the key to this successful unification of the medical profession was the emergence of specialization among doctors. It was not so much the simple fact that many doctors began to specialize. Specialization was a common development within all professions during the late nineteenth and early twentieth centuries. What was distinctive about medicine was that the profession was able to recognize and channel the drive to specialization in such a way that the profession became more unified rather than more diversified, as happened in law and engineering, for example.

New scientific and technical knowledge was at the basis of specialization in medicine. There were two phases to the change. During the 1870s and 1880s, the most ambitious American doctors and medical students went

to Vienna or Berlin to study. According to one study
of the relationship between American medicine and German
universities, between 30 and 40 percent of the most
prominent American doctors in the Gilded Age were trained
in Europe. Most went not to study basic medical science
but rather to do specialized post-graduate work,
primarily to gain clinical experience in a specialty.[4]
Those who went abroad during the 1870s and 1890s brought
home new knowledge and techniques from Vienna and Berlin.
But more importantly, American medical education began
to institutionalize this newly acquired knowledge. Thus,
the numbers going abroad began to decline somewhat in the
1890s and markedly after 1900.

Johns Hopkins University, under William H. Welch,
established the model. In 1893 it combined a research
hospital and a medical school to create a wholly new
institution staffed by full-time medical teachers.
Graduates from Johns Hopkins, graduates of German
universities, and a growing number of medical journals
all served to publicize the institutional model and to
sponsor the creation of similar medical schools. The

---

[4] Thomas Neville Bonner, American Doctors and German Universities; A Chapter in International Intellectual Relations, 1870-1914 (Lincoln, Neb., 1963), chap. 2.

elite medical schools were quickly becoming distinguished from the mass of proprietary medical schools by the specialized education they could provide. Such education produced dramatic improvements in medical knowledge and techniques, a fact which became very apparent in the 1890s when the acceptance of asepsis and antisepsis, combined with the earlier development of anesthesia, made surgery the first large-scale specialty. This development gave a significant impetus to the establishment of hospitals with standards sufficiently high that modern surgery could be performed in them. Once the investment in such hospitals had been made, the groundwork for a specialist-based profession had been created.[5]

All that remained was to unify the profession on terms acceptable to the specialists. In 1901 the American Medical Association, which had been a fairly ineffective body for half a century, adopted a federal structure. That is, it changed itself from an organization of individuals with a national perspective to a House of Delegates chosen from local and state affiliates. With this organizational innovation, the AMA became an effective advocate for the profession, or rather for the

---

[5] Stevens, American Medicine, pp. 34-74.

leading elements in the profession. The fact that the AMA was able to achieve this unity at a time when similar attempts in law and engineering were failing reflects the unity of aims and efforts that had emerged during the previous twenty years among local medical societies, licensing associations, and leading medical schools. They all agreed on the need to upgrade entrance standards to the profession, to specify the curricula in medical schools, to suppress the weakest proprietary schools, and to reduce the number of students graduating from medical schools.

All these efforts were carried on at the state level during the late nineteenth century and then transferred to the national level in 1904 when the revitalized AMA created a Council on Medical Education as a subsidiary organization. The Council gained the support of the Carnegie Foundation for the Advancement of Teaching for a focused investigation of medical schools throughout the country. This investigation produced the well-known Flexner Report, published in 1910. The report was uncompromising in its criticism of the existing state of many medical schools. The overriding message in the Report was the need to develop scientific excellence in medical schools. What this meant in practice was that marginal schools would be driven out of business and the number of doctors would cease to rise, two developments which did indeed occur the next decade.

There were other themes in the campaign against marginal medical schools besides the one stressed in the Flexner Report. A recent examination by Gerald E. Markowitz and David Karl Rosner of medical journals in the years before and just after the Report emphasizes that the desire to raise doctors' status and income was an important part of the campaign. Many doctors complained about their poverty and attributed it to the fact that the profession was "overcrowded," especially in Eastern states. According to Rosemary Stevens, the overcrowding argument was especially appealing to general practitioners, a large group in the profession whose support was essential to the success of the movement. The general practitioners benefited only indirectly from changes in medical education and from the emergence of specialists, and they had every reason to begin to fear the growing power and influence of the specialists. In the 1920s, conflict between general practitioners and specialists became the central issue within the AMA. But during the period that the Flexner Report had its greatest impact (1910-1920), the general practitioners supported the modernization efforts, probably because they thought the efforts would raise their status and incomes.[6]

By World War I the medical profession had greater organizational strength and cohesion than the legal profession and was far more willing to recognize explicitly the specialization which had been the hallmark of developments during the preceding thirty to forty years. Specialization could lead to unity in the medical profession because it was built on substantial increases in medical knowledge and techniques. These increases greatly enhanced the status and power of the profession, indirectly by increasing public respect for the profession and directly by providing sanction for controls on the number of doctors. The latter move increased the incomes of all physicians, whether specialists or not. No doctor who wanted to be progressive could resist the demand that he support institutions and reforms which were improving the quality of medical care. In addition, there was a clear

---

[6] Stevens, American Medicine, pp. 55-74; Gerald E. Markowitz and David Karl Rosner, "Doctors in Crisis: A Study of the Use of Medical Education Reform to Establish Modern Professional Elitism in Medicine," American Quarterly 25 (May 1973), 82-107; Abraham Flexner, Medical Education in the United States and Canada (New York, 1910); Richard H. Shryock, Medical Licensing in America, 1650-1965 (Baltimore, 1967); James G. Burrow, AMA: Voice of American Medicine (Baltimore, 1963); Forrest A. Walker,

proscription within the profession on allowing a hierarchy among the emerging specialties to develop. True, some specialists, for example, surgeons, were given greater deference than other specialists, for example, pediatricians. However, the differentials were never allowed to become great. Both the fact that all physicians under the new regime were trained in the same medical schools and experienced roughly the same internship and residency training, and the fact that major city hospitals recognized the legitimacy of all specialties the licensing boards were willing to certify, contributed to the unity of the profession. A potential split between the specialists and general practitioners was averted during the crucial years between 1900 and 1920, largely, it seems, because no one could deny the impressiveness of the new knowledge and techniques which had given birth to the new specialties.

****

"Compulsory Health Insurance: 'The Next Great Step in Social Legislation'," Journal of American History 56 (September 1969), 296-301; John C. Burnham, "Medical Specialists and Movements Toward Social Control in the Progressive Era: Three Examples," Jerry Israel, ed., Building the Organizational Society, Essays on Associational Activities in Modern America (New York, 1972), pp. 19-30.

In law the pattern was very different, although there too the emergence of specialization was directly linked to an organizational innovation in which the new specialists worked. But in the legal profession, the organizational innovation--the large law firm--was a response to the needs of another new urban industrial institution--the modern large corporation. The large law firm did not represent, as the general hospital did in medicine, the institutionalization of new scientific knowledge and techniques. The genuine specialists in the legal profession were a much smaller proportion of the total profession by 1920 than were their counterparts in the medical profession. This fact greatly hampered the legal elite's attempts to create the degree of unity and organizational strength that the medical elite was achieving.

Another important factor, closely linked to the fact that specialization in the law was not rooted in new scientific knowledge or techniques, was that clear hierarchical distinctions emerged among lawyers. These distinctions depended upon the types of practices lawyers had, the nature and social class of their clients, the size of their firms, the nature of their legal training, the physical location of their offices, the size of their

incomes, and, often, their ethnic and family connections.[7]
Such divisions certainly existed in medicine, but they
were overridden by one great source of unity: new and
effective scientific knowledge and techniques. No such
source of unity existed among lawyers. As a result,
such specialization as existed, whether among the upper
bar or the lower bar, was not formally recognized.
Though it existed as a blatant and obvious fact, it was
not given open recognition.

One contemporary observer, Alfred Z. Reed, who
wrote the legal profession's equivalent of the Flexner
Report, believed that the distinction between elite and
non-elite lawyers had become analogous to that between
physicians and other medical health professionals,
such as pharmacists, nurses, midwives, dentists, and
veterinarians. He urged elite lawyers to recognize
the reality of the distinctions within the profession,
believing that if they did so the legal profession could

---

[7] Joel Handler, The Lawyer and His Community (Madison, 1967), pp. 4-5; Jerome Carlin, Lawyer's Ethics: A Survey of the New York City Bar (New York, 1966), p. 169; Carlin, Lawyers on Their Own: A Study of Individual Practitioners in Chicago (New Brunswick, N. J., 1962); Jack Ladinsky, "Careers of Lawyers, Law Practice, and Legal Institutions," American Sociological Review 28 (February 1961), 47-54; Kenneth J. Reichstein, "Ambulance Chasing: A Case Study of Deviation and Control Within the

become as organizationally strong as the medical profession had.[8] But Reed was not nearly so influential as Flexner had been. The fiction was maintained that the practice of law was one thing, that anyone trained as a lawyer could perform the functions of anyone else trained as a lawyer. Attorneys gave lie to that premise everyday in their actions, in their private discussions among themselves, and in their treatment of fellow members of the bar, but that was no matter.

The legal elite had very good reasons for trying to preserve the conception of the bar which had grown up over the years. Their reasons were closely tied to their political and social views, views which in turn owed much to their self-conception and even to their personal style as lawyers. To them, the legal profession had a unique and valuable role to play as a mediating and stabilizing force in a society in the throes of rapid and often heedless change.

Legal Profession," Social Problems 13 (Summer 1965), 3-17; Wilbert E. Moore, The Professions: Roles and Rules (New York, 1970), pp. 90-91. Although all of these studies are based on the mid-twentieth-century bar, it is clear from contemporary testimony that they represent patterns going back at least to the turn of the century.

[8]Alfred Z. Reed, Training for the Public Profession of the Law: Historical Development and Principal Contemporary Problems of Legal Education in the United States with Some Account of Conditions in England and Canada (New York, 1921), pp. 216-217.

Elite lawyers never were willing to see themselves purely and simply as spokesmen for corporate interests. They preferred to think of themselves as preserving principles and institutions, such as private property and the rule of law. The profession's leading members were very touchy about the label "corporation lawyer," which became attached to so many of them in the years after 1890. A distinction that leading lawyers wished all their critics would make was neatly drawn by Elihu Root's biographer, Philip C. Jessup, when he summarized his impressions after hearing Root recount a major case. Root had become the counsel for Hill and Morgan rather than for Harriman in the Northern Securities case simply because Morgan's lawyer, Francis Lynde Stetson, had contacted him a few hours before Harriman had. Jessup decided he

> might describe it by saying that Mr. Root was not so much a corporation lawyer as a lawyer with corporate clients. He was the attorney for important affairs, and when those affairs were centered in the hands of corporations, he necessarily had corporate clients.[9]

---

[9] Notes on a conversation with Elihu Root, May 4, 1930, Box 243, Philip C. Jessup MSS, Library of Congress.

William Howard Taft made the same distinction in defending his choice of George W. Wickersham as Attorney General.

> The proposition that Wickersham is connected in any way with corporate interests is ridiculous. He has no financial interest in any of them. He is a corporation lawyer, but why the United States should not have the benefit of as good a lawyer as the corporations, I don't know.[10]

Taft recognized that "there are lawyers who are nothing but corporation promoters and who are so identified with the business of their corporation and so much interested financially in their profits that they are not lawyers at all."[11] But he knew Wickersham did not fall into that category. Wickersham's own position was made quite clear in a letter written to his son in law school.

> Never become a director of <u>any</u> company. A lawyer has no business to be a <u>director</u> in a company of which he is counsel. The only times I have departed from this rule--and they are only two or three instances--I have regretted it. . . . The failure to observe [this rule] has I believe contributed much to impair the position which lawyers once occupied in the public esteem.[12]

---

[10] William Howard Taft to E. F. Baldwin, December 24, 1908, W. H. Taft MSS, Series 8, Sec. War Per. Letterbook XXXIII, 254, as cited in James C. German, Jr., "Taft's Attorney General: George W. Wickersham," (Ph.D. dissertation, New York University, 1969), p. 15.

[11] Ibid.

[12] George W. Wickersham to Cornelius Wickersham, May 4, 1910, G. W. Wickersham MSS, as cited in German, "George W. Wickersham," p. 15n.

Philander Knox, who was closely identified with U.S. Steel, insisted on making the same distinction between a corporation lawyer and a lawyer with corporations as clients.

> My idea of a corporation lawyer is a man who gives his whole time to the service of a corporation and not a lawyer who may have corporations among his clients. It is not who a lawyer's clients are but the nature of the service he has rendered to them that determines the lawyer's character. If he has served corporations only to protect their legal rights he has performed a duty which is required of him by the obligations he has assumed to the community in entering his profession. If he has used his learning and influence to enable a corporation to evade the law or to perpetuate acts of injustice, he is morally culpable and violates his professional obligations as well. It is the moral quality of the act and not the identity of the client served that is to be taken into consideration.[13]

Elite lawyers insisted on the image of the independent lawyer protecting his clients whoever they might be, thereby ignoring the possible relevance of gross inequalities in wealth and power between potential clients. In so insisting, these lawyers were holding onto a conception of the lawyer's role that was more appropriate to a society of atomistic individuals than to an organizational society. By insisting that the

---

[13]Note unsigned and undated, but attributed to Knox, P. C. Knox MSS, Box 2, Library of Congress.

primary consideration for judging a lawyer was the moral quality of his acts, by defining morality in terms of professional ethics, Knox was claiming the prerogatives of professionalism established by nineteenth-century lawyers before the rise of specialization within the bar.

Elite lawyers could hang on to this view of their role, despite its many contradictions, partly because they could maintain considerable formal independence while performing their professional role. A striking and informative contrast with the engineering profession can be made in this regard.

****

Engineering, like law, was an old profession that modernized in the late nineteenth century. As Monte Calvert has shown, that modernization provoked a conflict among mechanical engineers between the "school men" and the "shop men." The shop men represented the older professional elite. They were often recruited from upper-class families seeking a tie to industrial culture that was not too blatantly entrepreneurial. Developing their professional skills in the small machine shops that produced tools and products on order, the shop men were the mainstay of the mechanical engineering profession until the late nineteenth century. Beginning about 1870, when universities started establishing engineering schools, a new group entered the profession. The engineering schools stressed the advantages of a solid grounding in mathematics; they also promoted the expansion of the profession by admitting large numbers of students with a middle-class or lower-middle-class background.

Between 1890 and 1910, a dispute raged between the school men and the shop men. The focus was on such issues as admission standards to engineering schools, the degree of proficiency in manual shop skills that should be required of a mechanical engineer, and the nature of the apprenticeship an engineer should serve. The shop men were not opposed to a technical education, for many of them had considerable technical education. They simply insisted that shop training was in many ways superior to technical training and that, in any case, shop training should definitely precede formal higher education. An important theme in the conflict seems to have been the image and social status of the profession. The shop men wanted to retain the image of the engineer as an autonomous independent professional, an entrepreneur perhaps, but certainly not a bureaucratic functionary.[14]

---

[14] Monte A. Calvert, The Mechanical Engineer in America, 1830-1910: Professional Cultures in Conflict (Baltimore, 1967).

The school men were not necessarily opposed to the image of the engineer as an autonomous independent professional. But they were not inclined to reverse the major employment trend in the profession, which was that increasing numbers of engineering school graduates were going to work in bureaucratic situations with no immediate expectation of a managerial or ownership role. Ultimately, a certain number could expect to move into management. But by then their independence as engineers would have been badly compromised, as such promotions were dependent upon internalizing the assumptions and aims of the firm rather than of the profession. Accompanying this move into bureaucratic work situations was a growing specialization, which often meant a lower level of competence was expected of any particular engineer. A further dimension of these changes was that the profession as a whole was suffering a general decline in status.

After 1900, engineers in all fields attempted to synthesize their business (or bureaucratic) and professional orientations. Among the mechanical engineers, this attempt took the form of the scientific management movement. Scientific management was not strongly supported by the school men. Shop men were stronger supporters because the movement promised an elite role for engineers, albeit a more bureaucratized and less personalized role than they would have preferred. The logical consequence of adopting scientific management would have been to place nearly all business decisions in the hands of the corporation planning department, where engineers would have control. But scientific management and the other less fully articulated parallel movements in the other branches of engineering never achieved the hopes of their supporters.

As Edwin T. Layton has made clear, such movements were severely circumscribed by strong pressures within the profession for engineers to accommodate themselves to the business rather than the professional orientation of their roles. The ideal career pattern, as emphasized both by the professors in the engineering schools and by the employers in the corporations, was to move into management positions, with the understanding that decisions there would be made as much according to business as engineering criteria. In fact, the scientific management and similar movements were a transitional reaction against this emerging pattern. But the movements were only a transitional phenomenon. By the 1920s, the various professional associations of engineers were strongly

influenced by ex-engineers who had moved into management.
These former engineers used their influence within the
associations to stifle anti-business discontent by, for
example, preventing the publication of articles critical
of public utility rates in engineering journals.[15]

****

In the legal profession, the old elite, as epitomized
by such men as Joseph H. Choate and Elihu Root, made a much
more graceful accommodation to new trends. The old elite
maintained control of the profession, while at the same
time promoting a number of innovations which significantly
changed the profession. A conflict of sorts did develop
between school men--such as Roscoe Pound, John H. Wigmore,
and William Draper Lewis in the elite law schools--and
elite practitioners. There are some parallels between that
conflict and the one within mechanical engineering. But,
for the most part, the school men in law had less influence
over the new generation of practitioners than their
counterparts had in engineering. The influence that the
school men did have in law was subtle. That influence,

---

[15] Ibid.; Edwin T. Layton, The Revolt of the Engineers; Social Responsibility and the American Engineering Profession (Cleveland, 1971).

combined with other trends to be discussed in later chapters, did lead to a fairly widespread adoption of many of the school men's viewpoints by the 1920s. But seen in retrospect, that development does not seem to have been so much a "victory" won by the school men as the end product of the working out of changes largely initiated by the old elite. The school men may have been ahead of the elite in seeing the full implications of the direction in which the profession was heading. But it is not accurate to say that a change analogous to the replacement of the "shop culture" with the "school culture" had occurred.

Why was law different? The main explanation can be found in a simple but powerful fact: whereas engineers increasingly became employees of businesses and their preferred career line led them into management, lawyers continued to work under professional supervision. Although some lawyers moved into corporation law departments, the elite of the profession headed the large law firms in major cities. Those lawyers who became corporation directors identified themselves first and foremost as lawyers rather than as businessmen, although of course the potential difference between the two orientations was smaller in law than in engineering.

The elite lawyers who formed the first large law firms were the men who changed the dominant image of the lawyer from the advocate to the counselor. They themselves usually retained the advocate's role. Choate and Root, for example, always thought of themselves as court lawyers, and they owed their public prominence in no small measure to the fact that they were advocates. The change in roles occurred among the younger men they took on first as associates and then as partners. But the important point is that the change occurred within law firms and not by the creation of new institutional arrangements for the practice of law.[16]

That lawyers were able to maintain greater professional autonomy than engineers seems traceable, paradoxically, to the same factor that helps explain the bar's relative organizational weakness and lack of unity

---

[16] As late as 1930, 94 percent of the lawyers, judges, and justices were listed by the Census as either in the "Professional Service" (87 percent) or "Public Service" (7 percent) categories. Of the 6 percent employed directly by businesses, more than half were in either railroad companies, insurance companies, or banking, brokerage, and real estate firms, indicating the immaturity of the corporation law department in manufacturing industries. In comparison, only 42 percent of engineers were listed in "Professional Service," a figure inflated by the fact that engineers in management were not counted as engineers. Bureau of the Census, Fifteenth Census, Vol. V., Population, General Report on Occupations.

vis-à-vis medicine: the lower level of technical knowledge among lawyers. In medicine, technical knowledge helped unify the profession and gave legitimacy to the doctors' desire to control such large organizations as the general hospital, which utilized their expertise. In engineering, there was less public consensus on the proper use of the profession's technical knowledge. Effective use of that knowledge did not require a close personal relationship with clients. An engineer's clients were much better organized and more powerful than a doctor's clients. Therefore, technical knowledge and the attendant specialization tended to make engineers sophisticated but replaceable cogs in the industrial machinery. Only by moving into decision-making positions in management could they rise above the level of replaceable parts.

Lawyers, at least elite lawyers, did not face that threat. Because their knowledge was less technical, that is, because the law was a less exact science, their personal reputations and legal and business contacts and experience counted for more. This was especially true in such complex matters as corporate reorganizations. Paul D. Cravath, a member of the New York financial bar, acknowledged that in most cases when a distinction between economic and legal questions could be made, it was not the duty of a lawyer to give advice to his client on economic questions.

> If you tell him what he may lawfully do, you may usually leave it to him to decide what he may wisely do. But in reorganizations, particularly if your clients are inexperienced in reorganization practice, it is often the duty of counsel to advise them both as to the practical and legal aspects of the questions presented for decision. A plan of reorganization, however lawful, will bring disappointment and discredit to its authors if its terms are not such as to command the support of security holders. It is quite as important to propose a plan which will be supported by the security holders as one which will be supported by the courts.[17]

It is significant that whereas Elihu Root's attitude was that "about half the practice of a decent lawyer consists in telling would-be clients that they are damned fools and should stop," a recent study of salaried lawyers in corporation law departments found very little sense of role ambiguity: they saw themselves as members of the corporate team, not as lawyers who happened to be working for a large organization.[18] But corporation

---

[17] Paul D. Cravath, "The Reorganization of Corporations; Bondholders' Protective Committees; Reorganization Committees; and the Voluntary Recapitalization of Corporations," in Francis Lynde Stetson et al., Some Legal Phases of Corporate Financing, Reorganization and Regulation (New York, 1917), pp. 153-154.

[18] Philip C. Jessup, Elihu Root, 2 vols. (New York, 1938), 1:133; John D. Donnell, The Corporate Counsel: A Role Study (Bloomington, Ind., 1970), p. 163.

law departments were slower to develop than engineering departments and typically have been responsible only for routine legal problems. Corporations retain independent firms for more important matters, especially those involving dealings with the financial community or with government, where contacts and experience count for as much as legal knowledge.

But in more strictly legal questions, personal knowledge and experience, as opposed to purely technical knowledge, are also important. This is largely traceable to the central role of the judge in determining what the law is and is not. The elite lawyer's role was to persuade the appellate judge to find a legal formula favoring his client. Judges could not be counted on to be predictable. But certain lawyers had developed the skill of gaining favorable rulings. Obviously, not just any similarly trained lawyer could achieve the same results. Hence, elite lawyers had good reason to support strongly the independence of the judiciary. For on it depended their continued independence, or at least the continuation of their accustomed performance of their professional role.

CHAPTER 4

CHANGES IN LEGAL TRAINING: FROM THE LAW OFFICE TO THE LAW SCHOOL

The modernization of the legal profession did not depend on dramatic advances in legal knowledge or techniques; rather it was an adaptive response to changes centered in the economy. But changes in legal education did affect the specific course that modernization took within the profession. During the 1890s, the law school replaced the law office as the primary locus of legal training. As a consequence, practitioners lost direct control over admission to the profession. The way was opened for the admission of men and women who might never have found a place in law offices because their ethnocultural background varied from that of most practitioners. This new group of urban immigrant lawyers became an important negative reference group for leading lawyers after 1900. At the same time, the expansion of law schools created the opportunity for a new specialty to emerge within the profession: the full-time law teacher-scholar. This new law professoriate, centered in university law schools, constructed a professional ideology. The practitioner elite was forced to confront and evaluate this ideology in its own attempts to preserve and increase the profession's social and political influence after 1900.

Until very late in the nineteenth century, the manner in which men and (rarely) women gained admission to the legal profession was something like the system described by New York lawyer Francis M. Finch:

> Men totally unfit registered their names as clerks and then picked up in a way both lazy and unsystematic enough of the Blackstone and Kent and enough of practice, through the copying of papers, to pass the very lazy and timid examination of a sudden committee drafted from a reluctant Bar. . . . He absorbed what law he knew rather than studied it.[1]

During the late Gilded Age, the law office was supplanted by the law school as the typical training locale for lawyers. Related to this change was an increasing standardization of bar examinations. The shift to law school education was most dramatic among the middle and lower strata of the bar. In fact, it

---

[1] Francis M. Finch, "Presidential Address," New York State Bar Association, Reports 24 (1901), 47. For a good summary of ante-bellum bar admission standards, see Lawrence M. Friedman, A History of American Law (New York, 1973), pp. 276-277.

occurred almost before the legal elite was aware of it. For elite lawyers, law school training had been a common experience throughout the nineteenth century. An examination of the obituaries of leading lawyers in the American Bar Association Reports, 1900-1911, reveals that a majority of these men had some college education and law school education; they often combined office training with law school work. The massive shift within the profession to law school training affected the elite, but less directly and less dramatically than it did the other strata of the bar.

By 1910 new members of the bar in highly urbanized states--even those not destined for the elite--almost always had law school backgrounds. Jerold Auerbach has estimated that in 1870, one-fourth of those admitted to the bar were law school graduates and in 1910 two-thirds were.[2] Only 18 percent of those presenting themselves for admission to the New York bar in 1900 had no law school training at all. By 1919 the figure was down to less than 3 percent.[3] New law schools were created

---

[2] Jerold S. Auerbach, "Enmity and Amity: Law Teachers and Practitioners, 1900-1922," Perspectives in American History 5 (1971), 573, citing American Law School Review 1 (1902), 14; Green Bag 15 (1903), 217; ABA, Reports 24 (1901), 399-401; ibid. 29 (1916), 678.

[3] New York State Bar Association, Reports 24 (1901), 52; ibid. 43 (1920), 323.

in large numbers to train aspiring lawyers. Many of these were proprietary law schools, often attracting night students who worked during the daytime. Other new law schools were located in universities.

A major issue emerged during the 1900 to 1920 period concerning the nature of the legal education to be provided in the university law schools. A small group of elite law schools, which aspired to set national standards, struggled successfully to impose their model on the majority of university law schools. That controversy revealed that the change in training from law office to law school had made legal education and admission to the bar much more subject to organization, disputation, control, and regulation than ever before.

****

Beginning in 1870, the United States Commissioner of Education kept records on the number of law schools and of law school students. These figures are summarized in table 1.[4] They show an initial surge of growth in law

---

[4] Summaries of the Commissioners Reports can be found in Alfred Z. Reed, <u>Training for the Public Profession of the Law: Historical Development and Principal Contemporary Problems of Legal Education in the United States with Some Account of Conditions in England and Canada</u> (New York, 1921) pp. 442-445; "Report of the Committee on Legal Education and Admission to the Bar," ABA, <u>Reports</u> 20 (1897), 387-388. The figures in the following discussion are drawn from these sources.

schools during the 1870s, as the number of schools increased almost two-thirds and the number of students nearly 90 percent. That growth leveled off during the 1880s, although the number of students grew at a rate twice that of the growth of schools, with most of that growth occurring at the end of the decade. In 1886-1887 there were 3,185 students in law schools, only fifty more than in 1880. By 1889-1890 that figure had jumped to 4,518. The economic downturn of the mid-1880s may help to explain the slow growth during that decade, although the more severe depressions of the 1870s and 1890s had no such apparent effect on law school enrollments.

TABLE 1

LAW SCHOOLS AND LAW STUDENTS

	1870	1880	1890	1900	1910	1920
Number of law schools	31	51	61	102	124	143
Number of law students	1,653	3,134	4,518	12,516	19,567	c.27,000

A more likely explanation for the slow growth during the 1880s is that several private colleges branched out into professional education before they were fully committed to such education. During the 1870s, twenty-six new schools were started, of which twenty were still in

operation in 1880, but only twelve in 1890. The great
majority of these schools were in Protestant or non-
sectarian colleges or universities. (See table 2.)
Seventeen such colleges had law departments in 1870;
this number grew to thirty in 1880 and dropped to twenty-
nine in 1890, despite the fact that twenty-two new
law schools were created during the 1880s. The new schools
created during the 1880s were primarily in state colleges,
either four-year institutions or expanded normal schools.
One-third of the law schools in operation in 1890 had been
created during the previous ten years. Their mortality
rate was quite low, indicating that student demand during
the 1880s was sufficient to sustain law schools in
institutions with a commitment to professional education.
Twenty of the twenty-two new schools were still in
operation in 1890 and eighteen in 1900.

TABLE 2

LAW SCHOOLS BY CATEGORIES

	1870	1880	1890	1900	1910	1920
Non-collegiate	3	5	11	24	37	48
State university	10	14	19	26	34	36
Private college or university	18	32	31	52	53	59
Total	31	51	61	102	124	143

All of these fitful beginnings turned into a floodtide in the 1890s. During that decade, forty-three new schools were started so that by 1900, 40 percent of the schools operating had been created during the previous ten years. The total number of law schools grew by two-thirds. Even more dramatic is the growth in the number of students. Their number climbed an astounding 177 percent, at a time when the bar as a whole was growing at a rate of 36 percent. There was some increase in the number of state university law schools, from fourteen to nineteen. But the most dramatic increases occurred in non-collegiate law schools, from eleven to twenty-four, and in private college law schools, from thirty-one to fifty-two. The latter had reached a plateau in their growth by mid-decade. In 1910, there were forty-four of them and in 1920 forty-three. On the other hand, the non-collegiate law schools continued to grow in numbers, reaching thirty-seven in 1910 and forty-eight in 1920.

A comparison of the figures on the growth of the profession and the increase in law schools and law school students clearly reveals that one form of training was substituted for another. The law schools did not contribute to any "overcrowding" of the profession. The decade of the most spectacular increases in law school attendance, the 1890s, witnessed a slower growth in the size of the profession than in each of the previous two decades. In the 1890s, the number of law students increased five times as fast as the number of lawyers. The first two decades of the twentieth century, when the law school was becoming firmly established as the normal locale of training, were the years of slowest growth in the profession of any years between 1870 and 1930. The rate was less than 1 percent between 1900 and 1910 and only 7 percent between 1910 and 1920. At the same time, those listed by the Census in "Professional Service" occupations increased by 45 percent between 1900 and 1910 and by 26.8 percent between 1910 and 1920. (See tables 3, 4, and 5.) Throughout the latter half of the nineteenth century, there had been a steady growth in the number of lawyers and in the proportion of lawyers to the general population. That growth reached a peak in 1900, declined for the next twenty years, and began to resume in the 1920s. Law schools made a parallel secular growth but did not become a truly significant factor in the growth of the profession as a whole until the 1890s.[5]

---

[5]Alba M. Edwards, Comparative Occupation Statistics for the United States, 1870 to 1940 (Washington: Bureau of the Census, 1943), p. 111.

TABLE 3

PROPORTION OF LAWYERS AND OTHER PROFESSIONALS
TO TOTAL POUPLATION

	1870	1880	1890	1900	1910	1920	1930
All professional service	165	91	72	64	54	49	38
Lawyers	954	783	702	664	802	866	764
Physicians	619	584	602	576	608	729	798
Engineers	5,620	7,120	2,225	1,753	1,035	776	543
Clergymen	888	777	714	681	780	829	827

[to aid in interpreting the table: the upper left hand cell means, for example, that in 1870 there was one professional for every 165 inhabitants of the nation. The lower the number, the greater the proportion of professionals to the total population]

TABLE 4

PERCENTAGE OF THOSE IN PROFESSIONAL
SERVICE WHO WERE LAWYERS

1870	1880	1890	1900	1910	1920	1930
12.2	11.7	10.2	9.7	6.7	5.6	4.9

TABLE 5

GROWTH RATE OF PROFESSIONS

(In Percentages)

	1870-80	1880-90	1890-00	1900-10	1910-20	1920-30
Total population	25.9	25.4	20.8	20.8	15.1	17.1
Professional service	60.7	59.4	34.5	45.0	26.8	49.9
Lawyers	53.4	39.7	36.0	.2	7.0	31.1
Physicians	33.1	22.4	26.0	14.5	-4.1	6.1
Clergymen	44.0	36.3	26.8	5.7	7.8	16.8
Dentists	54.2	42.0	69.5	33.8	40.3	26.5
Engineers	---	300.5	53.1	105.2	53.4	66.2
College professors	---	---	---	123.6	113.2	85.3

In fact, the growth in the profession during
the twenty-five years after the Civil War was probably
more of a factor in the emergence of law schools than
vice versa. That growth seems linked most closely
to the increasing urbanization of the profession, which
was in turn related to the changing function of the
law in an increasingly urbanized and industrialized
nation.

During the Gilded Age, the volume of reported
cases grew enormously, reflecting not only changes
in the nature of legal business but also the same
technological changes in printing and distribution
which contributed to the mass marketing of popular
magazines during these years. This development was both
a symptom and a cause of the growing complexity of
the law. Blackstone and Kent were becoming obsolete
as guides and no new updated compilations could fulfill the role they had once served. Theron G. Strong,
a leading lawyer who lived through this change, remarked near the end of the nineteenth century that
the emergence of a myriad of reported cases "has
virtually transformed the profession from a class
of lawyers able to practice without law books to a class

almost entirely dependent on the adjudged cases."[6]
As a consequence, systematic study rather than practical familiarity with the law in its actual operation was becoming more essential.

At the same time, law offices, especially in larger cities, were increasingly reluctant to take on law clerks to read law in their offices. The coming of the typewriter and the stenographer eliminated the routine jobs they had performed.[7] The new large firms continued to want apprentice lawyers, but they wanted men who had already had a grounding in the principles of the law.

The changing nature of universities and colleges and of their role in American life also contributed to the growth of law schools. In the ante-bellum period, colleges and universities required professional schools associated with them to be self-supporting. Teachers assessed and collected the fees and were responsible for keeping the school solvent. Harvard University,

---

[6] Theron G. Strong, Landmarks of a Lawyer's Lifetime (New York, 1914), p. 427, as quoted in George W. Martin, Causes and Conflicts: The Centennial History of the Bar of New York, 1870-1970 (Boston, 1970), p. 196.

[7] A good general discussion of the various reasons the law school supplemented the law office can be found in Preble Stolz, "Clinical Experience in American Legal Education: Why Has It Failed?" in Edward W. Kitch, ed., Clinical Education and the Law School of the Future (Chicago, 1970), pp. 54-76.

the University of Virginia, and the University of
Michigan were about the only exceptions to this pattern
before the 1870s. In 1878, Columbia put the law
faculty on a salaried basis and took over financial
management of the law department. Cornell followed suit
in 1887, the University of Pennsylvania in 1888, New
York University in 1889, and Northwestern in 1891,
confirming the new trend. Yale continued on the old
basis until 1904, apparently as a part of its general
reluctance to follow the new trends in legal education,
including the case method of instruction.[8]

The growth during the 1890s was certainly not due
to any innovations in legal education initiated during
that decade. One close student of the law school's
development, Alfred Z. Reed, concluded that the crucial
1890-1915 period witnessed no new ideas, but rather
an increasing emphasis on using existing machinery to
standardize and force into more general use devices
developed during the 1865-1890 period. He believed
the 1890 changes in legal training were due to "the
coming of a new and more imitative generation into power."[9]

---

[8] Reed, Training, pp. 44-45, 183-185; Elizabeth G. Brown, Legal Education at Michigan, 1859-1959 (Ann Arbor, 1959), p. 69.

[9] Reed, Training, pp. 392-393.

The changes Reed saw occurring in the 1890-1915 period utilized ideas generated during the previous quarter century and included more than just the switch in training from the law office to the law school. He included the following changes in his list as well: more active interest by the bar elite (that is, the ABA) in the subject of legal education, lengthening of the course to three years in the leading law schools and the adoption of a six-year academic and professional course in major universities, emergence of night law schools, acceptance by an increasing number of practitioners and law schools of the Harvard case method, and centralized state bar examinations.[10]

The newest idea in this list was the night law school. Strictly speaking, it was not a new idea. By the mid-1880s, there were three night law schools in Washington, D.C., for clerks in government departments. These were Columbia College, established in 1865 (now George Washington University Law School), Georgetown University Law School, and National University Law School. A Georgetown graduate introduced the idea outside of Washington for the first time in 1884,

---

[10]Ibid.

creating Northwestern College of Law in Portland, Oregon. The idea was first tried in a major metropolis in 1888, when the Metropolis Law School was formed in New York City. (It later was absorbed into New York University.) In Chicago, the Chicago College of Law (later the Chicago Kent Law School) was created as an affiliate of Lake Forest College. Also in 1888, the Baltimore University Law School (later absorbed into the University of Maryland) was created.[11]

The success of these innovations, which were major contributors to the upsurge in law school enrollments in the late 1880s, revealed the strong demand for evening and night instruction in major cities. An important ingredient in this demand were first- and second-generation immigrants. The steadily increasing ethnic mix within the profession was almost certainly due partially to the willingness of law schools to take in immigrants who might have found it difficult to gain admittance to a law office to read law, given the historic ethnic exclusiveness of the bar.

Between 1900 and 1910, the absolute number of native-born white lawyers with native-born parents went down, from about 86,000 to about 83,900, while

---

[11] Ibid., p. 397.

the number of first- or second-generation immigrant lawyers had increased from 27,200 to 30,100. In 1900, 75.6 percent of lawyers had native-born parents. In 1910, the figure was 73 percent and in 1920, it was 70.6 percent. In New York City, lawyers with native-born parents constituted 53.5 percent of the bar in 1900 and 44.6 percent in 1920. In Chicago, the figures were 54.3 percent and 44.6 percent respectively. Another way to state the New York-Chicago comparison which captures both their difference and their similarity is to note that between 1900 and 1920 in New York, native-born white lawyers with native-born parents increased by 20.3 percent, whereas first- and second-generation immigrant lawyers increased by 72.2 percent. In Chicago, the figures were a <u>decline</u> of 11.7 percent among native-born white lawyers with native-born parents and an increase of 28.4 percent among first- and second-generation immigrant lawyers.[12]

It should be emphasized that these trends in the ethnic mix of the bar were not unique to law among the

---

[12] Bureau of the Census, <u>12th Census of the United States</u>, Special Reports, Occupations (Washington, 1904); <u>13th Census of the United States</u>, Vol. IV, <u>Population</u>, Occupations (Washington, 1923).

professions. Whereas the total number of physicians increased 11 percent between 1900 and 1920, the native-born white physicians with native-born parents increased only 1.75 percent and the first- and second-generation immigrant physicians increased 27.3 percent. In 1900, 73.5 percent of the nation's physicians were native-born whites with native-born parents and by 1920 that percentage had slipped to 68.4. Thus, medicine remained only slightly less native than the law. Dentistry, a much faster growing profession (up 85.3 percent between 1900 and 1920), changed its ethnic mix from 73 percent with native-born parents in 1900 to 62.5 percent in 1920. The native-born with native-born parents segment of the profession grew at a rate of 61.8 percent during those two decades, whereas the first- and second-generation immigrant segment of the profession grew at a rate of 160.5 percent. That latter figure was surpassed in magnitude only among the engineers, who grew at a fantastic rate of 213.0 percent from 1900 to 1920. The interesting point about the growth in the engineering profession is that the ethnic mix did not change significantly, despite that great increase in total numbers. Engineers with native-born parents made up 66.4 percent of the profession in 1900 and 65.3 percent in 1920, having grown at a rate of 208 percent. First- and second-generation immigrants, by contrast, increased their numbers at a rate of 215 percent. The one profession in which contrary trends can be found is college teaching. Sixty-five percent of professors in 1910 had native-born parents, a proportion which increased to 70.4 percent by 1920.[13]

Focusing on individual cities, it would appear that the trends noted for lawyers in New York and Chicago also hold for other professionals. The number of doctors increased by 40.8 percent in New York between 1900 and 1920 (compared to 11.0 percent nationally). There was a marked difference between those with native-born parents, whose 13.0 percent increase was only slightly above the national rate for doctors, and first- and second-generation immigrants, who increased at a rate of 63.7 percent. In 1900, 45.4 percent of New York City doctors had native-born parents. By 1920, that percentage had dropped to 36.3. In Chicago, the growth rate was slower, as was also true among lawyers. But the same marked difference between those with

---

[13]Ibid.

native-born parents and first- and second-generation immigrants shows up. The total number of doctors in Chicago increased by 27.1 percent between 1900 and 1920; this gross figure masked the fact that those with native-born parents increased by only 5.8 percent and the first- and second-generation immigrants increased by 43.2 percent. In 1900 doctors with native-born parents comprised 48.9 percent of physicians in Chicago; in 1920, this figure was down to 40.4.[14]

What seems to have happened between 1900 and 1920 was that the sons of the white native middle class were choosing either the newer, more technical professions or college and university teaching in preference to the older professions. After 1920 this trend was reversed somewhat. The bar grew by 31 percent during the 1920s, at the same time that the general population was growing by 17.1 percent and all professional service occupations by 49.9 percent. During the 1920s the law definitively replaced the clergy and the medical profession as the fastest growing old profession. Physicians increased only 6 percent during the decade, and the clergy grew at a 17 percent rate. But the new professions were still outpacing the bar. Engineering grew at a

---

[14] Ibid.

rate of 66 percent and college teaching at a rate of 85 percent during the 1920s.[15]

Evening and night law schools undoubtedly contributed greatly to the resurgence of the bar's growth during the 1920s. These schools had increased steadily in number since the acceleration in their growth in the 1890s. Prior to the 1890s, the main barrier to their expansion had been the long-standing tradition that a law school needed a university or college affiliation in order to be recognized. That tradition was broken dramatically in 1891 as a consequence of the schism which split the Columbia University Law School and led to the creation of the New York Law School under the leadership of the followers of the departing Columbia dean, Theodore Dwight. The New York Law School almost immediately received a charter from the New York Board of Regents. The Board willingly granted the charter because the new school had such good credentials: Dwight was highly respected as a law professor, the new school had three former Columbia professors on its faculty, and they were able to create a Board of Trustees composed entirely of Columbia Law School graduates. But the long-term impact was to open the eyes of potential law school

---

[15]Edwards, Comparative Occupation Statistics, p. 111.

promoters with less prestigious credentials to the possibility of securing charters without dickering for a tie with a college.[16]

The 1891 dispute at Columbia was merely the opening round of a controversy over legal education which can be traced in the profession over the next thirty years. Columbia President Seth Low's decision to revise the Law School curriculum, which had caused the schism and the departure of Dwight's supporters, represented a conscious choice for an elitist conception of the purpose of legal education. In contrast, Dwight had wanted to give a sound knowledge of the law to the men of average ability who made up the larger proportion of the bar members. The eventual result of Low's decision was that the case method replaced Dwight's lecture-textbook method of instruction at Columbia. However, Low did not make instruction by the case method mandatory. In fact, there were not enough casebooks in print in 1891 to use them universally even if all the remaining professors had wanted or felt competent to use them.

---

[16] Reed, Training, p. 192; Columbia University Foundation for Research in Legal History, A History of the School of Law: Columbia University, ed. Julius Goebel (New York, 1955), pp. 152, 446n.

The immediate changes Low made were the following: (1) the various subjects were to be studied concurrently rather than serially; (2) public law study was made acceptable for the LL.B. (beginning Columbia's long tradition of close collaboration between the Political Science Department and the Law School); (3) the hours of instruction were adjusted to discourage work in law offices during the first two years and to facilitate though not necessarily to encourage such work in the third year; (4) a broader range of choice was offered in legal subjects; (5) three years was established as the standard legal course rather than the previous two.[17]

The advocates of the case method liked to argue that their curriculum effectively trained law students in legal thinking, whereas the old curriculum merely imparted legal knowledge. But in 1891, training in legal thinking was by no means universally desired by students or supported by practicing lawyers. Hence, there was a general

---

[17] Columbia Foundation for Research, *History of the Law School*, pp. 146, 152-155; William A. Keener to Hugh Nelson, February 13, 1895, W. A. Keener MSS, Columbia University Libraries.

exodus of students from Columbia to the New York Law School. Columbia's enrollment dropped from 623 in 1890-1891 to 315 in 1891-1892 and continued to decline, hitting a low point of 288 in 1894-1895, just at the time when law school enrollments nationally were increasing rapidly. The New York Law School immediately replaced Columbia as the second largest school in the nation, behind the University of Michigan, which had not yet shifted to the case method. The New York Law School sustained its initial success, becoming the largest in the nation by 1904-1905. The difference in the length of the required course, two years rather than three, probably accounted for part of the popularity of the new school, as did its willingness to adapt itself to the needs of those who found it necessary to work while studying.[18]

On the other hand, other law schools that switched to a three-year course found that the switch did not seriously affect their enrollment. Harvard led the way in 1878. Its enrollment went down slightly, but soon recovered. In 1870, when Christopher Columbus Langdell

---

[18] Columbia Foundation for Research, *History of the School of Law*, pp. 446n, 447n, 151-152.

took over the Harvard Law School, it had about 130 students, which was a large enrollment for the time. In 1895, when Langdell retired after having thoroughly modernized the school, lengthening the course of study, raising the entrance requirements, increasing the tuition, and establishing the case method, the enrollment was at 400.[19]

Harvard's development might be considered unusual, since in the mid-1890s 76 percent of its entering students were college graduates, compared to 42 percent for the University of California, the next highest institution, and 41 percent for Columbia.[20] However, Harvard was simply ten to fifteen years ahead of other schools. By 1917 only twenty-three law schools and by 1920 only sixteen had not yet switched over to the three-year curriculum; almost all these schools were in the South.[21]

---

[19]Arthur E. Sutherland, The Law at Harvard: A History of Ideas and Men, 1817-1967 (Cambridge, Mass., 1967), pp. 168-183.

[20]ABA, Reports 17 (1894), 397. There was no sharp difference between leading night schools and leading day schools in the percentage of students holding a college degree.

[21]Reed, Training, pp. 177-178. A good summary discussion of the triumph of the Harvard structure and approach in the elite schools is in Robert Stevens, "Two Cheers for 1870: The American Law School," Perspectives in American History 5 (1971), 430-441.

But the conflict between Columbia and the New York Law School did reflect a major tension in the law school world between a practical and an academic approach to legal training. To keep this conflict in perspective, it should be pointed out that American legal education never became as academically oriented as European legal education.[22] The issues in America concerned whether practice courts and legal aid clinics should be a part of the law school experience and the extent to which the details of local procedural rules and of local law should be taught. The dispute clearly divided the elite law schools and the night schools.

But even within the elite schools' national organization, the Association of American Law Schools (established in 1900), there was much discussion of these matters. State university law schools in the Midwest and Far West tended to argue that since their students usually went directly from the school to independent practice, some practical experience during law school would be desirable to give budding lawyers confidence and to fulfill the students' expectations that law

---

[22] This represents a long-standing distinctive feature of American legal education, going back to the earliest law schools during the ante-bellum period. Reed, *Training*, pp. 45-46.

school would prepare them as practitioners. Opposition to this argument came from schools such as Harvard and Columbia, whose graduates often went from the law school into a law office (on a salaried basis). Harlan Stone expressed the point of view of these schools:

> The practitioner spends his entire life in a legal clinic. We need not worry about his getting sufficient experience of that kind. He only spends three years in the scientific study of legal theory. After that his approach to the legal theory is purely haphazard. Now, it seems to me wholly a question of the economical use of time.[23]

By the time Stone spoke, this issue was something law school professors were fighting out among themselves, although seeking to gain allies among practitioners. In the 1890s, before law school professors were organized and before the legal elite had decided where it stood on legal education, the ABA's Committee on Legal Education and Admission to the Bar and the ABA's Section of Legal Education (created in 1893) kept a close watch on developments in legal training and earnestly debated how the elite could influence trends in the most favorable way.[24]

---

[23] Association of American Law Schools, *Proceedings* 16 (1916), 60.

[24] ABA, *Reports* 15 (1892), 318; 18 (1895), 315-316; 20 (1897), 361-364; 23 (1900), 467-468; 24 (1901), 399-403.

Elite lawyers were concerned about two main issues: (1) how to preserve the quality of admittees to the bar and (2) whether the case method should be the preferred method of instruction in the law schools. The debates over the case method in the Committee and the Section during the 1890s revealed a general consensus that the law school's task was to teach the principles of law. Several practitioners were skeptical that the case method could do that; some feared that the students would only learn which leading cases to refer to when preparing briefs. It was clear to all by the 1890s that the case law was becoming too voluminous for such training to be useful.

Beginning students seem to have had a similar reaction, at least initially, judging by the reminiscences of Allen Wardwell and Learned Hand, both of whom attended Harvard Law School in the 1890s. Wardwell remembered that they read and discussed cases in class, but because there was no explicit instruction in legal principles, it was possible to "go through half or two-thirds of the year sometimes without the faintest idea of what it was all about."[25]   Hand remembered

---

[25] Allen Wardwell, Oral Memoir, 1952, Columbia University, p. 28.

being similarly baffled. "They gave you no instructions. They just went through the case books. I remember reading a fifteenth century case on property. I hadn't any idea what the words meant."[26] But both Hand and Wardwell considered the method successful; after an extended period of initial confusion, both found "miraculously" and "by osmosis" that the subject began to make sense. Wardwell concluded that "without experiencing the other method, we were all sold on the Harvard method, not because we went there, but because it really did seem to sharpen up your wits if nothing else."[27]

By the end of the 1890s most of the skeptics in the legal elite, though they had usually learned by the old method, seem to have been persuaded by the evidence that students like Wardwell did seem better prepared than those taught principles directly via lecture and textbooks. In 1900, the ABA's Section of Legal Education helped create the Association of American Law Schools, an organization dedicated to spreading not only the case method but also the institutional arrangements (full-time

---

[26] Learned Hand, Oral Memoir, 1957, Columbia University, p. 25.

[27] Wardwell, Oral Memoir, p. 30.

faculty, three-year curriculum, adequate library) and the ideology ("the law ought to be systematized") of the elite law school professors. The professors went off in their own direction, and the ABA turned the main thrust of its organizational interest to other matters, maintaining a skeptical distance from and at times even an active hostility to the interests and enthusiasms of the professors. The legal elite had "checked out" the case method, approved it, and then lost interest in the wider implications of its adoption which the professors perceived.

Meanwhile, two systems of legal education grew up. The nationally-oriented elite universities developed a system based on full-time instructors and the case method, while the metropolitan evening and night schools followed a system based on part-time instructors and either textbooks or a combination of texts and casebooks. The existence of a divided profession ran counter to the ideology of the bar elite. But not until the 1920s did the organized bar actively intervene through a nationally-directed attempt to impose unity on law schools.[28]

---

[28] Auerbach, "Law Teachers and Practitioners," pp. 587-601 contains an excellent discussion of the effort in the early 1920s. The following account differs

More typical during the 1890-1920 period were attempts by state bar associations to control developments in legal education by standardizing bar examinations and by raising the educational requirements for those seeking to take the bar examinations. This movement reflected the strong preference for state-centered but nationally-coordinated action that was very characteristic of the bar elite's views during these years.

In 1894 New York established a state board of bar examiners. Other states soon followed suit, with strong encouragement from the ABA. In 1898 the ABA's Section of Legal Education was the scene of a lengthy discussion among existing state law examiners on how they were preparing and administering the exams. The examiners and their audience also swapped horror stories about older examination methods in the "bad old days." By 1900, nineteen states had state boards of examiners and a Conference of State Boards of Bar Examiners had been created, meeting annually at the same time as the ABA to coordinate policies and procedures, By 1906,

---

from Auerbach's in emphasizing the continuity of the bar elite's interest from the 1890s to the 1920s. The difference between the two periods concerned the issue of the legitimacy of national action rather than the desirability of raising standards. This is in no way to deny the importance of nativism as a motive of efforts in the early 1920s, which Auerbach emphasizes.

twenty-nine states had examination boards. As might be expected, the movement was strongest in the Northeast, but all sections of the country except the Far West were involved. The examiners tended to be judges and practitioners, and only rarely law school men.[29]

The state board system undoubtedly helped make permanent the trend toward law school as the locus of legal training. This effect was explicitly recognized by Franklin M. Danaher, the long-time head of the New York Board of Bar Examiners. He ascribed the fact that in his state 70 percent of the applicants for the state bar in the late 1890s had some law school training to the feeling among law students "that under the system of examinations established by the State Board, it is almost impossible to qualify unless they are fully prepared, and they know that they cannot get adequate preparation outside a law school."[30] The state board system may also have contributed to the slowdown in the growth of the profession after 1900, although even Danaher recognized there was a

---

[29] ABA, Reports 21 (1898); 23 (1900), 577; 29 (1906), 493.

[30] Ibid. 21 (1898), 538.

general feeling that the bar was cheaper and easier to enter than the other learned professions.[31]

The bar examination system was a solution more congenial to the practicing lawyer than to the elite law school professor. This point is made quite clear in an 1894 letter from Dwight's successor as Columbia Law School dean, William A. Keener, to Wall Street lawyer John B. Pine, who had suggested Columbia actively assist in directing the work of the new state board.

> I do not think that it would be advisable for us to have the examinations of the School conducted under the joint direction of the Board of Examiners and the Faculty. . . . We have just succeeded, after three years of great effort, in establishing the position that the Law School should be something more than a fitting school for the Bar, and should be national in its aims, not simply local. I feel that a move in the direction suggested by you would tend to cause us to be regarded simply as a means of gaining admission to the New York Bar, and therefore as nothing more than a fitting school for that Bar.[32]

Keener had good relations with the original board. These relations between the board and Columbia deteriorated during the next twenty years to the point that a public controversy arose between Danaher and Columbia's dean,

---

[31] Ibid.

[32] Keener to Pine, November 20, 1894, Keener MSS.

Harlan F. Stone. Danaher and Stone disagreed over the appropriateness of state bar examination questions, which Stone believed tested rote knowledge of petty details rather than legal reasoning.

State bar examinations were (and are) an imperfect test of an applicant's suitability for the profession. But it is not at all clear that any other standards are better indicators. The organized bar wrestled with this question at nearly every annual meeting of state and national bar associations from the mid-1890s through the early 1920s, when the ABA finally adopted a definitive policy and turned its attention to trying to implement that policy.

The issues in the thirty-year debate were whether law school training should be required, and if so, how many years; whether night schools and day schools should be treated the same; whether part-time study of law should be proscribed; whether prelegal collegiate education should be required; whether a post-law-school clerkship should be required; what the standards for the certification of law schools should be.[33] For the most part, the story of these proposals and debates belongs to the history of the bar elite's changing

---

[33] Edson R. Sunderland, *History of the American Bar Association and Its Work* (n.p., 1953), pp. 140-147.

perception of its profession's role, function, and public image and to the history of the bar association activists' efforts to create unified and active bar organizations.

The tempo of activity picked up markedly after about 1910 when the bar elite became very concerned that

> hundreds of young men apply for admission every year who are morally and intellectually incapable of the practice of law. Many of them seem to have attained such a knowledge of legal rules as enables them to pass the Bar exam. . . . Then they commence what they call the practice of law, and in many instances they come before us in a few years for disbarment. In the disbarment proceedings it clearly appears they are absolutely lacking in any conception of legal principles, or the obligation and duties which a lawyer assumes to the State, to his profession, and to his clients.[34]

As Elihu Root explained to the Washington Conference of Bar Association Delegates in 1922, in the old days of law office study, the aspiring lawyer "took in, through the pores of his skin, the way of thinking and of feeling, the standards of morality, of honor,

---

[34] New York State Bar Association, Reports 34 (1911), 236, quoting a letter from Justice Ingraham to John R. Dos Passos supporting a resolution calling for a compulsory clerkship and the elimination of the part-time study of law.

of equity, of justice, that prevailed in that office."[35]
Under the new regime of law schools and bar exams, there
was no assurance a lawyer would get such "moral instruction" in his training. To men like Root, this situation
was especially serious because increasing numbers of
immigrants were seeking admission to the profession.
The bar elite convinced itself that immigrants lacked
conceptions of and commitment to American ideals of
honesty and justice. In support of the two-year
prelegal higher education requirement passed by the
Washington Conference, the Chicago Bar Association
Record noted:

> the adoption of these standards of legal education is of peculiar importance to Chicago by
> reason of the large number of applicants for
> admission to the Bar who are of foreign birth. .
> . . In order to prepare them for that leadership
> in public sentiment and governmental matters
> that falls to the lot of lawyers, it is essential
> that they have a thorough knowledge of American
> institutions and ideals.[36]

Elihu Root made clear the depth of his feeling on the
matter:

> I do not want anybody to come to the Bar which
> I honor and revere, chartered by our government
> to aid in the administration of justice, who

---

[35] Elihu Root, Men and Policies; Addresses (Cambridge, Mass., 1925), p. 149.

[36] Chicago Bar Association Record 6 (January 1923), 1-2.

has not any conception of the moral qualities that underlie our free American institutions--and they are coming, today by the hundreds.[37]

The modernization and urbanization of the legal profession, one result of which was the shift in training from the law office to the law school, increased stratification within the bar. This inevitably led to differing conceptions of "professional ethics" within the profession.[38] At the same time, non-Anglo-Saxons increasingly sought and gained admission to the profession. When these circumstances were coupled with public criticism of the profession and of legal institutions during the progressive years, the bar elite's protectiveness of "their" profession fell rather easily into the latent nativist channels in their thought. Nativism came naturally for the bar elite not only because of their sociocultural prejudices, but also because they so closely identified their profession with the protection of American republicanism and American distinctiveness.

But bar leaders found themselves in an uncomfortable dilemma. A major tenet of their ideology was that

---

[37] Root, Men and Policies, p. 151.

[38] Jerome Carlin, Lawyer's Ethics: A Survey of the New York City Bar (New York, 1966), p. 165; Kenneth J. Reichstein, "Ambulance Chasing: A Case Study of Deviation and Control Within the Legal Profession," Social Problems 13 (Summer 1965), 3-17.

equality of opportunity was a reality in America, with the openness of their profession to men of character and talent serving as a prime example. Abraham Lincoln's career was frequently cited when the bar was in a mood of self-congratulation. Of course, this openness had always entailed a responsibility for the profession's leaders to police abuses. The rise of the law school meant that the informal methods of policing entry used in the nineteenth century were no longer available. More formal, organization-minded solutions were now both called for and much more possible. But precisely what the formal barriers to entry should be was never clear. If bar admission standards were raised too high, the law would come to resemble, in fact and in the public eye, more of a caste than the open profession it prided itself on being. This problem, along with the general weakness and lack of purpose in bar associations, kept the organized bar from taking a clear stand on bar admission standards until the 1920s, when new ideological currents were beginning to make an impression on the profession.

CHAPTER 5

RISE OF LARGE LAW FIRMS

The large law firm is the most striking manifestation of the organizational impulse in the twentieth-century legal profession. Its significance is indicated by the finding of sociologists that within the legal community of a large city today, the major indicator of a lawyer's status is the size of his firm.[1] Recognizing the importance of the large firm, Willard Hurst chose the transition in the lawyer's role from advocate to counselor as the basis for his periodization in the history of the modern bar. The advocate was either an independent practitioner or a member of a small firm; he did his lawyering in court; his legal practice was intimately involved with commerce, but his professional interests were not dominated by the needs of large business enterprises. In contrast, the counselor is typically a member of a large firm; he does his lawyering in his

---

[1]Richard S. Wells, "The Legal Profession and Politics," Midwest Journal of Politics 7 (May 1964), 176 citing Jerome Carlin, Current Research in the Sociology of the Legal Profession, mimeo (Bureau of Applied

office, offering advice; his legal practice is dominated by the needs of large corporations.

Hurst believed that the transition from advocate to counselor began during the 1870s. But he was vague about how long the transition lasted and when, precisely, the tone and ethos of the profession became dominated by the concerns and outlook of the counselor rather than by those of the advocate. Hurst also failed to clarify whether the transition from advocate to counselor, which occurred primarily among the bar elite, influenced only the elite or pervaded the entire profession. The clear implication of Hurst's account, however, was that the transition significantly influenced the entire profession.[2]

The trend toward large law firms was tied to the growth of corporate law practice and therefore to the trend toward large corporations. However, the two trends were not entirely parallel. There were two main

---

Social Research, Columbia University: August 1962), p. 21. Despite the importance of large firms, it should be pointed out that as late as the mid-1960s, more than half of all lawyers in private practice were practicing alone. According to a 1963 estimate, 57 percent were in one-member firms, 29 percent in two- to four-partner firms, and 14 percent in firms of five or more partners. See David F. Cavers, "Legal Education in Forward-Looking Perspective," in Geoffrey C. Hazard, ed., Law in a Changing America (Englewood Cliffs, 1968), pp. 154-155.

[2] James Willard Hurst, The Growth of American Law: The Law Makers (Boston, 1950), pp. 297-308.

reasons that they were not. Firstly, in the early years of corporation law practice, when individual entrepreneurs and investment bankers were the major clients, a large law firm was not necessary. Only when industrial corporations requiring continuous legal supervision became the main clients did corporation law practice require large law firms. That requirement was not firmly established until World War I or immediately thereafter. Consequently, in the 1920s there was a quantum jump in both the size and number of large law firms.

Secondly, the pace at which leading lawyers bureaucratized their firms was influenced by cultural factors as well as by the requirements of their corporate clients. There was nothing in the early history of the development of large corporations that would have prevented large law firms. Rather, leading lawyers were slow to bureaucratize their firms partly because they were reluctant to model their professional practice after the organizational trends increasingly dominant in the economy and society.

Elihu Root's career exemplifies this reluctance. He developed a reputation as a leading old-style advocate and court lawyer in the New York City bar during the final decades of the nineteenth century, before he entered McKinley's Cabinet in 1899 as Secretary of War. In 1900, when he considered returning from government service to private practice, he was approached by several leading firms as a potential partner. He turned down a "generous offer" from the Cravath firm, one of the originators of the modern large firm organizational model. In a letter to William D. Guthrie of that firm, Root explained that

> too great and profitable a practice deprives one of the time and opportunity to really do his best in anything. I feel, as I know you do, that it would be much more satisfactory to make less money and get more satisfaction out of doing things considerately and thoroughly.[3]

The pace and specialization of a large firm prevented the kind of law practice Root, already a very wealthy man, desired. Root was true to his resolve. When he returned to practice between his stints in Washington in 1904-1905 and again after finally leaving public

---

[3] Elihu Root to William D. Guthrie, May 22, 1900, copy in Philip C. Jessup MSS, Box 252, Library of Congress. See also E. Root to Langdon Parker Marvin, November 19, 1903, copy in Jessup MSS, Box 252. Marvin was in the firm of Carter & Ledyard, another leading turn-of-the-century Wall Street firm. As it turned out, Root decided to remain in McKinley's Cabinet in 1900.

service in 1915, Root was "of counsel" to his son's firm and not a partner in the firm.

As Root suggested, Guthrie very likely sympathized with him. The Cravath firm's historian tells us that Guthrie, "the most driving and keenly analytical of any of the firm's many partners," resisted the innovations in staff organization made by Paul D. Cravath in the late 1890s. Rather than using the young law school graduates whom Cravath brought into the firm as associates, for example, Guthrie relied on his own older assistants.[4]

The resistance of Root and Guthrie to the confining embrace of a large firm might be dismissed as individual idiosyncracies. But there is evidence that prior to the 1920s, a firm could engage in an active corporate practice yet, by deliberate choice, remain small. The history of two of the largest post-World War II New York City firms, Shearman, Sterling & Wright, and Davis, Polk, Wardwell, Sunderland, & Kiendl, convincingly demonstrate this point.

The Shearman, Sterling firm was the largest firm that sociologist Erwin Smigel found in the late 1950s when he conducted a study of law factories, using fifty or more

---

[4]Robert T. Swaine, The Cravath Firm, 3 vols. (New York, 1946-1948), 1:359, 776-778. When Guthrie withdrew from the firm in 1906, it was no surprise.

partners and associates as his criterion for a large firm. He found twenty-one such firms in New York City and seventeen in other cities in 1959.[5] The largest firm, Shearman, Sterling & Wright, had thirty-five partners and ninety associates. The Davis, Polk firm was near the top, with thirty partners and sixty-five associates.

An examination of Hubbell's Legal Directory from the 1870s to the 1920s reveals that neither firm had as many as four partners and associates until the 1910s. Certainly, neither could be considered a "major" firm, in terms of size, until the 1920s.[6] Before that decade, Shearman, Sterling & Wright was a small firm with a distinguished reputation. In 1892 it had three partners, in 1903 two partners. Despite its small size, the firm had a long list of distinguished clients, including the National City Bank, Edward H. Harriman,

---

[5] Erwin O. Smigel, "The Impact of Recruitment on the Organization of the Large Law Firm," American Sociological Review 25 (February 1960), 58. In a recount in 1968, Smigel found 34 such firms, 11 of which had more than 100 partners and associates, in New York. Shearman & Sterling was the largest firm, with 169 attorneys. Smigel, The Wall Street Lawyer (Bloomington, Ind., 1969, 2nd ed.), pp. 358-359.

[6] Hubbell's was consulted for the following years: 1872, 1882, 1892, 1903, 1914, 1924. Those years were chosen on the basis of the availability of Hubbell's in the Stanford Law Library. They were the best dates for obtaining samples as close as possible to ten-year intervals.

James J. Hill, and the American Sugar Refining Company. It handled many large probate and real estate cases, and its partners served as executors and trustees of many large estates. The firm was active in railroad reorganizations and in bank and other corporate consolidations. It was retained as counsel on a regular basis by several important companies, including Amalgamated Copper Company and Consolidated Gas Company. The partners held a number of directorships in leading corporations. John Sterling, who was the office lawyer and rarely appeared in court, served as a director at one time or another of the National City Bank, the Consolidated Gas Company, the New York Edison Company, the New York Trust Company, and the Great American Insurance Company, among others.[7]

By 1914 the firm had expanded to two associates and three partners. By 1924 the firm had grown dramatically to thirteen partners. The senior partner was John A. Garver, Sterling's biographer, who had been with the firm since at least the early 1890s. But no Shearman or Sterling was to be found among the list of thirteen partners in 1924.

---

[7] John A. Garver, John William Sterling (New Haven, 1929), pp. 76-78; Morton Keller, In Defense of Yesterday: James M. Beck and the Politics of Conservatism, 1861-1936 (New York, 1958), p. 67.

The Davis, Polk firm traces its origins to the 1850s. It was founded by Francis N. Bangs, a Yale Law School graduate who specialized in trial work and participated actively in the Association of the Bar of the City of New York, after its founding in 1870.[8] The lawyer responsible for advancing the firm to its prominent status in the New York bar was Francis Lynde Stetson, well known as J. P. Morgan's lawyer, who joined the firm in 1880. In 1887 the firm, under the name of Bangs, Stetson, Tracy & MacVeagh, began working for the Morgan firm. That connection, and Stetson's Democratic political ties, brought the firm much legal business. Besides work for Morgan, the firm handled the legal affairs of the Erie Railroad, the Guaranty Trust Company, the International Paper Company, and others. Grover Cleveland was counsel for the firm between his two terms as President.

Stetson was an extremely skilled corporation lawyer, but he resisted the trend toward large law firms. He was more law-minded than commercial- or organization-minded, preferring the informality of a small office;

---

[8] Beryl H. Levy, *Corporation Lawyer--Saint or Sinner? The New Role of the Lawyer in Modern Society* (New York, 1961), p. 32.

he was also reluctant to assign his clients to other partners or associates. Stetson did, however, make it a practice to retain someone, such as John Stanchfield or Francis Wellman, who specialized in trying cases, because he considered the firm too small and too busy to try its own cases. He followed this practice even though both Stetson and his partner Frederick B. Jennings had gained wide experience in trial practice before becoming corporation lawyers, Stetson serving for a time as the Corporation Counsel for New York City.[9]

Hence, the firm did not join the ranks of truly large firms until 1919, when Stetson had become senile and Jennings and Russell had gone into partial retirement. By 1924, under the name of Stetson, Jennings, Russell & Davis, the firm had fourteen partners. But until the 1920s, as long-time partner Lansing P. Reed reflected years later, "the firm was a firm only in name."[10]

Additional evidence of the resistance among leading lawyers to innovations in firm organization and operation

---

[9] William Harbaugh, *Lawyer's Lawyer; The Life of John W. Davis* (New York, 1973), p. 186, drawing on the firm's privately printed history; Levy, *Corporation Lawyer*, pp. 70-73; Allen Wardwell, Oral Memoir, 1952, Columbia University, pp. 38-41.

[10] Harbaugh, *Lawyer's Lawyer*, p. 187.

can be found in stories about the reluctance to utilize modern inventions and business innovations. One lawyer of the old school, Charles F. Southmayd of Evarts, Southmayd & Choate, one of the most distinguished late nineteenth-century New York City law firms, was reported to have boasted until his dying day that he never traveled on the elevated railroad although taking it instead of a surface car would have cut thirty minutes off the four-mile journey between his home and office. Southmayd, who died in 1912, never once rode in an automobile and abandoned the surface lines when they converted from horses to electric motors. From then on, he took horsedrawn cabs. Assuming the credibility of these stories, it is not surprising that his partner Joseph H. Choate remarked about him at his death, "I hardly observed any change in his appearance, his dress, his manners, or mode of conversation from the time I first knew him in 1855."[11]

Southmayd was undoubtedly an extreme case. More typical was the situation at Sullivan & Cromwell, another leading Wall Street firm. Through the years, the firm appeared to make some concessions to progress. A wall

---

[11] Frederick C. Hicks, ed., <u>Arguments and Addresses of Joseph Hodges Choate</u> (St. Paul, 1926), pp. 150-152.

phone was installed in 1881 and desk phones about 1900; stenographers were introduced into the office in the late 1890s, to replace the occasional male stenographer who had been called in previously when one of the partners fell behind in his correspondence.[12] But the firm's lawyers ignored such advances, according to John Foster Dulles, who joined the firm as a clerk in 1911. Dulles reports that although the office had a telephone switchboard and operator, neither telephones nor stenographers were fully accepted. "Some of the older partners felt that the only dignified way of communication between members of the legal profession was for them to write each other in Spencerian script, and to have the message thus expressed delivered by hand." Dulles thought these lawyers considered both telephone messages and dictation an affront to their sense of privacy and decorum.[13]

Amusing as these stories are, they should not be dismissed simply as examples of a quaint cultural lag. They illustrate a tension between professional-mindedness

---

[12] Arthur H. Dean, William Nelson Cromwell, 1854-1848; An American Pioneer in Corporation, Comparative and International Law (New York, 1957), pp. 23-29.

[13] John Foster Dulles, "Foreword," in Dean, William Nelson Cromwell, p. iii.

and commercial- (or organizational-, or bureaucratic-) mindedness, a tension that was introduced into the world of the legal elite by the law-factory type of organization. This tension helps explain why the institutionalization and formalization of the truly large law firm lagged behind the growth of their corporate clients. So long as the economic necessity for large firms could be resisted, many though not all leading lawyers did resist. By the 1920s such resistance was no longer economically feasible. From then on, Judge Learned Hand's statement that "sometimes I feel sorry for lawyers, they seem to me to be so earnest and to work so hard, and when all is said and done to get very little out of life, except, perhaps, money," would seem increasingly on the mark when applied to lawyers in large firms.[14]

Evidence from the 1920s to the present indicates that the law factory has been especially grinding on younger lawyers. It has subjected them to long hours of work, taught them to give instant obedience to the hard-driving perfectionists so typical among the senior partners, and trained them to expect verbal abuse rarely

---

[14] Learned Hand to Felix Frankfurther, July 27, 1921, Frankfurter MSS, Box 63, Library of Congress.

balanced by praise for work well done.[15] The analytical powers and brilliance of the senior partners often has overawed young lawyers in the firm, who have had to spend the first two or three years working long and hard simply to prove themselves. Winthrop Aldrich told his biographer that his most vivid recollection from his early years around 1910 with Bryne, Cutcheon & Taylor in New York was that he had to prove himself to James Bryne as a man of initiative, ingenuity, and technical competence.[16] That Aldrich was the son of powerful U.S. Senator Nelson Aldrich suggests that in this particular, at least, his experience must have been typical. After those first few gruelling years, the main motivation for hard work became the desire to earn a partnership, a prize available to fewer than half of the associates taken into the firm in any given year.

No wonder Roscoe Pound remarked in 1926 that "I have seen more than one student who seems to me particularly suited for [legal aid work] get into the treadmill of a big office and have most of the milk of human kindness squeezed out of him therein."[17] A more recent student

---

[15] Swaine, *Cravath Firm*, 2:124-132.

[16] Arthur M. Johnson, *Winthrop W. Aldrich: Lawyer, Banker, Diplomat* (Boston, 1968), pp. 36-39.

[17] Pound to John S. Bradbury, October 8, 1926, Pound MSS, Paige Box 11, Harvard Law School Library.

of large law firms has "grievingly observed" that
although the younger lawyers grumble, the appeal of
money and prestige induces them to submit to team
discipline. Their individual personalities are ground
down. "They practice under someone else's aegis; and
the world, more likely than not, will hear no more about
them as notable simple personalities."[18]

The large firm, after all, has viewed all associates
and partners as employees. It has not permitted them to
have their own clients, as distinct from the firm's.[19]
It has also demanded intense loyalty, even of those who
have no assurance of becoming partners, often restricting
the civic and political life of its members and demanding
conformity in life style, especially in dress, manner,
and choice of residence.[20] One bar association enthusiast
complained in 1924:

> The fault I find with the overgrown law firm is
> that it virtually stands between the public and
> the profession on the one side and its own junior
> partners and law clerks on the other side. The

---

[18] Levy, Corporation Lawyer, p. 94.

[19] Ibid., pp. 92-93; Swaine, Cravath Firm, 2:2-10.

[20] Richard A. Watson and Rondal G. Downing, The Politics of the Bench and the Bar; Judicial Selection Under the Missouri Nonpartisan Court Plan (New York, 1969), p. 76; Smigel, "Large Law Firm," pp. 58, 62.

heads of the firm patronize the bar association, but the others are too busy to take a day off to consider professional affairs. A lawyer cannot sell himself as employe[e] by the year to any firm and yet be in a position fully to discharge his duties to the community and to the state as a lawyer should.[21]

Such loyalty and team spirit have been demanded even though the scale of the large firm has not permitted intimate contact between partners and associates, or even among all partners. To facilitate cohesion, the firm has relied upon the ethnic, social, and educational similarities of firm members, as well as upon the assurance that senior partners will be recruited from within the firm.[22]

Although the young lawyers in the large firm have gone along with a system that promised them substantial material rewards, they have often felt dissatisfied. One lawyer reported in 1932 to his former law school professor that in ten years of working for

---

[21] Herbert Harley, "Organizing the Bar for Public Service," *Journal of American Judicature Society* 8 (October 1924), 75.

[22] Edwin C. Austin, "Some Comments on Large Law Firms," *The Practical Lawyer* 3 (April 1957), 12-15; Roger B. Siddall, *A Survey of Large Law Firms in the United States* (New York, 1955), p. 34; Smigel, "Large Law Firms," p. 57. Smigel found in the late 1950s that of the 468 partners in the 20 large New York firms, 71 percent were from Harvard, Yale, or Columbia Law School and 32 percent were listed in or belonged to families in the Social Register.

a large New York firm, he had noticed that "there are a great number of young men who are dissatisfied spiritually, who have no respect for the older men for whom they work, who become more cynical, caring less and less each year to make more out of themselves than machines." It was the grinding hard work, long hours, and the lack of any higher aim than money and prestige which produced this cynicism and alienation.[23] This same young man lamented publicly (but anonymously) in Scribners, "If there had been one real effort to strangle an injustice, one trial to overcome wrong at some personal sacrifice, a trying attention to banish some error--but I recall none."[24]

Despite this numbing philistine atmosphere, the large law firms have never become fully bureaucratized or commercialized. The tension between professionalism and commercialism-bureaucratism which slowed their emergence has remained, although the balance has tipped in the direction of commercialism. The one full-scale

---

[23] Harrison S. Dimmitt to Zechariah C. Chaffee, Jr., February 12, 1932, copy in Frankfurter MSS, Box 152.

[24] Harrison S. Dimmitt [William Maybree Downing], "Life in the United States: New York Lawyer," Scribners, January 1932, p. 23.

scholarly study of Wall Street law firms, conducted by sociologist Erwin Smigel, concluded that, contrary to the popular image, the firms were "underbureaucratized."[25] From extensive interviews, Smigel found that supervision in the firms was loose and that written rules and procedures were only slightly developed. Lawyers' written and unwritten professional rules and professional self-control rather than bureaucratic rules and supervision explained the large firms' flexibility and success in meeting corporate clients' demands for quality legal service. Smigel also found a general cultural resistance to organizational innovation. The firms he studied were old and conservative and proud of being so. The older, more conservative partners often seemed to Smigel to think of themselves as akin to small-town general practitioners; they did not like the notion of a segmented, departmentalized, hierarchical organization, seeing it as not quite professional.[26] It may even be the case that organizational control of lawyers does not extend fully to their relationship with clients. Sociologist Joel Handler suspects that individual partners in the large firms

---

[25] Smigel, Wall Street Lawyer, passim.

[26] Smigel, "Large Law Firm," p. 62.

have their own clients, in the sense that if the firm dissolves or the partner leaves, "his" clients will follow him.[27]

Such under-bureaucratization may be due not only to the professionalism in the role identities of the senior partners, as Smigel suggested; it may also represent an accommodation by the firms to internal strains and conflicts. One study of a large Pittsburgh firm has concluded that loose supervision and lack of written rules and procedures were not merely reflective of the smooth functioning that professional identity permitted in large firms; rather these conditions were necessary to mitigate the alienation and conflict produced among junior partners and associates by the clash of professional and organizational goals, needs, and attitudes. As has been emphasized above, the younger associates in the firm felt this alienation and these conflicts especially strongly. To the firm they brought an ideology that combined capitalist individualism and high-minded professionalism, then felt frustrated because the firm's organizational and business goals did not wholly square with that ideology. From this perspective, loose and informal means of supervision

---

[27] Joel Handler, <u>The Lawyer and His Community</u> (Madison, 1967), p. 170n.

appear as a kind of "professional-minded" compensation for the general practice in large firms of, for example, allocating shares of fees in approximate proportion to the business attracted to the firm rather than in proportion to time spent or the difficulty of cases.[28]

On the other hand, the professionalism of younger associates should not be exaggerated. In addition to the testimony of disgruntled law school professors about the crass material ambitions of even the best law school students, the few sociological studies of elite law school seniors which have been conducted (in the late 1950s) clearly reveal them to have a much lower commitment to their profession and a much less well established set of preferences for specialized work than was found among medical students.[29]

****

If the tension between professionalism and commercialism in large firms has been visible to social scientists in the post-World War II period, it is even

---

[28] William Delany and Alan H. Finegold, "Wall Street Lawyer in the Provinces," Administrative Science Quarterly 15 (June 1970), 197-198; Wilbert E. Moore, The Professions: Roles and Rules (New York, 1970), p. 194.

[29] William A. Glaser, "Doctors and Politics," American Journal of Sociology 66 (November 1960), 233; Smigel, "Large Law Firm," p. 60.

more visible to the historian of the transition period, between 1870 and 1920, when the structure of the large firms was being created. The history of that transition is very complex, not the least because so many firms were involved (although only a tiny percentage of the entire bar) and because there was a great deal of experimentation and diversity, reflecting the personal tastes of the many strong-willed lawyers in those firms.

In order to develop some sense of chronology, <u>Hubbell's Legal Directory</u> was examined at ten-year intervals between the 1870s and 1920s to see how many large firms existed in major cities.[30] That evidence provides objective data on the external features of

---

[30] Certain problems and limitations of the source should be mentioned. <u>Hubbell's</u> was probably the major directory in this period. It began publication in 1870, with 1872 being the first year it contained an adequate listing of attorneys. For some reason or other, some major firms may not have been listed. Indeed, there were a few cases in which a firm appeared, say, in 1903, then disappeared in 1914 and reappeared in 1924. There were also a few cases in which large firms were not listed in the main city directory section but announced themselves in the advertising section at the end. A careful check of both sections was made for each year sampled. The number of such anomalies turned out to be sufficiently small as not to cause concern. Another limitation is that some firms may have only listed partners and omitted the names of associates, thus distorting their true size. But such a large number of firms did list associates that it does not seem the figures understate the story of the development of large firms. Identifying firms which were continuous with

large firm development, to supplement evidence on internal development gleaned from biographies, memoirs, and the few available firm histories.

A list of all firms with at least four members (any combination of partners and associates) was compiled. For the purposes of this study, these firms were considered "large firms." By present-day standards, a four-member firm is not very large, although only a minority of lawyers are in such firms. But four was found to be a good indicator for the period under study. In 1872, only 15 such firms were listed in Hubbell's. There were 39 by 1882, 87 in 1892, 210 in 1903, 445 in 1914, and by 1924 the number was well over 1,000.

---

previously listed firms, but whose firm name changed over the ten years between samples, was another problem. Firms were considered continuous if their personnel, especially the senior partners, remained substantially the same between sample years. In marginal cases, attention was paid to the firm's office and cable addresses, good clues to continuity. Since the cable address was a one-word identifier, it was especially useful. Another potential problem is that by sampling at ten-year intervals, firms which happened to be down in size in a sample year would have been missed, and firm members who joined and then left firms in between sample years would be omitted from the list of major-firm partners that was compiled. This is a problem of unknown magnitude, although it tends to make the list of major firms and major-firm members biased in the direction of firms and partners with some continuity as large firms.

Using the large-firm list as a base, a second category, that of "major firms," was created. Such firms had to have at some time at least seven partners or a combination of at least twelve partners and associates. They also had to maintain themselves as large firms over a ten-year period (that is, they had to appear on two consecutive lists of large firms). There was one exception: if a firm appeared on the large-firm list for the first time in the 1920s, it was considered a "major firm" only if it had at least ten partners. These numbers are, of course, arbitrary. They can be defended because they help tell the story of the emergence of the truly large firm. In 1872 there were no major firms listed in <u>Hubbell's</u>. There were 3 in 1882, 4 in 1892, 8 in 1903, 33 in 1914, and by 1924 more than 100.

The figures on large firms (four or more members) roughly indicate the chronology of the development of corporation law as a specialty--"roughly" because such a specialty did not require a minimum number of members, especially in the early years, and because a large firm did not necessarily have a primarily corporate clientele. However, the likelihood was very high. Such specialization developed first in New York City between the 1870s and 1890s. It was firmly established in the ten largest cities in the country by the early 1900s and in all metropolitan cities by the mid-1910s.

But a corporation law specialty did not necessarily require a law factory. Whether or not a law factory was required depended upon the size and complexity of the businesses being counseled and the specific nature of the legal business involved. Beginning in the 1890s in New York City, the law factory form of organization developed to meet the changing needs of the leading corporations in America. The figures on the major firms tell in broad outline the story of the development of law factories.

Ten cities were identified which had an especially high density of large or major firms during the period. These cities, ranked according to number of major firms in the 1920s, were New York, Chicago, Boston, Cleveland, Detroit, Philadelphia, Buffalo, Kansas City, Milwaukee, and Cincinnati.[31] Ninety-one firms in these ten cities were identified as large enough to be considered "major firms" at some time

---

[31] These cities were chosen because of their consistent appearance among the top ten cities in the fifty-year period. By the 1920s several of the cities at the bottom of the list were being eclipsed by such cities as Los Angeles, San Francisco, Baltimore, St. Louis, Pittsburgh, and Ft. Worth. In addition, Toledo and Providence were just outside the top ten throughout much of the fifty-year period.

during this period; 1064 lawyers were identified as partners in these firms or their predecessor firms, so long as the predecessor firm was of large-firm size. Thirty-eight of these ninety-one firms and 464 of the 1064 partners were in New York City, indicating its clear leadership in the development of law factories. Chicago had seventeen major firms. Boston had nine, Cleveland eight, Detroit and Philadelphia five, Buffalo three, Kansas City two, and Milwaukee and Cincinnati one each.

New York's leadership is even more dramatic when we consider the date that these ninety-one firms joined either the "large-firm" or the "major-firm" lists. As table 6 below shows, until 1892 there were no large firms outside New York City that would later become major firms (hereafter referred to as "future major firms"). In New York, three of the future major firms existed as large firms in 1872. In 1882, eight were large, including three which had attained major-firm size. It was not until 1903 that any firms outside New York City joined the major-firm list, as table 7 shows.

TABLE 6

NUMBER OF FUTURE MAJOR FIRMS OF AT LEAST LARGE FIRM SIZE, BY YEAR, FOR TOP TEN CITIES

Cities	1872	1882	1892	1903	1914	1924
New York	3	8	15	22	33	38
Chicago	0	0	2	7	12	17
Boston	0	0	2	4	6	9
Cleveland	0	0	1	4	6	8
Detroit	0	0	1	3	5	5
Philadelphia	0	0	1	2	3	5
Kansas City	0	0	1	2	3	3
Buffalo	0	0	1	2	3	3
Milwaukee	0	0	1	2	2	2
Cincinnati	0	0	1	1	1	1
Total	3	8	26	49	74	91

TABLE 7

NUMBER OF MAJOR FIRMS, BY YEAR, FOR TOP TEN CITIES

Cities	1872	1882	1892	1903	1914	1924
New York	0	3	4	5	11	34
Chicago	0	0	0	1	3	17
Boston	0	0	0	1	3	8
Cleveland	0	0	0	0	2	8
Detroit	0	0	0	0	0	5
Philadelphia	0	0	0	0	0	5
Kansas City	0	0	0	1	2	2
Buffalo	0	0	0	0	0	3
Milwaukee	0	0	0	0	1	1
Cincinnati	0	0	0	0	0	1
Total	0	3	4	8	22	84

The importance of the turn-of-the-century merger movement to the formation of large firms is suggested by the fact that by 1903 more than half of the ninety-one future major firms were established as large firms. There were forty-nine. More than half of these forty-nine (twenty-seven) were outside New York City. If we examine all the large firms in the top ten cities, whether they eventually became major firms or not, we find that of the fifty-eight large firms on the 1892 list, forty-four were new firms. (See tables 8 and 9.) Of those forty-four, twenty-five were in New York. The increase by 1903 is dramatic. There were now 141 large firms in the top ten cities, 104 of which had not been on the 1892 list. Of these 104 new large firms, over half (sixty-four) were outside New York. The growth in large firms continued, but its rate leveled off. In 1914 there were 216 large firms in the top ten cities, of which 132 had not been on the 1903 list.

TABLE 8

TOTAL NUMBER OF LARGE FIRMS, BY YEAR,
FOR TOP TEN CITIES

Cities	1872	1882	1892	1903	1914
New York	10	23	39	64	85
Chicago	2	2	4	23	41
Boston	0	2	2	13	18
Cleveland	0	0	2	8	13
Detroit	0	1	3	6	12
Philadelphia	0	0	1	5	12
Kansas City	0	0	1	8	13
Buffalo	0	0	3	4	7
Milwaukee	1	2	1	4	7
Cincinnati	1	1	2	6	8
Total	14	31	58	141	216

TABLE 9

TOTAL NUMBER OF <u>NEW</u> LARGE FIRMS,
BY YEAR, FOR TOP TEN CITIES

Cities	1872	1882	1892	1903	1914
New York	10	18	25	40	48
Chicago	2	2	4	20	31
Boston	0	2	2	11	9
Cleveland	0	0	2	6	9
Detroit	0	1	3	6	5
Philadelphia	0	0	1	4	10
Kansas City	0	0	1	7	8
Buffalo	0	0	3	3	5
Milwaukee	1	2	1	3	3
Cincinnati	1	1	2	4	4
Total	14	26	44	104	132

The importance of the 1920s to the establishment of major firms is indicated by the fact that in 1914 only twenty-two of the ninety-one firms had yet attained major-firm size (see table 7). In 1924, eighty-four had, nearly a fourfold increase. Even in New York, the increase in major firms was threefold, from eleven to thirty-four. Seven firms which had attained major-firm size in earlier years dropped back to large-firm size by the 1920s, a clear sign of how tenuous the institutionalization of the major firm was prior to the 1920s: four of the firms were in New York (representing three of the four major firms on the 1892 list) and one each in Boston, Kansas City, and Milwaukee.

Outside the top ten cities, the pattern was similar, although on a smaller scale and lagging a few years behind. By 1914, 106 cities not among the top ten had at least one large firm (see table 10). There were 229 such firms in these 106 cities, compared to 216 large firms in the top ten cities, marking the first time a majority of such firms were found outside the top ten cities. Eleven of these 229 were major firms. They were located in Birmingham, Los Angeles (two), San Francisco, Toledo, Pittsburgh (a thirteen-partner firm), Providence, Dallas, Ft. Worth (two), and Charleston, West Virginia. This represented a significant increase over 1903, when fifty-two cities not in the top ten had had sixty-nine large firms, none of which fell in the major-firm category and only two of which (in Baltimore and Columbus) had as many as seven members. In 1892 only twenty-two cities not in the top ten had had twenty-nine large firms, only six of which had more than four members, including one Utica, New York firm with six partners.

TABLE 10

DEVELOPMENT OF LARGE FIRMS
OUTSIDE TOP TEN CITIES

	1882	1892	1903	1914
4-member firms	5	23	50	121
5-member firms	3	3	14	53
6-member firms	0	3	3	26
7-9-member firms	0	0	2	23
10-14-member firms	0	0	0	6
Total firms	8	29	69	229
Total cities	8	22	52	106

****

Besides showing clearly the leadership of New York City, the tables reveal interesting patterns for particular cities. Philadelphia is especially conspicuous for its relative slowness to develop large law firms. On the other hand, several cities stand out because large firms developed relatively early in them, for example, Cincinnati and Milwaukee. In addition, Cleveland and Kansas City, although not particularly early in developing large firms, were conspicuous because the firms that did appear were extremely large for their time.[32]

Cincinnati and Milwaukee each had one large firm in 1872, at a time when New York and Chicago were the only other cities among the top ten with any large firms. The Cincinnati firm (Lincoln, Smith & Warnock) did not appear on the 1882 large-firm list. Similarly, the one firm on the 1882 list (King, Thompson & Maxwell) did not appear on the 1892 list. Not until the 1890s did firms develop which were able to maintain themselves as large firms. Both of the large firms appearing on the Cincinnati

---

[32]These figures confirm the information Lord Bryce received from his informants: "The custom of forming legal partnerships is one which prevails much more extensively in some parts of the Union than in others. In Boston and New York, for instance, it is common, and I think in the Western cities. . . in Philadelphia one is told that it is rather the exception." James Bryce, American Commonwealth, 2 vols. (New York, 1910, rev. ed.), 2:667.

list in 1892 (Harmon, Colston, Goldsmith & Hoadly; Paxton & Warrington) appeared on the large-firm list every subsequent decade, with the former becoming Cincinnati's one major firm in the 1920s, having retained the same firm name over the years. Milwaukee's one large firm (Finches, Lynde & Miller) in 1872 did appear on the 1882 list, but disappeared from the large-firm lists after that. The two new firms on the 1882 list (Cotzhausen, Sylvester & Scheiber; Davis, Riess & Shepard) were absent from the 1892 list. In the 1890s in Milwaukee, as in Cincinnati, a large firm appeared which was able to maintain itself and to become in the 1920s a major firm (Winkler, Flanders, Smith, Bottum & Vilas, which changed its name to Bottum, Hudnall, Lecher & McNamara in the 1920s).

The first Kansas City firm to appear on the large-firm list (Lathrop, Morrow & Fox in 1892) is noteworthy because it early became one of the largest firms in the nation. It had only four members in 1892; but in 1903 it had grown to fourteen members (seven partners and seven associates under the firm name Lathrop, Morrow, Fox & Moore) making it, along with the New York firm of Carter, Hughes & Dwight, the largest firm in <u>Hubbell's Directory</u> that year. The Lathrop firm grew to ten partners in 1914 and then to fifteen members (seven partners and eight associates) in 1924, retaining its firm name from the early 1900s throughout this period.

Even more impressive than the record of the Lathrop firm, since it was alone in attaining such size in Kansas City, is the size of several of the major firms in Cleveland. On the 1924 list there was one twenty-nine-partner firm (Squire, Sanders & Dempsey), one nineteen-partner firm (Tolles, Hogsett, Ginn & Morley), two fifteen-member firms (White, Cannon & Spieth with eight partners; Dustin, McKeehan, Merrick, Arter & Steward with seven partners), and one ten-partner firm (Bulkley, Hauxhurst, Jamison & Sharp). Several of these firms had been fairly large in the 1914 list as well. No New York City firm, even in the 1920s, was as large as the two largest Cleveland firms, although Sullivan & Cromwell with seventeen partners was close.

Cities with a precocious record of large-firm development seem to have been predominantly Midwestern cities. Several Midwestern cities besides Cincinnati, Milwaukee, Kansas City, and Cleveland were congenial to large firms earlier than cities of similar size in other regions. Columbus and Toledo in Ohio and St. Paul and St. Louis all present similar patterns, although their growth was not sufficient to get them into the top ten cities. On the other hand, several non-Midwestern cities outside the top ten, notably Baltimore, Providence, and Syracuse, had similar patterns.

In general, however, it seems accurate to say that a particularly open and inventive brand of professionalism among lawyers developed in the Midwest. This is shown by other evidence besides the record of large firms. Chicago, for example, was noteworthy in the early support its organized bar gave to reform efforts in the administration of justice and in the delivery of legal services.[33] Chicago pioneered in the juvenile and in the municipal court movements. The Chicago bar supported the public defender movement at a time when the New York City bar elite viewed it with suspicion.[34] Cleveland initiated the crime survey movement in the 1920s, when it called in a Harvard Law School team to study its police force and the administration of justice in its courts.[35] In so

---

[33] For example, Roscoe Pound, who was a close observer of the organized bar and of efforts to reform the administration of justice, reported, "I think the livest local bar association in the country is the Chicago Bar Association." Pound to William B. Cockley, March 2, 1917, R. Pound MSS, Paige Box 8. See also James Willard Hurst, The Growth of American Law, pp. 154-163.

[34] "Report of the Committee on the Defense of Poor Persons Accused of Crime," Chicago Bar Association, Reports 42 (1915), 65.

[35] Felix Frankfurter and Roscoe Pound, Criminal Justice in Cleveland (Cleveland, 1922).

doing, Cleveland was taking over the lead from Chicago, where the civic elite crime commission movement had developed most fully during the progressive period.[36] Chicago was also the home base for the American Judicature Society, which played an important, although probably not crucial, role in publicizing the judicial council movement during the 1920s.

A combination of economic, social, and cultural factors explains Midwestern professionalism. Economic activity in the region had increased to the point that large firms were feasible. Urbanization, with its attendant problems, had also increased, to the point that an innovative approach to law reform seemed called for. Compared to the Eastern bar elite, the Midwestern bar elite was newer and less aristocratic, because most leading lawyers in the various Midwestern cities came not from the upper class of those cities but rather from elsewhere in the Midwestern region.

---

[36] Mark H. Haller, "Urban Crime and Criminal Justice: The Chicago Case," Journal of American History 57 (December 1970), 619-635; David R. Johnson, "Crime Fighting Reform in Chicago, An Analysis of its Leadership, 1919-1927" (M.A. thesis, University of Chicago 1966).

Another factor explaining the newer, less aristocratic character of the Midwestern legal elite was a greater variety in educational backgrounds than was found in the Eastern bar elite. A college education and law school training were less "mandatory," at least prior to 1900. In addition, the number of lawyers in truly large firms or with an exclusively corporate clientele before the 1920s was never large enough in itself to constitute a viable bar elite. Hence, the elite was relatively inclusive and heterogeneous, maintaining, at the same time, its "standards." Finally, Midwestern professionalism reflected general features of Midwestern regionalism, at least among the upper and middle classes, in this period. It is the Midwest, after all, that we identify with the more open and innovative aspects of the progressive movement, whether we think those aspects signify "democracy" or "elitism."[37]

---

[37] Careers of leading lawyers reported in obituaries in the ABA <u>Reports</u> between 1900-1911 confirm these impressions. Only 4 percent of Chicago lawyers had been born in that city and only another 24 percent elsewhere in Illinois. In comparison, 84 percent of Philadelphia lawyers had been born in that city or elsewhere in Pennsylvania, and 63 percent of Boston lawyers had been born in that city or elsewhere in Massachusetts. New York City had a mixed pattern, with 42 percent born in that city or elsewhere in New York state. Interestingly, the major Midwestern cities outside Chicago (Cincinnati, Cleveland, Kansas City, and Milwaukee) had a pattern very similar to

The contrast between the Midwestern cities and Eastern cities is strongest in the cases of Philadelphia and Boston and weakest in the case of New York City. New York's elite was recruited from a wide region and was not notably home-grown. A college education and law school training was also not so "mandatory" a requirement before 1900. On the other hand, the absolute number of lawyers in large firms and with an exclusive corporate practice was always much greater in New York City, a factor which contributed to a greater homogeneity among leading lawyers and a greater social exclusiveness. In addition, the cultural traditions of the general urban elite in New York City had a long heritage, creating a predilection to aristocratic demeanor among the leaders of New York's bar.[38]

Boston's, with 61 percent born either in the home city or state. However, the non-exclusiveness of the Midwestern bar elite is reflected in the fact that only 35 percent had ever even attended law school, whereas 89 percent of the Boston lawyers appearing in the ABA obituaries had attended law school. In Chicago, success depended much more on law school attendance than it did elsewhere in the Midwest. Of Chicago lawyers in the ABA obituaries, 40 percent had graduated from law school and 56 percent had attended. The 40 percent figure compares favorably with the 42 percent of Boston elite lawyers who had graduated from law school. However, only 60 percent of the Chicago lawyers had ever attended an undergraduate college, compared to 85 percent of the Boston lawyers.

[38] As mentioned above, only 42 percent of New York City lawyers whose careers were summarized in ABA obituaries between 1900-1911 were born in either New York

The contrasts between New York, Philadelphia, and Boston are instructive. Throughout the period of this study, Philadelphia produced only five major firms, while New York produced thirty-eight and Boston, a smaller city, produced nine. Cleveland with eight and Detroit with five produced as many or more than Philadelphia, and more of Detroit's firms were established earlier. No Philadelphia firm appears on a large-firm list until the 1890s. The 1892 firm was Biddle & Ward, with five partners and one associate. Significantly, the firm maintained a New York City office as well. In 1892 eleven cities had more large firms than Philadelphia: New York (39), Chicago (4), St. Paul (3), Toledo (3), Detroit (3), Buffalo (3), Boston (2), San Francisco (2), Hartford (2), Columbus (2), Cincinnati (2), and Cleveland (2). The second major Philadelphia firm to appear on the large-firm list was Howson & Howson, which specialized in patent

---

City or New York state, compared to 63 percent of the Boston lawyers born in that city or Massachusetts and 84 percent of the Philadelphia lawyers born in that city or Pennsylvania. Only 63 percent of the New York City lawyers had a college degree, compared to 74 percent in Philadelphia and Boston. Twenty-eight percent of the New York City lawyers had never attended college, compared to 21 percent of the Philadelphia lawyers and 15 percent of the Boston lawyers. Only about half as many of the New York City lawyers had ever attended law school compared to the Boston lawyers. The figures were 46 percent and 89 percent respectively. Interestingly, only 42 percent of the Philadelphia lawyers had ever attended law school--reflecting no doubt the stronger hold that the clerkship system had in that city than elsewhere.

law. Throughout the period the firm maintained offices in New York and Washington as well as Philadelphia; it was impossible to determine which city was truly the "home" city, so it was counted as a separate major firm in both New York and Philadelphia.

The bar elite in Philadelphia, in contrast to New York, had longer historic ties to the city's first families, those families which made their fortunes in the eighteenth and early nineteenth centuries. The strength of the family-firm tradition as well as certain other traditions peculiar to the Philadelphia upper-class milieu seem to have militated against the early creation of large firms. Digby Blatzell, the social historian of Philadelphia's upper class, has noted that no Proper Philadelphia lawyer has ever been named to the U.S. Supreme Court. To explain this fact, he notes the apparent absence among upper-class Philadelphia lawyers of any strong "itch" for public office. He also cites a disinclination for the sustained abstract reasoning so characteristic of the Boston-Harvard tradition, where the family-firm tradition among the legal elite also was long-standing, but where the involvement in national politics came earlier. Baltzell believes the avoidance of abstractions is a clue to the values and attitudes of

the Philadelphia upper class as a whole and not just of
Philadelphia lawyers.[39]

One eminent Philadelphia lawyer who fits this pattern very well was John G. Johnson, one of the most highly regarded appellate court attorneys, especially in antitrust cases, during the late nineteenth and early twentieth centuries. He served as a counsel in the E. C. Knight, Northern Securities, Standard Oil, American Tobacco, and U.S. Steel antitrust cases. Johnson was rumored to have refused both a seat on the Supreme Court in 1892 and the position of U.S. Attorney General under McKinley in 1901, because--so Johnson's biographer believes--Johnson did not want to give up his large income (somewhere between $100,000 and $200,000 per year) and was reluctant to desert clients in the middle of cases.

Johnson displayed signs of what can be called an anti-organizational personal style that may have been characteristic of the nineteenth-century Philadelphia upper class. He never established a partnership, although he did employ young lawyers to assist him as his business

---

[39]E. Digby Baltzell, <u>Philadelphia Gentlemen; The Making of A National Upper Class</u> (Glencoe, Ill., 1958), p. 146.

grew. One lawyer, Frank P. Prichard, was associated with him for thirty-seven years, between 1883 and 1917, but always as an employee, not as a partner. Johnson avoided bar association activities, preferring to devote himself to home, work, and his extensive art collection. He also had a set policy of refusing all offers of business directorships.[40]

As a sign of the winds of economic change which were eventually to blow over Philadelphia, several of the younger men in Johnson's office did leave the law for high business positions.[41] By the 1920s, Philadelphia had joined the national trend toward large law firms. Economic pressures were making the parochial attitudes of the Philadelphia legal elite increasingly anachronistic. The Biddle firm (now Biddle, Paul, Dawson & Yocum) had eleven members in 1924. One other firm (Roberts & Montgomery) was the same size and three firms were larger. Dickson, Beitler & McCouch, with sixteen partners, was a very large firm by the national standards of the 1920s.

---

[40] Barnie F. Winkelman, <u>John G. Johnson</u> (Philadelphia, 1942), pp. 113, 117, 187, 189, 197.

[41] Ibid., p. 189.

To illustrate the special flavor of Philadelphia's upper class and to compare it to the upper class of Boston and New York, Baltzell quotes three apocryphal letters of introduction supposedly carried by young job-seekers from New York, Boston, and Philadelphia. The letters are worth repeating here because they accurately capture important differences among the legal elites of the three cities, differences which served as effective barriers to the creation of a truly national bar elite until at least the 1920s.

The Philadelphian's letter read:

Sir, allow me to introduce Mr. Rittenhouse Palmer Penn. His grandfather on his mother's side was a colonel in the Revolution, and on his father's side he is connected with two of the most exclusive families in our city. He is related by marriage to the Philadelphia Lady who married Count Taugenichts, and his family has always lived on Walnut Street. If you should see fit to employ him, I feel certain that his very desirable social connections will render him of great value to you.[42]

"Very desirable social connections" have always been important credentials for admittance to the bar elite, no matter what the city; but their value seems to have been

---

[42] Baltzell, Philadelphia Gentlemen, p. 31, quoting Robert Douglas Bowden, Boies Penrose (New York, 1937), pp. 7-8.

especially pronounced in Philadelphia.[43] It is suggestive, for example, that Pennsylvania retained a clerkship requirement long after most other states abandoned it and that Pennsylvania's bar was long organized on a county basis with a weak state bar--that is, the Philadelphia bar did not perform the same function as the New York City bar in stimulating a state bar movement.

The Boston bar long demonstrated a similar lack of interest in promoting a state bar association in Massachusetts. But this was because of the national, indeed the international, orientation of the Boston bar elite, an orientation directly traceable to the Boston upper class' historic identification with the city's reputation as the cultural capital of the nation. The Bostonian's letter reflects this:

> Permit me to introduce Mr. Jones who graduated with highest honors in the classics and political economy at Harvard, and later took a degree at Berlin. He speaks and writes French and German, and if you employ him, I am sure his learning will make his services extremely valuable to you.[44]

---

[43] William Miller, "American Lawyers in Business and Politics," Yale Law Journal 60 (January 1951), 66-76; Gary B. Nash, "The Philadelphia Bench and Bar, 1800-1861," Comparative Studies in Society and History 7 (January 1965), pp. 203-220.

[44] Baltzell, Philadelphia Gentlemen, p. 31.

A bachelor's degree from an Ivy League college, attendance at Harvard Law School, and frequently an LL.B. were very common among the Boston bar elite during the Gilded Age. The elite was also conspicuously Boston-bred. All of these factors seem to have encouraged the Boston elite to be national-minded. Very likely, also, Boston's ties to the New York bar, facilitated by the close connection that developed during the Gilded Age between the Harvard Law School and New York, encouraged the early emergence of large firms. Significantly, the two earliest major firms in Boston--Moorfield Storey's firm and Louis D. Brandeis' firm, both of which appeared on the large-firm list for the first time in the 1890s--had important connections outside the city and had partners with national reputations.

Moorfield Storey's firm was formed in 1887 at the instigation of Charles Francis Adams, who wanted Storey to establish a firm to manage the legal business of the Union Pacific. The firm soon became involved in a wide range of corporate reorganizations and securities issues.[45]

Brandeis, who never was fully accepted into the Boston legal elite because he was Jewish, was the true

---

[45] Mark A. DeWolfe Howe, <u>Portrait of an Independent, Moorfield Storey, 1845-1929</u> (Boston and New York, 1932), pp. 183-186.

pioneer of modern forms of law firm organization in Boston. He was the first Boston lawyer to organize his office on the basis of taking bright young men quickly into partnership.[46] Beginning in 1881, he made it a practice to hire as salaried assistants those Harvard Law School graduates who stood high in their class.[47] That this was very rare in Boston in the 1880s is witnessed by Samuel Williston's report that no one in his Harvard class of 1888 was able to obtain a salaried position for his first year's work in an office.[48]

When Brandeis answered the complaints of several of the younger men in his firm in 1896 that their labors were contributing only to the firm's reputation, not to their own, he had to look to New York for examples to prove his point that a lawyer could earn a reputation even though his name did not appear in the firm designation. Pointing to the Evarts, Choate & Beaman firm,

---

[46] Samuel Williston, Life and Law (Boston, 1941), p. 112.

[47] Louis D. Brandeis to Christopher Columbus Langdell, December 30, 1889, in Brandeis, Letters of Louis D. Brandeis; Urban Reformer, ed. Melvin I. Urofsky and David W. Levy (Albany, 1971), p. 86. For additional details on Brandeis' practice, see Urofsky, A Mind of One Piece, Louis D. Brandeis and American Reform (New York, 1971), pp. 26-29 or the standard biography: Alpheus T. Mason, Brandeis: A Free Man's Life (New York, 1946), pp. 56-95.

[48] Williston, Life and Law, p. 104.

formerly Evarts, Southmayd & Choate, Brandeis argued that "Beaman [Charles C. Beaman, Jr.] was known everywhere before [Charles F.] Southmayd's retirement gave his name a place in the firm--and Treadwell Cleveland is now reaching the point of reputation which Beaman had a few years ago." Brandeis also pointed to Alexander & Green, where "John J. McCook reached the pinnacle in 1886" although his name was not in the firm designation.[49] Significantly, Brandeis also appealed to the argument of inevitability and efficiency (the two seeming to be the same in his thinking) to convince his young associates.

> The organization of large offices is becoming more and more a business--and hence also a professional necessity,--if properly planned and administered--it must result in the greatest success to the individual members both pecuniarily and in reputation.[50]

In the early 1890s many of the most distinguished lawyers in Boston were still practicing in one-partner firms. They may have had juniors in their offices, but they did not form partnerships. A list of such eminent lawyers would have included Richard Olney, Robert M. Morse,

---

[49] Brandeis to William Harrison Dunbar, August 19, 1896, in Brandeis, *Letters; Urban Reformer*, p. 125.

[50] Ibid., p. 124.

Solomon Lincoln, Lewis S. Dabney, Josiah H. Benton, and Augustus Russ. Many of these men were still engaged in trial work. Important railroads, such as the Union Pacific and the Chicago, Burlington & Quincy, still had their main offices in Boston, as New York had not yet taken over control of lines originally built largely by New England capital.[51]

But by the late 1890s, the pattern of corporate and legal business was clearly changing and the beginnings of the institutionalization of the major firm could be seen in New York at least. With its strong national orientation, the Boston bar elite would follow the New York pattern, to a greater extent than the bar elite of many other cities.

****

The tenor of developments in New York is suggested by the apocryphal letter of introduction from the New York man:

> The bearer, Mr. Brown, is the young fellow who took hold of Street and Company's Chicago branch a few years ago and built it up to one hundred thousand a year. He also made a great hit as Jackson & Company's representative in London. He's a hustler all right and you'll make no mistake if you take him on.[52]

---

[51] Williston, <u>Life and Law</u>, pp. 110-112.

[52] Baltzell, <u>Philadelphia Gentlemen</u>, p. 31.

The letter accurately reflects the "self-made man" character of the New York bar elite, not in the sense of rags-to-riches, but in the sense that these men had a history of moving around and making their own place within the elite. They were often from out of town and, in the early years, it was not uncommon for them to change firms. The only false note in the letter is that because it was written for a businessman rather than a lawyer, it is unduly commercial and does not reflect the sense of professionalism that had developed in New York.

Despite its leadership in the development of large firms, the New York legal scene in the Gilded Age was still presided over by the great advocates who fought prominent cases through the courts. These included such tense, dramatic contests as the Tweed trials, the arguments over the constitutionality of the income tax, the Beecher trial, and a series of contested wills of major fortunes. These advocates were generally remembered for their personal characteristics rather than for their legal erudition.[53] For example, in commenting upon

---

[53] Elting E. Morison, Turmoil and Tradition; A Study of the Life and Times of Henry L. Stimson (Boston, 1960), p. 64; Austin, "Large Law Firms," p. 9; Robert T. Swaine, "Impact of Big Business on the Profession: An Answer to Critics of the Modern Bar," American Bar Association Journal 35 (February 1949), 91-92.

Joseph H. Choate, probably foremost among New York lawyers during the Gilded Age, the New York *Tribune* emphasized his courtroom manner rather than his legal arguments:

> His method goes right home to the human heart. . . . He puts on no lofty airs, but often speaks with his hands in his pockets. He does not strive to stir up dark passions. While he is always a little keener, a little firmer, and more witty than the man in the box or on the bench, yet he is always a brother man to him.[54]

Yet, Choate was a partner in Evarts, Southmayd & Choate, one of the few firms to appear on the large-firm list every decade from the 1870s to the 1920s. The firm was one of the earliest to join the major-firm list, in 1882. As if to underline Choate's and the firm's transitional status, it failed to grow beyond the eight partners it listed in 1882, falling back to seven in 1892 as Evarts, Choate & Beaman, and to four in 1903 as Evarts, Tracy & Sherman, after the death of the two senior partners and the departure of Choate to London as the American Ambassador to the Court of St. James. The firm had four partners again in 1914 as Evarts, Choate & Sherman (the name Choate referring to Joseph, Jr.) and then was back up to six in 1924 as Evarts, Choate,

---

[54] Edward Sandford Martin, *Life of Joseph Hodges Choate*, 2 vols. (New York, 1921), 1:445; see also 2:80-83.

Sherman and Leon. The transition generation in New York may have institutionalized the <u>large</u> firm in order to service the needs of its corporate clients, but it did not institutionalize the <u>major</u> firm. That development required lawyers with a temperament, professional outlook, and set of ambitions somewhat different from Choate's.

Among the new generation was Charles Evans Hughes. In 1883 the young Hughes entered the firm of Chamberlain, Carter & Hornblower, which had listed four partners in the 1882 <u>Hubbell's Directory</u>. The firm was small and unhurried enough that Hughes was able to do some essentially <u>pro bono</u> work, as counsel in a long court fight by a poor client who was trying to regain custody of his children.[55] Hughes remembered this situation as typical of the best firms in New York in the early 1880s.

> In those days, with the exception of the few who specialized in conveyancing, searching of titles and incidental matters relating to real property, the best law firms were engaged in general practice, with many cases in the courts, and the most highly prized professional opportunities in New York City still lay in advocacy. . . . the office arrangements even of the best

---

[55] Charles Evans Hughes, <u>The Autobiographical Notes of Charles Evans Hughes</u>, ed. David J. Danelski and Joseph S. Tulchin (Cambridge, Mass., 1973), pp. 64-65.

> firms were very simple. Large retinues of law
> clerks, secretaries and various helpers . . .
> were unknown. Important court papers (when
> not printed) were still written by a copyist
> whose "copper-plate" work was greatly admired.
> . . . The Firm had a single stenographer and
> there was but one telephone which was placed
> in the outer hall of the office.[56]

But the firm was destined to become one of the largest firms in New York and also to serve as a "seed" firm for a number of other developing major firms. In 1892 (as Carter, Hughes & Dwight, eight partners and six associates), it was the largest firm in the nation.

The growth of Chamberlain, Carter & Hornblower during the 1880s was primarily due to Walter S. Carter, who not only brought most of the business into the firm and managed the office, but also established the practice of hiring a few outstanding graduates of leading law schools immediately after their graduation, with an eye to retaining a few of them as partners. The firm became a spawning ground for future eminent New York City law firms. In addition to Carter and Daniel H. Chamberlain, the Reconstruction Governor of South Carolina, the other senior partner in the firm was William B. Hornblower, who left in 1887 with James Bryne to form his own firm,

---

[56] Ibid., pp. 63, 75.

Hornblower, Bryne & Taylor, taking with him the business he had been handling, the Grant and Ward receivership and New York Life Insurance Company's legal affairs. Hornblower was later nominated to the Supreme Court by President Cleveland, although political opposition blocked his confirmation. His firm joined the list of major firms in the 1910s as Hornblower, Miller & Potter, with nine partners. By 1914 Bryne had gone on to form his own firm, Bryne & Cutcheon, with six partners.

At the same time Hughes entered the Chamberlain, Carter & Hornblower firm, two future prominent Wall Street lawyers, Henry W. Taft (William Howard Taft's brother) and George W. Wickersham (Taft's Attorney General), were leaving. Wickersham went to Strong & Cadwalader, where he specialized in corporate reorganizations and served as a legal counsel for several major railroad and subway construction projects. Taft teamed up with William D. Page in Page & Taft and later joined Wickersham's firm, which in 1914 became Cadwalader, Wickersham & Taft, with eight members in the firm. As an indication of the true size of such a firm, it had a legal staff of fifteen who were not firm members and a non-legal staff of twenty-nine.[57] Cadwalader, Wickersham & Taft became one of the handful of leading firms in the "financial bar" in New York, handling legal business including corporate reorganizations, for a wide range of financial institutions, such as August Belmont and Company, Ladenburg, Thalmann and Company, Vermilye and Company, Robert Winthrop and Company, Real Estate Trust Company, the Manhattan Trust Company, Speyer and Company, and William A. Read and Company.[58]

Another member of the Chamberlain, Carter & Hornblower firm who was leaving just at the time Hughes entered the firm was Lloyd W. Bowers, who had been the managing clerk and who went to Chicago, becoming the General Counsel for the Chicago, Milwaukee and St. Paul Railroad and later for the Chicago and Northwestern Railroad. He also served as Solicitor General under

---

[57] In addition to Hubbell's, see Henry W. Taft, A Century and a Half at the New York Bar (New York, 1938), p. 176n; James C. German, Jr., "Taft's Attorney General: George W. Wickersham" (Ph.D. dissertation, New York University, 1969), pp. 3-5. Hubbell's 1914 directory still listed the firm as Strong & Cadwalader and listed it as having seven partners and no associates, indicating that the Directory had been made up from information received in 1913.

[58] Taft, Century and a Half, pp. 191-200.

Taft and was rumored as a Supreme Court candidate before his death in 1910.[59]

Other prominent members of the Chamberlain, Carter & Hornblower firm in its formative years included Robert Grier Monroe, grandson of Supreme Court Justice Grier; Starr J. Murphy, who went on to become the personal counsel to John D. Rockefeller; John W. Houston, described as "one of Harvard's brainiest products;" George W. Schurman, the brother of President Schurman of Cornell, who stayed with the firm until his death in 1931; Frederick R. Kellogg, who developed a high reputation at the New York bar and formed his own major firm (Kellogg & Beckwith in 1903, Kellogg, Emery, Boston & Cuthell in 1914, and Kellogg, Emery, Inness-Brown & Cuthell in 1924), and John A. Garver and Ralph S. Rounds, who went on to head such prominent firms as Shearman & Sterling and Rounds, Hatch, Dillingham & Debevoise respectively.[60]

Probably the most well known ex-partner in the Chamberlain, Carter & Hornblower firm, at least in the

---

[59] Beerits Memorandum, "Ancestry and Early Life," pp. 18-19, Charles Evans Hughes MSS, Box 165, Library of Congress.

[60] Ibid.; Otto E. Koegel, <u>Walter S. Carter, Collector of Young Masters; or, The Progenitor of Many Law Firms</u> (New York, 1953), pp. 103-106.

lore of the profession, was Paul D. Cravath. He was
described by one historian as "a law-office organizer
in the same way as the magnates he represented were
corporation organizers." That is, he established "a
law factory system which paralleled those of his clients'
enterprises" and his system became the "prototype for
other gilt-edge law offices."[61] Cravath joined
Chamberlain, Carter & Hornblower on the recommendation
of Charles Evans Hughes, who described him to Walter S.
Carter as the best man in the Columbia Law School.[62]
In 1888 his name was added to the firm's name, when it
became Carter, Hughes & Cravath. An important client
of the firm was George Westinghouse. His business,
combined with all their other legal business, kept the
firm so busy that it operated two offices. Hughes, who
handled most of the court work for the firm, worked day
and night and took no vacation between 1888 and 1891.
The pace was too much for Hughes, who went into semi-
retirement for two years as a law school professor at
Cornell Law School.[63] But Cravath, a robust and

---

[61] Levy, Corporpation Lawyer, p. 88.
[62] Beerits Memorandum, pp. 18-19, Hughes MSS.
[63] Ibid.

humorless man, thrived on the hard work. In 1899 he moved to the firm of Seward, Guthrie & Steele as a partner, taking with him the business of the Westinghouse interests and the law office system Carter had pioneered.[64]

The firm Cravath joined, which had been Blatchford, Seward, Griswold & DaCosta until 1884 and Seward, Guthrie & Steele thereafter, had, according to the firm's historian, already begun to build up a significant corporate practice. In 1885 it had for the first time assumed primary responsibility for the consummation of a major railroad reorganization, that of the Denver and Rio Grande Railway Corporation. In the 1890s corporate work became, for the first time, the main work of the firm. The demands of such work helped entrench the changes in firm organization which Cravath brought with him and then perfected.

Prior to Cravath's arrival, the firm had been staffed by friends of the partners, of colleagues at the bar, and of clients, and most of them stayed only a few months. These men had not been much help in the important corporate matters which were increasingly dominating the firm's work. These men had not been paid and had been

---

[64]Hughes, Autobiographical Notes, pp. 72-87.

allowed to seek clients of their own. The lack of system and organization in the firm is revealed by the fact that in 1884 the firm employed no filing clerk and did not even have the semblance of a filing system. Though it did employ stenographers and copyists, it did not yet use typewriters. Even at the Carter firm in the late 1880s, the staff was minimal and the young law school graduates were thought of as part of the clerical force.[65]

Cravath changed all that. He hired only young lawyers who had graduated from both college and law school, preferably with high scholastic marks from elite universities. Cravath also preferred men with forceful personalities and rugged physiques, recognizing that the new type of corporate law practice required hard work from high-strung, tense, and driving personalities. The young lawyers were paid and were not allowed to work for anyone but the firm. In return, they gained the experience of working on the major reorganizations and securities issues which were, by the late 1890s, almost the exclusive work of the firm. The firm acted as counsel for such financial houses as Kuhn, Loeb and Company,

---

[65]Ibid., pp. 64-65, 75; Swaine, *Cravath Firm*, 1:370-372, 657-658, 364-365.

Speyer and Company, and the City of London Contract Corporation. During the great merger movement, the firm acted as counsel for the bankers who formed the American Steel and Wire Company, the American Bridge Company, the American Hide and Leather Company, and the International Steam Pump Company. It was during these years that the transition from advocate to counsel occurred, as reorganization and securities issues became more and more matters confined to the conference room rather than the courts.[66]

Thus, by the late 1890s and early 1900s, Cravath was creating a system of law office organization which would, when it became the general rule in the 1920s, make nearly impossible the kind of career he and his young colleagues on the Carter firm had known. They had established major reputations as young men. For example, Hughes was only twenty-six and Cravath twenty-five when they were made partners in Carter's firm in 1888. These men had been able to move easily from firm to firm, often creating new firms themselves and carrying their clients with them. In addition, they often became known by the

---

[66]Swaine, Cravath Firm, 1:657-658, 423-436, 633-642 370-372.

public, sometimes because, like Hughes, they were active in court practice, sometimes because they became involved in urban, state, or national politics. But the Cravath system, once institutionalized, churned out anonymous organization men, steadfastly loyal to the firm that had hired them fresh out of law school, moving only if the firm informed them it could not advance them to partnership.

A young lawyer in his third year with the Cravath firm, Mason Bigelow, was moved to complain in 1915 about his position in a revealing letter to his law school dean, Harlan Fiske Stone. He had worked on a wide variety of matters, including corporate organizations and reorganizations, underwriting of securities, wills, partnership agreements, construction contracts, and real estate transactions. In some of these matters, he had been given considerable personal responsibility. He had no complaints about the character of the work. But he wanted to leave the firm because "the number of older men in the office is so large that the outlook for advancement is not favorable, and . . . another office might, therefore, offer greater advantages."[67] Bigelow was not even listed

---

[67] Mason Bigelow to Harlan Fiske Stone, January 6, 1915, H. F. Stone MSS, Miscellaneous Correspondence, Columbia University Library.

as an associate of the Cravath firm in Hubbell's, its practice being to list only the partners. Stone advised Bigelow to look into Bowers & Sands, a five-partner firm.

By the 1920s the system Cravath had initiated was well established and regularized. The managing clerks of the leading law firms had even entered into a gentlemen's agreement after World War I to eliminate the practice that had grown up of competitive bidding for the services of the most promising law school graduates. They established uniform beginning salaries and agreed not to pirate employees away from each other.[68]

It took some time, however, for the Cravath system to spread. Allen Wardwell, who went into Francis Lynde Stetson's firm right after graduating from Harvard Law School in the late 1890s, reported that at first he was not paid. For several years, he did routine work only a cut above that of a clerk, not moving into corporation work until around 1904.[69] By 1905 William Draper Lewis was reporting that there was a heavy demand from large law offices for the best graduates of elite law schools,

---

[68] Swaine, Cravath Firm, 2:2-10; Smigel, "Large Law Firm," p. 61.

[69] Wardwell, Oral Memoir, p. 42.

"and oftentimes at very fair salaries."[70] "Oftentimes," not "always." John Foster Dulles reported that in 1911, when he was hired as a law clerk with Sullivan & Cromwell, another firm in the financial bar, he was paid only $50 per month.[71] One law firm historian's impression is that the customary starting salary for law school graduates in New York City in 1910 was $600 per year, which would accord with Dulles' experience. By the late 1920s, that figure had grown to $2400.[72] Apparently, the agreement among managing clerks to eliminate competitive bidding was confined to New York, judging by a letter in 1925 to Felix Frankfurter from a partner in Hale & Dorr, a leading Boston firm with long-standing ties to Harvard. The letter reflects a surprising ignorance about the correct level of competitive bidding for law school graduates.

> If we have to pay more than $1200 a year to get really first-class men in the School, we will, of course, do so. I am advised that to some extent good men go to New York rather than Boston

---

[70] ABA, Reports 28 (1905), 553.

[71] Dulles, "Foreword," in Dean, William Nelson Cromwell, pp. i-ii. Dulles' case may have been a little unusual since he did not have an Ivy League law degree. He had to rely on a letter of introduction from his grandfather, John W. Foster, Secretary of State in Benjamin Harrison's administration, who had read law with Cromwell's former partner in 1857.

[72] Swaine, "Impact of Big Business," p. 168.

because they get up to $2,000 or perhaps more to begin with. If we ought to pay that much, we will.[73]

****

During the 1920s, the new demands of corporation law practice greatly increased the number of truly large law firms. In the early days of corporation law practices, railroads, banks, and insurance companies had often been the most important clients of leading lawyers. As Willard Hurst has noted, the history of corporation law in the late nineteenth and early twentieth centuries reflects this fact. Corporation law legislation in this period was aimed at developing and perfecting the enabling type of corporation statute. This was largely the work of a small group of "financial venturers" and their lawyers, who saw advantages to themselves in the development of large corporations.

> Symbol of the self-styled responsible leadership of this interest was J. P. Morgan. Morgan perceived an expanding market for limited-commitment investments in a growing upper middle class of increasing affluence and in the financial intermediaries--insurance companies and banks--on which this class relied. Morgan needed a larger stock in trade--corporate shares and bonds--to realize the potentials of this market. To some degree he also saw the need to maintain investing

---

[73] Joseph N. Welch to Felix Frankfurter, November 27, 1925, Frankfurter MSS, Box 111.

confidence in this broader market. Confidence
meant that the investment banker should use his
strategic command of capital to police against
unsettling competition; entry to industrial
markets should be barred to rash newcomers, and
those already in should be persuaded or pressured
to accept reasonably stabilized market shares.
This investment banker's approach put first
priority on a corporate structure which allowed
creation of large aggregations of capital and
centralized inside control of corporation
finances--both to take advantage of the investment market and to determine the conditions of
change and stability. This demand found willing
cooperation in the states which pioneered in
the new type of corporation acts.[74]

A large corps of lawyers might enable a corporation to manage the legal questions in this kind of financial maneuvering in a more efficient way. But a few extremely knowledgeable counselors from a relatively small firm could do the job well also. In any case, so long as the largest corporations were railroads, the risks were not all that great. As Paul D. Cravath explained,

> Voluntary reorganizations are . . . comparatively
> infrequent in the case of railroad companies.
> The business of a railroad company is not apt
> to suffer seriously from a receivership. Indeed
> a railroad often emerges from foreclosures and
> receivership materially strengthened by the
> purging process through which it has passed.
> Not so with the average industrial corporation,
> whose business, goodwill and trade position are
> apt to be shattered by the effects of even the

---

[74] James Willard Hurst, <u>The Legitimacy of the Business Corporation in the Law of the United States, 1780-1970</u> (Charlottesville, Va., 1970), pp. 72-73.

most successful receivership or the most expeditious foreclosure. While in the case of a railroad, liquidation is usually impossible, if the affairs of an insolvent industrial corporation once get into the courts there is always the danger that creditors will force liquidation, preferring the cash proceeds of liquidation to the securities of a reorganized company. Consequently, sensible men, in dealing with an insolvent industrial corporation, make every effort to accomplish a voluntary readjustment.[75]

Hence, it is not a great surprise that Victor Morawetz, who had been a Cravath firm partner since 1887 and who was generally recognized, along with Francis Lynde Stetson, as one of the two leading railroad reorganizing lawyers in the 1890s and who was Andrew Carnegie's personal lawyer, withdrew from that budding law factory in 1896 to become the General Counsel for two railroads--so he could have more free time.[76]

Industrial corporations required more continuous legal supervision. In part this was due to the need for financial security cited by Cravath. In part it was due

---

[75]Paul D. Cravath, "The Reorganization of Corporations; Bondholders' and Stockholders' Protective Committees; Reorganization Committees; and the Voluntary Recapitalization of Corporations," in Francis Lynde Stetson et al., Some Legal Phases of Corporate Financing, Reorganization and Regulation (New York, 1917), pp. 211-212.

[76]Swaine, Cravath Firm, 1:383, 490, 562-564. He became General Counsel for the Atchison, Topeka and Santa Fe and for the Norfolk and Western, both of which he had helped reorganize. Morawetz is a good example of a professional-minded lawyer in the transition period. He published two books on political economy and the law,

to the increased volume of government regulations that industrial corporations became subject to from about 1914 on.[77] In part, it was because the production and organizational needs of industrial corporations generated a new spirit in the business world, a spirit which Hurst believes corporation law reflected from at least the 1920s on. He sees Andrew Carnegie symbolizing the new spirit, despite Carnegie's personal hostility to the corporation device.

> Carnegie saw the mission and the profits of business, not in financial maneuver, but in production regularly increased and made more profitable by investing in the best methods that developing technology and managerial skills could devise. Moreover, he held before him the vision of constantly expanding markets, which he would command by hard-driving competition in quality and price supported by technical and managerial efficiency. The promise of lasting growth and gain Carnegie saw, not in materials or money, but in large-scale organization; organization was the new factor of production. As the country moved into an expanding economy through the 1920's, prevailing

---

served on many committees for the Association of the Bar of the City of New York, and was a cofounder of the American Law Institute in the 1920s.

[77] Austin, "Large Law Firms," pp. 10-15; Swaine, "Impact of Big Business," pp. 89-92, 168-171.

opinion shared this faith in the key importance of energy and skill in business direction. The new corporation acts--designed to allow full scope to vigorous policy direction and management at the center--were consistent in structure with this faith in the productivity of such organization.[78]

Leading lawyers never completely succumbed to this new faith, partly because they continued to concentrate on the financial rather than the production side of the businesses they counseled[79] and partly because their professional predilections and social ideology remained essentially anti-organizational. However, the demands of their corporate clients by the 1920s clearly required the continuous and detailed supervision possible only

---

[78] Hurst, *Legitimacy of the Business Corporation*, pp. 74-75. This same theme has been emphasized by the "entrepreneurial school" of business historians, of whom Alfred Dupont Chandler is probably the dean. See his *Strategy and Structure: Chapters in the History of the Industrial Enterprise* (Cambridge, Mass., 1962). As Chandler's book makes clear, Alfred Dupont Sloan is probably a better symbol of the new spirit than Andrew Carnegie.

[79] Swaine, *Cravath Firm*, 2:432-433 and Dean, *William Nelson Cromwell*, pp. 59-74 makes this clear for two of the most important firms in the 1920s.

in the law factories.[80] From then on, the term "corporation lawyer" became unambiguously the designation for a lawyer who practiced in a large law firm.

---

[80] Swaine, "Impact of Big Business," p. 91; Swaine, Cravath Firm, 2:319-326; Robert A. Gordon, Business Leadership in the Large Corporation (Washington, 1945), pp. 260-265. Most railroads and insurance companies did have their own law departments, but they primarily handled routine matters. Apparently only a few other corporations established law departments before the 1930s. See John D. Donnell, The Corporate Counsel: A Role Study (Bloomington, Ind., 1970), p. 28; Taft, A Century and a Half, pp. 175, 193. For additional data, see chap. 3, fn. 16, above.

PART III

IDEOLOGY AND ORGANIZATIONAL STRUCTURE
OF PROFESSIONALISM

CHAPTER 6

THE BAR ASSOCIATION MOVEMENT, 1870-1900

Julius Cohen, a young member of the New York City legal elite who was dedicated to making bar organizations and bar self-government more effective, noted in 1916 an apparent conflict in the thinking of bar leaders. When he examined bar association reports from the late nineteenth and early twentieth centuries, he found statements of what he called the individualist viewpoint and at the same time statements of the need to establish guild-like and state-directed controls over admission to the legal profession.

> In their conception of the relationship of the individual to the State, the lawyers of the previous generation believed thoroughly that the State existed primarily for the development and progress of the individual, yet they fought the same individualistic philosophy when it took the shape of the Indiana constitutional provision that "every person of good moral character" was of right entitled to practice law.[1]

---

[1] Julius Henry Cohen, The Law: Business or Profession? (New York, 1916), pp. 126-127. Bar leaders may well have disagreed with Cohen's belief that their views were contradictory. Individualism does not necessarily imply an indifference to standards of expertise. Nevertheless, Cohen did perceptively note a major dualism in bar elite thought.

Indeed, the record of bar associations provides ambiguous and even contradictory evidence of the bar elite's participation in the development of the organizational society. From the 1870s on, there was a definite movement to establish and then expand bar associations, a movement that acquired special momentum in the 1890s. Leading lawyers were often very active in these associations, contributing their valuable time to serve as officers and as committee members in the associations' attempts to gain influence over the organization and functioning of the profession and the administration of justice.

Yet, despite this evidence of commitment and activity by the most prominent members of the profession, there is a distinct aura of triviality and ineffectualness surrounding the functioning of bar associations throughout the 1870 to 1930 period. The national organization, the American Bar Association, was able to enlist only a minority of the bar; state and local associations, while more inclusive, were not representative bodies either. There was not much cooperation among bar associations at different levels. Although the associations restricted themselves to narrowly professional concerns, the problems they addressed were rarely eliminated and only partially ameliorated.[2]

For example, there were numerous complaints throughout the period about such matters as overcrowded dockets, delays in the courts, mediocre lower court judges, irrational procedural rules, and shyster lawyers. Throughout the period, the same complaints were made, virtually the same remedies proposed. But there was a distinct trend toward working out a comprehensive reform plan to replace the piecemeal approach of the past. There was also a trend away from personalizing the issues and toward bureaucratizing the issues,

---

[2]Willard Hurst's judgment on bar associations can be considered authoritative:
"The record of the ABA might fairly be taken to measure the most sustained work of the organized bar in law reform and revision. One could not accurately or fairly label this record reactionary or radical, conservative or liberal, in the ordinary meaning of any of these terms. It was not a record of a comprehensive, long-range program, though on particular fronts the Association put forth organized, coherent activity. Certainly it was not the record of a pressure group that could show energy, internal discipline, or staff work comparable to the activity of the contemporary spokesman organizations for industry, commerce, labor or agriculture. As a pressure group, the lawyers were crude amateurs. With few exceptions they busied themselves with matters which they took up in isolation from the social context, and matters which were generally of secondary social importance, concerning issues merely incidental to the basic institutions and powers of the time. The ABA's most important contributions to law

from decreeing that the problems in the administration of justice resulted from the low character of men in the bar and on the bench, to deciding that the problems were technical ones which continuous administration by experts, usually experts with university credentials, could resolve. However, these trends emerged slowly and cannot be described as consistent features of bar elite ideology until the 1920s, the same decade that large law firms became fully institutionalized.

Several questions need to be asked about bar association history. What was the original impetus for bar association development, and what kept associations active and expansion-minded? Why were associations so ineffective, even within the narrow circle of activity they permitted themselves? Why did leading members of the profession persist in supporting associations that seemed unable to produce major changes? Why, given their experience, did the bar leaders' analysis of the problems in the administration of justice and their proposed solutions to those problems change so slowly?

---

    reform developed slowly. They concerned the regu-
    lation of the legal profession itself, the pro-
    cedure of the courts, and the enactment of uniform
    laws among the states."
James Willard Hurst, <u>The Growth of American Law: The Law Makers</u> (Boston, 1950), p. 361. Hurst did not attempt to analyze the reasons behind the organized bar's spotty record.

To answer these questions requires a combination of structural and ideological analysis. Taken together, the answers provide a summary of the professional outlooks of the bar elite in the 1870-1930 period.

The history of the modern organized bar is traditionally dated with the founding of the Association of the Bar of the City of New York (ABCNY) in 1870. The ABCNY was the first of several big-city bar associations established in the 1870s as part of the general revival of organizational activity among lawyers in the Gilded Age. For example, the Chicago Bar Association held its first meeting in November 1873. The Bar Association of Cleveland was established in 1873, the Bar Association of St. Louis in 1874, the Boston Bar Association in 1877.

These city bar associations in turn stimulated the creation of state bar associations. For instance, in 1876 the ABCNY queried lawyers around New York state about whether a state bar was desirable. When the lawyers responded favorably, an organizational meeting was held in November 1876. Not only did the New York state bar prove viable, but it also stimulated the formation of city and county bar associations throughout the rest of the state during the next few years.[3] By the mid-1880s the bar of all the industrial northeastern and north central states had been organized at the city, county, and state levels. However, the pattern varied from state to state. The county associations were especially strong in Pennsylvania and Massachusetts, while the state associations were weak. In other states, the city and state associations were stronger than the county associations. Outside the industrial areas, bar association organization proceeded more slowly. But by the 1890s, bar associations were sufficiently dense across the country that nearly all practicing lawyers could have been members.[4]

In fact, however, only a minority were members.[5] Partially, this was by design. The early bar associations were not open membership associations. They all

---

[3] George W. Martin, Causes and Conflicts: The Centennial History of the Association of the Bar of New York, 1870-1970 (Boston, 1970), pp. 131-133.

[4] In 1890 there were 20 state and territorial associations and 168 local associations; in 1900 there were 40 state and territorial associations and 258 local associations. ABA, Reports 23 (1900), 644-665.

[5] No one has calculated percentage figures for state or local bar associations. The ABA counted 0.9 percent in 1880, 1.05 percent in 1890, and 1.3 percent in 1900. By 1920, after an active recruiting effort, the figure was raised to 9 percent. In 1915 Harlan F. Stone reported

made admission to membership dependent upon recommendation by current members and a screening process. Even if they had been open membership associations, it is doubtful that they would have attracted significantly larger numbers, at least during the Gilded Age. Even this early, the bar was sufficiently stratified that social distance worked against the creation of thoroughgoing professional fellowship.[6]

Properly speaking, the bar association movement of the 1870s represented a revival; but it was a revival based on a weak tradition of bar organization. The few bar associations of the colonial and early national periods were not very strong or active; they came close to disappearing in the 1830s and 1840s. The primary reason for the bar's historic organizational weakness was that professional life was well regulated without bar associations. The judiciary established the guidelines for legal practice and proclaimed the authoritative

---

that only 35 percent of the 17,000 lawyers in New York City were members of any bar association. Stone, <u>Law and its Administration</u> (New York, 1915), p. 174.

[6] Numerous complaints about the low quality of the bar made by the bar elite at early bar association meetings testify to this stratification.

word on acceptable legal knowledge. Bar associations served primarily as social clubs and occasionally as lobbying associations for higher bar admission standards. This situation contrasted markedly with that in the medical profession, where the lack of a dominant authority to arbitrate among competing claims to professional expertise in the ante-bellum period led to the proliferation of medical societies, each dedicated to the advancement of its particular medical persuasion.[7]

The revival of bar associations from the 1870s on was, most fundamentally, a response by a self-proclaimed urban professional elite to their perception that the judiciary was no longer satisfactorily performing its regulatory function. The elite believed that popular control, mediated through political parties, had been

---

[7] Maxwell Bloomfield, "Lawyers and Public Criticism: Challenge and Response in Nineteenth-Century America," American Journal of Legal History 15 (October 1971), 269-277; William R. Johnson, "Educational and Professional Life Styles: Law and Medicine in the Nineteenth Century," History of Education Quarterly 14 (Summer 1974), 185-208. Both Bloomfield and Johnson persuasively refute the guild history interpretation, which argued that the period from 1765 to 1830 was the golden age of bar self-government and the period from 1830 to 1870 witnessed a temporary setback to professionalism due to the successful onslaughts of the leveling spirit of Jacksonian democracy. According to the guild history interpretation, the bar's historic sense of professionalism was being revived in the 1870s, albeit under altered socioeconomic conditions. See Roscoe Pound, The Lawyer from Antiquity to Modern Times

substituted for judicial control. Many in the elite viewed the practice of electing rather than appointing judges as the major cause of this loss of professional self-regulation. Elected judges, they believed, were so beholden to political parties and popular favor that they were indifferent to the necessity of protecting the rule of law and the good name of the profession. In the view of the elite, the evidence was all around them: public criticism of the profession and of the administration of justice seemed to be increasing, the quality of the lower bar seemed to be decreasing, judges seemed unable to control delays in either lower court proceedings or in the appellate process or to make the substantive law more certain and less contradictory. Scandals involving corruption and bribery on the judicial bench seemed to be occurring more frequently, and the scope of judicial review over legislation continued to be a lively issue of public debate. In part, the elite believed, increased public interest in the functioning of the legal system was stimulated by a sensation-seeking press. But more

---

(St. Paul, 1953), pp. 221-362; Charles Warren, A History of the American Bar (Boston, 1911), pp. 39-145, 188-239, 292-324; Hurst, Growth of American Law, pp. 277, 366; Stone, Law and Its Administration, pp. 162-165.

fundamentally, the increased public interest reflected what the elite saw as undue politicization of the profession. They wanted to reverse this politicization, not by returning control of the profession to an apolitical judiciary, since that was impractical, but by purifying the profession from within.[8]

In the words of Henry Nicoll, speaking at the first organizational meeting of the Association of the Bar of the City of New York, "all that is intelligent, all that is honest, all that is honorable in this Profession" had to be gathered together in order that the influence of the best might be able "to create a spirit of professional brotherhood, to create in the members of our profession a regard for the profession."[9] Nicoll traced the debasement of the bar to the New York state constitution of 1846, which created an elected judiciary in place of the previously appointed bench and made entry

---

[8] Audra L. Prewitt, "American Lawyers and Social Ferment: Prelude to Progressivism, 1870-1900" (Ph.D. dissertation, Northwestern University, 1973), pp. 29-70 has a good discussion of the ideas expressed by the founders of modern bar associations. The founders of ABCNY managed to include nearly all these ideas when explaining the need for their new association. See Martin, Causes and Conflicts, pp. 3-15.

[9] Ibid., pp. 31-32.

to the bar much easier by eliminating waiting periods and making examinations much easier.[10]

In other states the diagnoses and the ambitions were similar. Hailing the creation of the Chicago Bar Association, an editorial in the Chicago Legal News looked forward to "a thorough organization of the bar of this State, [by which] the standard of professional conduct could be elevated, and the disreputable shysters who now disgrace the profession could be driven from it."[11] The Executive Committee of the Chicago association phrased its intentions somewhat more elegantly.

> It has been deemed advisable that in Chicago some action should be taken by the profession to elevate its character. It is believed that the organized action and influence of the legal profession, properly exerted, will lead to the creation of more intimate relations between its members than now exist, and will, at the same time, sustain the profession in its proper position in the community, and thereby enable it, in many ways, to promote its own interests and the welfare of the public.[12]

To make the point very clear, the Committee declared as the standard for membership that "only those who have

---

[10] Ibid.

[11] Chicago Legal News, December 6, 1973, p. 89.

[12] Ibid., April 18, 1874, p. 242.

established a character of honor and industry in the profession will be recommended."[13]

The bar association movement was a manifestation in professional-minded terms of the same impulse which inspired the elite-directed reform movements of the late nineteenth century. Bar association leaders frequently were active in urban reform movements and in Mugwump state and national movements, which expressed themes similar to those expressed by the bar associations. These themes included alarm at the moral tone that public and professional life seemed to be assuming in the modern city, a diagnosis that politics and a crude materialism were responsible for this debasement, and a conviction that the solution was for men of the best sort to organize themselves so that they could oversee the operation of public and professional life. The civic elite's assumption seemed to be that quality would be recognized and deferred to if only it would make itself active and visible.[14]

---

[13] Ibid.

[14] Geoffrey Blodgett, The Gentle Reformers: Massachusetts Democrats in the Cleveland Era (Cambridge, Mass., 1966), pp. 23-29, 118, 139-140; Bloomfield, "Lawyers and Public Criticism," pp. 276-277.

Bar associations themselves rarely became directly involved in urban reform, except in such professional issues as the composition of the judiciary or the organization of the court system. But the dividing line between bar association activity and urban reform by bar association members was not always entirely clear. For example, although the ABCNY as a corporate body did not actually play a leading role in the campaign against Boss Tweed, the public got the opposite impression because so many of the prosecution leaders, the most prominent of whom was Samuel Tilden, were ABCNY members. The Association confined its official activity to opposing the nomination of Thomas A. Ledwith, Tweed's candidate for the New York Supreme Court in 1871, and to memorializing the state legislature to investigate charges of corruption against sitting Supreme Court judges.[15] The reluctance of the Association itself to engage in non-professional reform exasperated some of its "natural allies" such as William Travers Jerome, the District Attorney in the Seth Low administration, and John Jay Chapman, a major figure in

---

[15]Martin, Causes and Conflicts, pp. 68-74.

the City Club. Chapman, for example, publicly referred to the ABCNY as a "docile set of men."[16]

The reluctance of bar associations to engage in political issues stemmed from a variety of factors. Although some members of the elite were interested in taking over the national and in some areas the state organizations of the Republican party, they were generally reluctant to engage in the dreary details of lobbying and political maneuvering necessary to gain a positive hearing from state legislatures. The continuing localism of partisan political organization was a significant factor; the bar elite preferred a more exalted perspective.

Elihu Root, who was more active politically than most of the bar elite, declined the suggestion that he seek the New York governorship in 1904.

> The real duty proposed is one of State politics and the real burden to be assumed is the infinite multitude and mass of political details. . . I contemplate this with perfect loathing and disgust. . . . It would mean the permanent abandonment of my profession and my position at the

---

[16]The Nation, December 7, 1905, p. 454 and The Political Nursery, June 1898, as cited in Richard S. Skolnik, "The Crystallization of Reform in New York City, 1890-1917" (Ph.D. dissertation, Yale University, 1964), p. 324.

> Bar, the breaking up of my home to myself and my family, an exile for four years from the associations which make life worth living, and in exchange the complete surrender and devotion of my life to sordid details of local politics throughout the State.[17]

This disdain for the details of political maneuvering certainly retarded the development of a coherent strategy among the bar elite for pursuing its aims. This disdain also led, in the conservative crisis of the 1890s, to the conclusion among the elite that its major source of political power lay in its access to the courts, especially the federal courts.

Whether or not the political will could be summoned forth, it is not clear that bar association leaders had even thought through the kinds of solutions they preferred. The bar elite's ideas on such matters as raising standards and disciplining the bar were distressingly vague. Leading lawyers clearly would have

---

[17] Root to Henry Cabot Lodge, August 18, 1904, Root MSS, Box 184, Library of Congress. Robert D. Marcus, <u>Grand Old Party; Political Structure in the Gilded Age 1880-1896</u> (New York, 1971) provides abundant evidence on the localism of party organization. ABA presidents regularly called on their brethren to devote themselves more to the politics of their state legislatures. See the following presidential addresses in ABA, <u>Reports</u>: John Randolph Tucker, 16 (1893), 203; Alton B. Parker, 30 (1907), 392; Charles F. Manderson (1900), reprinted in <u>American Law Review</u> 34 (Sept.-Oct. 1900), 660-663. It is worth noting that many corporation lawyers found the details of their practice equally wearisome, a fact which

preferred the rest of the bar to fit their mold. However, they did not have a sociologically sophisticated understanding of why standards were as they were; at least they did not profess to any such understanding. Instead, they personalized the explanation, attributing the non-elite's standards to character defects or, in the case of first- or second-generation immigrants, to the lack of an in-bred understanding of American institutions. In advancing such an explanation and in defining for themselves their own standards of professional behavior, the legal elite was building its own social unity, which was an essential first step.

Social unity was essential because political issues, even those primarily professional in character, threatened to force leading lawyers to choose between partisan and professional loyalties. Certain professional issues, such as changing the methods of selecting judges or changing the admission standards of the bar, posed problems because these issues had or threatened to have consequences for the existing party structures. The judiciary was an important patronage plum to the parties, and

---

did not prevent that new specialty from growing rapidly during these same years.

a continued influx of ambitious, hungry young lawyers was an important source of manpower. So long as bar association members remained even marginally active in partisan politics, the unity and effectiveness of the associations was problematical. Although many leading lawyers shared a Mugwumpish aversion to blind partisan loyalty, they tended to approach politics in a more practical spirit than did the academic, literary, and journalistic representatives of the elite reform impulse.[18]

Therefore, a major goal of all bar associations was to establish a sense of professional community within the vaguely defined group of leading lawyers whom they considered their constituency. This effort preceded the other major focus of bar association activity, the attempt to establish the legitimacy of professional self-regulation.

In the late nineteenth century, the effort to create a functioning sense of professional community was for

---

[18] Evidence of this practical-minded approach to party loyalty by leading lawyers from both parties can be found in Francis Lynde Stetson to E. M. Shepard, September 17, 1893, E. M. Shepard MSS, Miscellaneous Correspondence, Columbia University Library, and in P. C. Jessup, notes on conversation with Elihu Root, November 5, 1934, Jessup MSS, Box 243, Library of Congress.

many bar associations their only ongoing activity. Except for its active involvement in the campaign to prevent adoption of a civil code in New York in the 1880s, the ABCNY, for example, concentrated on social activities and the maintenance of a library. The three committees which the ABCNY had appointed at its founding, the committee on amendment of the law, the committee on the judiciary, and the committee on grievances, all failed to function after the first few years.[19]

When the Chicago Bar Association reached the end of its first year, the Chicago Legal News summarized the Association's work by emphasizing its social function: "This association is doing much to cultivate a friendly and social feeling between the members of the bar."[20] Daily luncheons were held in the bar association's rooms, and there was an annual dinner to

---

[19] Martin, Causes and Conflicts, pp. 46-47. See pp. 143-157 for a thorough discussion of the fight against the civil code. James Grafton Rogers, "History of the American Bar Association," American Bar Association Journal 39 (August 1953), 662 concludes that a yearning for social contact and the need for library facilities were the major raison d'être of bar associations in the 1870s and 1880s.

[20] Chicago Legal News, October 5, 1874, p. 13.

which were invited many judges and members of the bar from surrounding states. But monthly business meetings were poorly attended, and the Association was little more than a fraternal organization until the late 1880s, when it became more activist in such areas as legal education, judicial elections, and legal ethics.[21]

An interesting insight into the balance between social functions and substantive activities of a state bar association can be gained from the remarks of 1905 Ohio Bar Association President James O. Troup. At the beginning of the annual meeting, he proposed that the Association restrict itself to one session a day, beginning at 9:30 in the morning. It seems that the delightful surroundings of Put-in-Bay, Ohio, where the Association had met yearly since 1888, had created "a tendency among the members to neglect meetings of the Association" in favor of "sitting on the veranda smoking, visiting, and wandering around."[22] Later, in his presidential address, Troup made clear that he had no desire to

---

[21] Ibid., December 19, 1874, pp. 101, 104; Herman Kogan, The First Century: The Chicago Bar Association, 1874-1974 (Chicago, 1974), pp. 40, 43-47, 63.

[22] Ohio State Bar Association, Proceedings 26 (1905), 9.

change the social tone of the meetings. He believed that the presence of wives and daughters at the meetings, which had become traditional, was helping, "more than anything else . . . to accomplish one of the express objects of the Association, viz., 'the cultivation of sociability among members of the bar'; a sociability which is elevating our manhood, sweetning our toil, and forever abolishing the asperities which formerly marred the conduct of professional business."[23] But there was the business side, which Troup did not want to neglect. He proudly reviewed the accomplishments of the state bar during its first twenty-five years. These included stimulating reform in court structure, cooperating with the Supreme Court in establishing educational requirements for bar admission, succeeding partially in codifying civil law (note the contrast with the ABCNY), successfully lobbying for statutory reforms such as improved election laws and corporation laws, facilitating the taking of a case to the appellate level, and raising salaries of Supreme Court judges.[24]

---

[23]Ibid., p. 87.
[24]Ibid., pp. 81-86.

These various social and substantive activities of city and state bar associations were not trivial functions, and they spoke to a strongly felt need. But they do reveal the sharp limits on the organization-mindedness of the bar elite during the Gilded Age.

At the national level, the American Bar Association reveals the same patterns. It was established in 1878 by seventy-five elite lawyers from major cities. Prominent in this group were Simeon E. Baldwin and other lawyer members of the American Social Science Association, an organization that sought to create a cosmopolitan elite. The ABA founders seem to have been interested in extending that general movement into their professional life. Baldwin, who is widely credited as the founder of the ABA, came from a prominent New Haven family of lawyer-politicians. Although he was a corporation lawyer, he preferred to think of himself as a gentleman scholar and lawyer-politician of the old school. His myriad associational activities were devoted to protecting old and new professions against the claims of popular democracy and commercialism.[25]

---

[25]Frederick H. Jackson, Simeon Eben Baldwin--Lawyer, Social Scientist, Statesman (New York, 1955), passim. I am indebted to Sally Flocks' stimulating reinterpretation of the meaning of Baldwin's professional activities in her

The ABA was also part of the national reconciliation between the North and the South. The first eleven annual meetings were held at Saratoga Springs, New York. During these eleven years, membership slowly climbed to 750. During the next thirteen years, alternate meetings were held at Saratoga Springs and major cities. Saratoga was a convenient meeting point for the Northern and Southern legal elite because by 1878, it had become the usual summer resort for many eminent Southern lawyers. Southerners played an important role in the new association: six of the first ten presidents were from the Southern or border states, including the first one, James O. Broadhead of St. Louis. Other leading Southern lawyers were active in the Association.[26]

Moorfield Storey of Boston, ABA president 1895-1896, emphasized that participating in the Association served to establish national lines of communication among the bar elite.

Yale University seminar paper, "Status Revolution and Professionalization: The Case of Simeon E. Baldwin," in author's possession.

[26] Francis Rawle, "Presidential Address," ABA, Reports 26 (1903), 261-262.

> The position of president of the Bar Association brought me into relationship with leading lawyers all over the country and kept me more or less busy during the term of office in attending meetings of Bar Associations in other States. It was a very agreeable, if somewhat exacting position and gave me a standing at the bar all over the country which otherwise I might not have attained.[27]

This national legal elite in the making remained a small group for many years. The annual meeting, which was about the only activity of the Association for its first fifteen years, drew an average attendance of 113 during its first ten years. Attendance did not reach 200 for a single meeting until 1891 when, for the second time, the Association met someplace other than Saratoga Springs. That year 202 attended the meeting in Boston. Membership totals were higher than attendance, but still not very impressive, new members averaging eighty-six per year during the first eleven years and somewhat higher

---

[27] Mark A. DeWolfe Howe, *Portrait of an Independent, Moorfield Storey, 1845-1929* (Boston and New York, 1932), p. 188, quoting from Storey's autobiography. Ironically, in 1912 Storey found himself trying to combat one of the implications of this focus on social unity among the national bar elite when he opposed the expulsion of black lawyer W. H. Lewis, a U.S. Assistant Attorney General, who had been admitted as a member before the admission committee discovered his race. At that time, S. S. Gregory of Chicago was ABA president. He printed an open letter replying to Storey, arguing that the ABA was as much a social as a professional organization, that its success depended on the social intercourse of members at the annual meeting, and that it was clearly the intention

thereafter. The association could boast 1,110 members when it convened in Boston in 1891.[28]

A shared cosmopolitanism and urbanism helped to unite ABA members. This can be illustrated by the high percentage of ABA members who were from major cities in the 1890s. In 1892, for example, 83 percent of the New York state members were from New York City (including Brooklyn). Of the Illinois members, 92 percent were from Chicago or Evanston. All twenty-four of the Louisiana members were from New Orleans. Of the Massachusetts members, 70 percent were from Boston and many of the remaining 30 percent came from Boston suburbs. Among the ten leading states in the Association, only Pennsylvania, Ohio and Wisconsin drew less than 60 percent of their membership from the two largest cities in

---

of the founders as well as many of the present members not to admit anyone from "that class of persons." Gregory was supported by an editorial in the Bench and Bar, which pointed out that other social and professional organizations lawyers belonged to had exclusion policies. The Union League Club of New York City barred Jews; the ABCNY barred women. The legal periodical noted that no one had protested those bars because "delicacy and gentility forbid." See Charles J. Bonaparte MSS, Box 188, Library of Congress, for copies of these items and others on the Lewis episode. See also ABA, Reports 37 (1912), 11-16, 93-95.

[28] ABA, Reports. The annual reports provide a complete list of all those registering at the annual meeting and full membership lists. See also Edson R. Sunderland, History of the American Bar Association and Its Work (n.p., 1953), pp. 39-41.

the state. In 1892 Philadelphia and Pittsburgh accounted for 56 percent of Pennsylvania's members; Milwaukee for only 33 percent of Wisconsin's; Cincinnati and Cleveland for 49 percent of Ohio's. Ohio's figures are distorted by the large number of medium-sized cities in the state, which accounted for most of the remaining 51 percent. Pennsylvania's special status seems to have derived from its long history of strong county bar associations and from the conservatism of the Philadelphia bar, a conservatism which revealed itself in the slowness to create large law firms and the weakness of the city bar association. These same percentage figures hold when ABA membership lists are examined in 1901, 1910, and 1920.[29] The small-town and rural lawyers were not attracted to the national association. State associations had higher percentages of non-urban members, but they depended upon the interest of urban lawyers for their effectiveness.

Not surprisingly, the tasks bar associations set for themselves were primarily designed to cope with the transformations in professional life brought about by urbanization. Taken together, these transformations were

---

[29] ABA, Reports.

seen by bar leaders as indicative of a deterioration in the standards of the urban bar. The three most important committees established by the ABA at its original meeting succinctly defined the tasks: improving the quality of judges, improving the quality of legal education, and encouraging more uniformity in commercial law in the various states.[30] The committees actually did very little. But they were symbolic of the main concerns of the bar elite and did define the directions in which the ABA moved when it became more active in the 1890s.

Although common urbanism helped to unite bar leaders at the national level, the growing split between urban and rural lawyers impaired possibilities for overall unity within the profession and contributed to the overall weakness of bar organizations. The history of professions in the twentieth century suggests that unless a profession can be united at the national level, its organizational effectiveness will be significantly diminished. National standards are much more convincing

---

[30]Max Radin, "The Achievements of the American Bar Association: A Sixty Year Record," American Bar Association Journal 25 (November 1939), 906-907.

to state legislatures or to others whose agreement is
needed. If the ABA had adopted a federal structure, the
organization would have been stronger. But efforts to
federalize the ABA progressed slowly, in large part
because non-urban lawyers remained indifferent to the
ABA. As early as 1879, state bar associations were
given the privilege of appointing delegates to the ABA
meetings. However, relatively few states even bothered
to take this minimal step. In 1880 only one state sent
a delegate; in 1887 seven states sent representatives,
in 1893 sixteen, in 1902 twenty-nine.[31] This same
weakness existed at the state level, where ties between
state and local bar associations were very tenuous.[32]
The rural-urban split was also important because many
of the lawyer-legislators were from rural districts.
To the extent that they felt a social and professional

---

[31] Sunderland, History of ABA, pp. 43-44. From 1887 to 1911, lists of local and state bar associations and their officers were published in the ABA's annual report. In 1912 local associations were omitted and only state associations listed. Between 1900 and 1914, summaries of major activities and addresses to state bar associations were published in the ABA's annual report.

[32] Margaret F. Sommer, "The Ohio State Bar Association: The First Generation, 1880-1912" (Ph.D. dissertation, Ohio State University, 1972), pp. 70-71 makes this clear for a typical industrial state.

distance from the urban lawyers who were pressing reforms on them through their bar associations, they were likely to resist such pressures.[33]

Another barrier to national bar organization was the fact that the legal system of each state was separate from that of other states. Only lawyers who practiced regularly in federal courts or who had clients doing business in several states could hope to gain in any immediate sense from national bar organization. Pointing out this lack of a strong national orientation among lawyers is just another way of emphasizing that the legal profession, unlike most other professions, did not modernize on the basis of any new universalistic technical principles. Those who advocated the case method of legal

---

[33] Corinne L. Gilb, Hidden Hierarchies: The Professions and Government (New York, 1966), pp. 218-221 cites several mid-twentieth-century studies that show lawyer-legislators vote more according to political party or regional interest than according to bar association policy. These studies offer the following reasons: (1) the career experiences and backgrounds of lawyer-legislators and bar association leaders differ; (2) the lawyer-legislators tend to identify themselves as politicians rather than as lawyers; or, if they do identify with the profession, they consider themselves more representative than bar association leaders of the majority of lawyers. If these trends can be found in the twentieth century, they almost certainly were stronger in the nineteenth century.

education tried to remedy this. In leading institutions such as Harvard, Columbia, Michigan, Northwestern, and the University of Chicago, professors deliberately created national law schools, only incidentally serving the needs of those who wanted to practice in the local jurisdiction. The degree of success that such schools had in imposing their standards on non-elite schools was a good index of the strength of the nationalizing potentialities in the legal profession. Success was modest, at least until the 1930s, and then probably increased as much because the depression hurt non-endowed law schools as for any other reason.[34]

The record of professional association activity indicates that throughout the 1870s and 1880s leading members of the urban bar felt that the profession and the administration of justice were not sufficiently well regulated and that informal means of social cohesion among the legal elite were no longer effective. They were more willing to act on the second concern, the lack of social cohesion. They focused on promoting social

---

[34] Robert Stevens, "Two Cheers for 1870: The American Law School," *Perspectives in American History* 5 (1971), 493-504.

cohesion rather than substantive reforms for three reasons. Without social cohesion, professional self-regulation could not even be attempted. Reforms in the administration of justice were bound to be resisted by political parties, and the legal elite recognized the organized bar's political weakness. Finally, continuous professional self-government required thinking about the bench and bar in bureaucratic terms. Although leading lawyers were quite willing to support measures like civil service reform, they were unwilling to rationalize their own profession along similar lines. They hoped urban reform efforts would purify politics and make continuous professional self-government unnecessary.

However, by the 1890s sufficient social unity had been achieved that the bar elite was prepared to move onto the next stage in associational development. In addition, in that decade substantive issues arose which began to teach the need for and to provide experience in more successful organizational techniques. For these reasons, bar association activity and effectiveness increased perceptibly during the 1890s. By 1900 the ABA had 1,540 members, an increase of 64 percent over its 1890 membership. As significant as the increase was, it was equally significant that it resulted from a deliberate policy. The Association moved its annual meeting from Saratoga Springs in alternate years, beginning in 1891 when it met in Boston. In 1893 it met in Milwaukee, two years later in Detroit, then in Cleveland, Buffalo, and Denver. After the 1902 meeting, Saratoga Springs was abandoned altogether. Attendance figures were consistently higher in the cities than at the resort, and, even more important, many new members from the host city and its vicinity joined the membership rolls. True, some of the new members failed to renew, but the net gains of the new policy were unmistakable.[35]

The most tangible signs of the new activism during the 1890s were two organizational innovations in the ABA. The first was the creation of the Commission for Uniform State Laws, the second was the creation inside the Association of permanent sections devoted to specialized topics of concern to particular segments of the profession.

The bar elite's common interest in greater uniformity of laws as between the states, especially of commercial law, had been an important factor in their original

---

[35] ABA, Reports 13-24 (1890-1901). See especially 18 (1895), 46-52 for a debate on the meeting site.

desire for unity. When Judge Gustave Koerner of Illinois replied to Simeon E. Baldwin's call to form the ABA in 1878, Koerner expressed a strong interest in uniform state laws.

> While in our diversified states an entire uniformity of the laws would be hardly attainable, if even desirable, yet no lawyer of any experience can have failed to regret the great diversity in our commercial law, and laws of contract generally in the different states. To assimilate the laws of the states particularly in that regard is highly desirable, and perhaps nothing would promote this object better than a national association.[36]

As was typical of the early years, the organization took no concrete action during its first twelve years, though members did express interest in uniform state laws at the annual meetings in 1879, 1882, 1886, and 1888.[37] The uniform laws movement was stimulated not only by a desire to unify the commercial law as an aid to interstate business, but also by a desire to prevent federal action. That is, the evils of diversity in state laws were attacked partially to forestall enlargement of the scope of federal control. The tangible fear was that if federal action became the norm, a

---

[36] Sunderland, History of ABA, pp. 12-13. Sunderland gives no source for the letter.

[37] ABA, Reports 2 (1879), 194-208; 5 (1882), 283-286; 9 (1886), 294-319; 11 (1888), 50-58, 307-321.

bureaucratic agency outside the control of the legal elite would be created in Washington.[38]

Finally, in 1889 a Special Committee on Uniform State Laws was appointed by the ABA. This was only the third special committee in the Association's history. The first was the Special Committee on Uncertainty in Judicial Administration, appointed in 1884; the second was the Special Committee on the Classification of the Law, appointed in 1888. The resolution creating the uniform laws committee proposed that it look into the need for uniform laws in four areas: marriage and divorce, descent and distribution of property, acknowledgement of deeds, and execution and probate of wills.[39] Separate standing committees of the Association had looked into these various areas in previous years, but the committees had not come up with any concrete suggestions.[40]

---

[38] Samuel Williston, Life and Law (Boston, 1941), p. 218. Williston spoke from experience as a drafter of four of the early uniform acts. See also Charles F. Libby, "Presidential Address," ABA, Reports 33 (1910), 350.

[39] M. Louise Rutherford, The Influence of the American Bar Association on Public Opinion and Legislation (Philadelphia, 1937), p. 276.

[40] Sunderland, History of ABA, pp. 50-54.

While the ABA Special Committee on Uniform State Laws was trying to decide how to carry out its mandate, the New York legislature passed the key legislation, thereby breaking the logjam in the movement. Thus legislation created in 1890 a three-man board of Commissioners for the Promotion of Uniformity of Legislation in the United States. In response, the ABA Special Committee urged that prestigious ABA committees be formed in each state to lobby for the creation of similar commissions by the various state legislatures.[41]

By 1892, when the first annual National Conference of the Commissioners on Uniform State Laws was held in conjunction with the ABA annual meeting (as it has been ever since), eight states had appointed commissioners. This number included not only the major industrial states of Pennsylvania, New Jersey, Michigan, and Massachusetts, as might have been expected, but also the Southern states of Georgia and Mississippi, indicating a truly national interest in the subject. Eleven more states sent commissioners in 1893, three more in 1894, seven more in 1895,

---

[41] Ibid.

and most of the remaining states in the next few years.[42] The ABA converted its special committee into a standing committee, chaired during the early years by Lyman D. Brewster of Danbury, Connecticut. The new committee and the National Conference worked very closely together. Their personnel were different in the early years but became almost identical by 1910.

In 1896 Brewster reported to the ABA that the work of the committee and the conference had so far been "deliberate, conservative and entirely on judicial lines. That is to say, it works to promote the symmetry, unity, and harmony of the law as a science."[43] He undoubtedly considered the law to be a science in the same sense that Joseph H. Choate, the eminent New York advocate, used the term when he summarized the viewpoint of his generation of elite lawyers: "We love the law because among all the learned professions, it is the only one that involves the study and pursuit of a stable and exact science."[44] The operative word for Choate was stable,

---

[42] ABA, Reports 15-18 (1892-1895); Rutherford, Influence of ABA, pp. 277-279.

[43] ABA, Reports 19 (1896), 407.

[44] Frederick C. Hicks, ed., Arguments and Addresses of Joseph Hodges Choate (St. Paul, 1926), p. 798.

as he made clear when he contrasted the law to theology and medicine.

> Theology . . . was once considered an immutable science . . . but now upon what unhappy times have we fallen, in which the props of our faith are being knocked from under us day by day . . . And then as to medicine, how its practice and its theories succeed each other in rapid revolution, so that what were good methods and healing doses and saving prescriptions a generation ago are now condemned as poisons and nostrums. Meanwhile the common law like a nursing father makes void the part where fault is and preserves the rest, as it has been doing for centuries, and we are busy applying to each new case as it arises, the same principles, the same rules of right and justice, which have been established for many generations.[45]

The uniform law commissioners were trying to live up to the spirit of this conception of the law. They were not seeking reform, but merely trying to make the common law more workable by making it uniform between the states. As Brewster assured the ABA in 1898, "the subjects on which the Commissioners are called to act . . . are few. The acts, so far proposed, are still fewer, and none of them novel."[46] Brewster did admit that this meant partial codification, the putting into statutory shape of the whole law on a particular subject, since "tinkering," which he defined as the attempt to

---

[45] Ibid., pp. 798-799.

[46] ABA, Reports 21 (1898), 331.

reconcile the law of various states, would not work, as it would produce bad laws based on senseless compromises. Thus, the commissioners strongly recommended that the states completely scrap their old laws and adopt the uniform model law.[47]

The first such model statute was the Negotiable Instruments Act of 1896, which was actually an adaptation of the 1882 English Bills of Exchange Act. The new act was immediately adopted in four states and by 1899 it was adopted in sixteen states. Each subsequent year a few more states joined in, so that by 1905 thirty states or territories had a uniform negotiable instruments law on their books.[48]

There was opposition to the law in several states. In Michigan, for example, the law was opposed on the grounds that it intruded on the practice of the legal profession. It was argued that after the law of commerical paper had been codified, the average man would not need a lawyer to collect a note. As might be expected, this oppostion came from the middle and lower strata of the bar, and not from the elite lawyers, who

---

[47] Ibid., pp. 327-328.
[48] Ibid., 20-28 (1897-1905).

were generally enthusiastic about the movement. The elite argued that although the law would eliminate many of the disputed questions which had arisen because of differences between various state laws, it would facilitate trade between the states and make transaction of business less complicated and more certain. The supporters also liked to point out that law is made *by* not *for* lawyers, that lawyers are supposed to put the interests of clients first. In any case, the supporters argued, no amount of codification would ever eliminate litigation and deprive lawyers of a livelihood. The Michigan legislature adopted the act in 1905.[49]

To a later generation of lawyers, the Negotiable Instruments Act and subsequent model uniform acts--the Sales Act of 1906 (never so widely adopted), the Warehouse Receipts Act, the Bills of Lading Act (1909), the Stock Transfer Act (1909), and the Conditional Sales Act (1918)--had several glaring deficiencies. The main fault was that they were not all entirely consistent with one another. Discrepancies among the acts were a major

---

[49] George [sic?] M. Bates, "Negotiable Instruments Act in Michigan Legislature," American Law Review 37 (November-December 1903), 876-879.

barrier to any one jurisdiction adopting all of them. In those which did, conflicting court interpretations of various provisions made them dissimilar acts in the different states, thereby nullifying the original purpose of the acts. For example, it was calculated that by 1940, 80 of the 198 sections of the Negotiable Instruments Act had different meanings in different states. Hence the need for a second-generation act, the Uniform Commerical Code.[50] This incomplete rationalization, especially the failure to create links among the various episodes of rationalization (the separate acts), was very typical of the bar elite's earliest forays into the bureaucratic organization of their profession.

The other major national organizational innovation of the 1890s, beyond the National Conference of Commissioners on Uniform State Laws, was the establishment of sections within the ABA. Sections were semi-autonomous bodies within the main association. They held their meetings

---

[50] William A. Schnader, "The Uniform Commerical Code," Harvard Review 3 (Fall-Winter 1965), 55-57. The National Conference of Commissioners on Uniform State Laws (CUSL) became an important body in bar circles for reasons other than its substantive activities. Its annual meeting, held a few days before the ABA annual meeting, became the locus of much bar politics, and activity in the CUSL became a common stepping-stone to an ABA leadership role. Rogers, "History of the ABA," 661.

at the time of the annual ABA meeting, but they had their own officers and by-laws and pursued their own policies. They were expected to develop proposals for the ABA to accept or reject, although in practice, consensus has been achieved, if at all, via behind-the-scenes communication between section leaders and national officers.[51] Besides indicating the greater organizational maturity of the ABA, the sections illustrate the specific professional concerns which generated a large specialized following in the 1890s.

Not surprisingly, one major area of concern was legal education and the standards of admission. The Section of Legal Education and Admission to the Bar was created within the ABA in 1893 and soon supplanted the standing committee which had been ineffectually discussing legal education since the founding of the Association.[52] At the time the Section was created, at least sixteen states--most of them in the South but also a few in more urban and industrial sections--had no requirements for any specified period of study or legal education prior to application for admission to the bar.[53] The Section

---

[51] Gilb, Hidden Hierarchies, p. 170.

[52] Sunderland, History of ABA, pp. 28-31.

[53] Cohen, Law: Business or Profession?, p. 135.

devoted its energies not to raising the admission standards in the various states, an effort which did engage the attention of several state bar associations, but instead to encouraging the emergence of quality law schools. In other words, the response of the Section was typical of an earlier pattern of ABA activity: the initial effort was made to create a set of national standards on which the elite could agree.

In the early years there was substantial disagreement, centering primarily on the case method. (The story of this dispute will be told in a later chapter.) There were a number of subsidiary issues which became topics for discussion in the Section. What should be the relationship between law school and undergraduate education? Should law school students spend much time learning the civil and criminal procedural rules of the jurisdiction in which the law school was located? How could legal education be shaped so that it upheld the place of law in society?[54] The Section provided a setting in which practitioners and professors could exchange ideas and take each other's measure. The practitioners tended to

---

[54]These and other topics were the subject of papers read to the Section during the 1890s. The reading of papers typically provoked long and serious discussion.

run the Section, although they were very sympathetic to the attempt of the professors to make law-school teaching a respected full-time professional specialty. The Section took the lead in 1900 in creating the Association of American Law Schools, which became the professional association for law professors.

The early history of the Section of Legal Education clearly illustrated the ABA's habit of responding to events rather than taking the initiative itself. In the 1890s legal education was obviously shifting from the law office to the law school, for complex reasons having very little to do with the activities of the bar elite. The shift was a dramatic manifestation of the general trend that had produced the modern bar association: the breakdown of older, more person-centered forms of professional control, overseen by judges who could make informed and binding decisions in cases of dispute or uncertainty.

Closely associated with changes in legal education during the 1890s were changes in admission procedures in the states. The trend was toward bureaucratic state examination boards to replace both ad hoc local boards and the diploma privilege. There was a general recognition that state-wide examinations were a useful indirect control on the quality of legal education, since there were otherwise no controls on those who wanted to create law schools.[55] New York took the lead when its State Board of Examiners held its first examination in January 1895.[56] The ABA sought to coordinate this movement in the various states by encouraging both bar examiners and those active in the bar examination movement to meet with the Section of Legal Education. In 1904 the Conference of State Boards of Bar Examiners was created. It held its meetings concurrently with the ABA. The rationalization of bar admission procedures, which the state bar examination movement represented, opened up the very sensitive issue of who should write the examination questions, and what standards of legal education they should conform to.[57]

One organizational innovation that failed during the 1890s was the National Bar Association, which was based on a federal structure. It enlisted prominent lawyers, especially from the West and South, who believed a more centralized national body was needed. Like the

---

[55] Radin, "Achievements of ABA," January 1940, pp. 19-20.

[56] ABA, Reports 19 (1896), 550.

[57] See chap. 9 below for discussion of law school professors' criticism of bar examination questions.

ABA, the National Bar Association focused on promoting uniformity in state laws. But the National Bar Association was short-lived. It probably suffered from the weakness of the state and local associations. The legal profession simply was not ready for a national association of bar association delegates. In the 1890s a national association still had to depend upon the cosmopolitan and national-minded urban elite. When the New York City and Boston bar associations made clear their allegiance to the ABA, the National Bar Association lost its access to the most organization-minded segments of the profession. The National Bar Association was also handicapped because it had to focus its interests and energies. Those lawyers interested in bar associations were interested for a wide diversity of reasons. When the ABA began to experiment with creating sections, it was able to tap this diversity in a way that a struggling new association could not. When the ABA began working on legal education and admission standards, it was probably taking a crucial step, for at least some members of most local and state associations were passionately interested in that issue.[58]

---

[58] Norbert Brockman, "The National Bar Association, 1888-1893: The Failure of Early Bar Federation," American Journal of Legal History 10 (April 1966), 122-127;

Activities on the state and local level in the 1890s are more difficult to summarize. At the local level, the Association of the Bar of the City of New York took steps that paralleled the ABA activities. It converted its grievance committee to a continuous investigative body by appointing a permanent part-time attorney to the committee in 1897. Shortly thereafter, the volume of complaints made and of actions taken increased enormously. Presumably the increase was an artifact of the organizational innovation rather than a reflection of a sudden deterioration in standards among the New York bar.[59]

In Illinois, the state and Chicago bar associations began working together in 1894 to persuade the state Supreme Court to change its admission rules to create a state board of bar examiners, to raise the requirement of law study from two years to three, to eliminate the diploma privilege, and to require that all candidates for the bar be high school graduates. The memorials to

---

Alfred Z. Reed, <u>Training for the Public Profession of the Law: Historical Development and Principal Contemporary Problems of Legal Education in the United States with Some Account of Conditions in England and Canada</u> (New York, 1921), pp. 211-212.

[59]Martin, <u>Causes and Conflicts</u>, pp. 353-367.

the court explained that such other states as New York, Massachusetts, Michigan, Ohio, Minnesota, and Wisconsin were enacting such changes and that unsupervised law schools were springing up all over. A man could enroll in a law school for two years and be allowed to take the bar exam, without having actually studied much. In 1897 the court agreed to the proposed changes.[60]

Why did national, state, and local bar associations become more active and more effective in the 1890s? Part of the answer has been suggested above. There were changes in the structure of the profession. For example, when legal education moved from the office to the school, the issues of uniform and quasi-bureaucratic standards for law schools and bar admission became more important than they had been. There were also changes in the law business of leading lawyers which suggested the need for reform. For example, such lawyers discovered from their day-to-day practice that the commercial law of the various states needed to be made uniform. These structural changes fed a growing anxiety within the bar elite about the major social changes that urbanization and

---

[60] Illinois State Bar Association, *Proceedings* 22 (1898), 122-129.

industrialization were bringing. The legal elite was beginning to lose its previous optimism about its own role and about the role of the law and legal institutions in the emerging new social order.

The bar elite sensed that the old rules of the political, economic, cultural, and social order were being questioned and that everyone seemed to be taking sides. This sense of social change, which, objectively speaking, reflected an accumulation of changes at least two decades in the making, was heightened by several developments peculiar to the 1890s. The depression raised serious questions about the permanence and stability of the existing economic system, questions which were heightened by the challenge of radicalism and labor activism. Coxey's army, the Pullman boycott, the Homestead strike, and even the Populist and Bryanite movements received anxious attention at ABA meetings. These events of the 1890s confirmed the fears of leading lawyers about the political and social trends of the times. They agreed that ways had to be found to limit the powers of legislative bodies, labor unions, and popular movements, but they were not of one mind about the proper means. The more cautious lawyers were concerned that the traditional balancing role of the legal system not be compromised.

They feared any moves which might make it appear that the system was intervening more heavily on one side than the other in contemporary disputes. On the other hand, the more alarmed lawyers argued that novel times demand that the law be creative. In their view, if there was popular disrespect for the legal system, it was because irresponsible men had attracted the public's attention. Therefore, they argued, the bar had a major education effort before it to restore the balance.[61]

The increase in bar association activity in the 1890s was only one of the responses bar leaders made to the challenges they perceived. Both the general and the special purpose urban reform movements in which many bar leaders were active began to turn away from occasional reform campaigns and toward a more bureaucratic conception of the urban reform task. At the same time bar leaders shored up their traditional defenses by formulating constitutional doctrines the courts would accept as

---

[61] Arnold M. Paul, Conservative Crisis and the Rule of Law (Ithaca, 1960) is the classic account of the conservative bar elite's reaction to what they perceived as a majoritarian threat in the 1890s. Paul bases his interpretation on the congruence between themes emphasized in speeches to the ABA and in the major U.S. Supreme Court decisions in the 1890s. A recent revisionist work is Prewitt, "American Lawyers and Social Ferment," pp. 71-151, which presents evidence of moderate-liberal resistance among some leading lawyers to the concept of judicial supremacy in the 1890s.

bulwarks of property against majoritarian threats. These activities have been examined in detail by other historians and will not be reviewed here.[62] The point to be made is that bar association activity cannot be considered in a political vacuum. It was only one in a series of responses the bar elite made. Bar association activity needs to be understood within this broader context.

From this broader perspective, the significance of bar associations is that they provided a forum within which leading lawyers could define the issues of the day in professional terms. In their bar association speeches, the lawyers began to tell themselves that not only their profession but also the rule of law itself was under attack. Insofar as the attacks focused on real weaknesses within the profession or the administration of

---

[62] See, for example, Skolnik, "Reform in New York City," partially summarized in Skolnik, "Civic Group Progressivism in New York City," New York History 51 (July 1970), 411-439; Samuel P. Hays, "The Politics of Reform in Municipal Government in the Progressive Era," Pacific Northwest Quarterly 55 (October 1964), 157-169; Bonnie R. Fox, "Philadelphia Progressives; A Test of the Hofstadter-Hays Theses," Pennsylvania History 34 (October 1967), 372-394; David B. Tyack, "City Schools: Centralization of Control at the Turn of the Century," in Jerry Israel, ed., Building the Organizational Society, Essays on Associational Activities in Modern America (New York, 1972), pp. 1-16; William H. Issel, "Modernization in Philadelphia School Reform, 1882-1905," Pennsylvania Magazine of History and Biography 94 (July 1970), 358-383;

justice, bar associations could play an important role in reforming and modernizing the profession and the courts. Beyond that organizational role, individual lawyers were exhorted to become active in political and public educational activities through which they could defend the profession, the rule of law, and core American institutions (primarily private property) from their attackers.

After 1900 bar associations continued to play the role they forged for themselves in the 1890s. The sections and national associations on legal education and uniform laws continued to function. Codes of ethics were adopted and grievance committees became more activist. The administration of justice in the lower courts received increasing attention as public criticisms of the court system grew through the progressive period and as some members of the profession, especially the younger lawyers trained at elite law schools, took up the banner of professional rationalization, at least in this limited sphere.

Elinor M. Gersman, "Progressive Reform of the St. Louis School Board, 1897," History of Education Quarterly 10 (Spring 1970), 3-21; David C. Hammack, "The Centralization of New York City's Public School System, 1896: A Social Analysis of a Decision." (M.A. thesis, Columbia University, 1969).

Although the lawyers' emphasis on the administration of justice was a real response to public criticisms, it was a selective response to that criticism. Lay critics of the profession launched a two-pronged assault on the legal system. One prong was aimed at the abuses in the lower courts; the other prong was aimed at trends in appellate-level court decisions, especially the spread of the substantive due process doctrine and the restrictions on police power. Some leading lawyers cautioned the courts to be prudent in these matters; but for the most part they dealt with the issue by wishing it would go away and by assuring each other in bar association meetings that lay critics simply did not understand the mysteries of the law. When the judicial recall issue erupted after 1910 and public criticism could no longer be ignored, the organized bar mounted its first massive propaganda campaign to defeat judicial recall proposals in the states. The campaign was organized at the national level within the ABA.

All of these post-1900 activities, as modest as they were in terms of the ambitions they revealed, represented an increased tempo of activity and a heightened sense of professional self-consciousness. Bar associations

at all levels actively sought, with some success, to
increase their membership and to publicize their aims
and activities.

CHAPTER 7

THE BAR ASSOCIATION MOVEMENT, 1900-1920

As befitted a conservative profession, there were no sharp breaks in the shift of the bar elite's ideology from a nineteenth- to a twentieth century conception of professionalism. Insofar as the transition can be dated 1905 marked the approximate beginning of the final stage in the shift from the genteel tradition approach to bar organization activity to the more rationalized and self-consciously political approach of the twentieth century. In the genteel tradition approach, the bar elite tried to reshape the profession in its own image, relying on force of example and on legislative and court-ordered coercion. Beginning in the 1890s, and increasingly after about 1905, the elite shifted its focus away from reshaping the profession to preserving and strengthening the role of the profession and of the courts vis-à-vis competing institutions and forces in the society.

In adopting a more defensive and quasi-corporatist position, the bar elite was responding to what it perceived as the trend of the times. In the words of one

Philadelphia lawyer, "one of the most individualistic races that has ever lived" was "being moulded by a community or communistic or socialistic set of ideas."[1] These were the abstract terms that leading lawyers used to describe the process Willard Hurst has referred to as the shift in the growing edge of the law from the actions of the courts to those of legislatures, and, eventually, to those of administrative agencies as well.[2]

For a variety of reasons, conservative lawyers sought ways to stem this process. They often opposed the ends that much social and some economic legislation was designed to achieve. Such laws were often a threat to their pocketbooks, a threat they preferred to interpret in class terms rather than individual terms, labelling it as an attack on the historic prerogatives of property. They also opposed legislation in the belief that attempts to solve social problems by legislative fiat were bound to fail, given human nature and the laws of economics, and that most ills legislation was designed to ameliorate

---

[1] Charles L. McKeehan, "Educational Requirements for Admission to the Bar," Pennsylvania Bar Association, Report 28 (1922), 350-351.

[2] James Willard Hurst, The Growth of American Law: The Law Makers (Boston, 1950), pp. 187-188.

were better "dealt with by such great conserving and uplifting forces as the home, the school, the church, public opinion, and what Edmund Burke, in a profound phrase, termed 'the enlightened spirit of self interest.'"[3] Finally, they opposed the growth of legislative power because they perceived it as a threat to judicial power. Elihu Root explained the conservative elite's perceptions of this danger.

> One of the chief objects of the judiciary is to act as a check on the exercise of legislative power. Without such a check our property, our liberty, and our lives would be completely subject to legislative tyranny, because it is only through the application of judicial power that the constitutional limitations which make up our bills of rights can be enforced.[4]

Although there were occasional mutterings about the influence of socialist ideas, and terms like "socialism" and "communism" were bandied about without any clear conception of their meaning other than that they were vaguely anti-individualistic, most leading lawyers recognized that the main impetus behind the surge of legislation lay within the middle class. As ABA

---

[3] McKeehan, "Educational Requirements for Admission to the Bar," pp. 350-351.

[4] Root to Judge C. M. Thomas, September 1, 1925, copy in P. C. Jessup MSS, Box 253, Library of Congress.

President Edmund Wetmore of New York explained, the increasing reliance on legislative solutions "springs primarily from the enlargement of the sympathies, the increased desire to relieve suffering and want, the benevolence, the altruistic spirit that evolution and modern conditions have developed among the ever increasing class of the well-to-do in an age of increasing wealth and prosperity."[5] What Wetmore and other leading lawyers feared about this trend was that the enlarged sympathies of the middle class would not be counter-balanced by concerns about the effect of statutory enactments on such historic national character traits as individual initiative, industriousness, and voluntary group action. Like Wetmore, most lawyers believed that in any case social problems could rarely be solved by legislation and that the primary result of an increasing reliance on legislation would be an erosion of traditional means of social control, including such institutional means as the courts and such non-institutional means as the spirit of individualism.

---

[5] Edmund Wetmore, "Presidential Address," ABA, Reports 24 (1901), 236. For an expression of similar views, see George R. Peck, "Presidential Address," ibid. 29 (1906), 310-318. Peck was a leading Chicago attorney.

Substantive due process and the uniform laws movement in the 1890s had begun the bar elite's counterattack. However, the scope of the uniform laws movement was narrow, confined largely to technical details of commercial law. Substantive due process was not narrow; but it was essentially negative and had to be defended by referring to a laissez faire ideology that was increasingly becoming a political liability. Public controversies over U.S. Supreme Court decisions during the progressive period pointed this up, especially after the <u>Lochner</u> decision, which was widely criticized as indicative of the hidebound laissez faire conservatism of the Court.[6]

Sustained public criticism of Supreme Court decisions greatly alarmed leading lawyers. After observing several years of such criticisms, Francis Lynde Stetson, J. P. Morgan's lawyer, confided that he had always regretted the Supreme Court's income tax decision in 1895 "because I regarded popular confidence in our highest court as of more consequence than the enactment or the repeal of an

---

[6] Barbara C. Steidle, "Conservative Progressives: A Study of the Attitudes and Role of Bar and Bench, 1905-1912," (Ph.D. dissertation, Rutgers University, 1969), pp. 314-317 discusses the progressive period criticisms of Supreme Court decisions.

income tax." Because he knew feeling continued to run high on the issue, he refused to join Joseph H. Choate, William D. Guthrie, and several other members of the New York City bar elite in public opposition to the income tax amendment, although he privately opposed an income tax as "inquisitorial."[7]

Lawyers feared that public respect for the bench and bar was seriously declining. Andrew A. Bruce warned that although the middle-class majority had "no great sympathy for organized labor nor for its grievances . . . they are nevertheless almost as skeptical of the courts as even organized labor itself." Bruce perceived that "there is everywhere to be found the conviction that our lawyers and our judges are behind the age; that they fail to recognize the basic needs of a growing civilization; that they are shrouded in a formalism."[8] Theodore Roosevelt spoke for the middle-class sentiment when he complained that "the man . . . attacking us is usually . . . either a great lawyer, or a paid editor who takes

---

[7] Francis L. Stetson to E. R. A. Seligman, March 3, 1911, Seligman MSS, Miscellaneous Correspondence, Columbia University Library.

[8] Andrew Alexander Bruce, "The Judge as a Political Factor," Green Bag 19 (November 1907), 667-668.

his commands from the financiers and his arguments from their attorneys."[9] By 1915 William Howard Taft, who complained privately that "the condition of the Supreme Court is pitiable," began his book Ethics in Service by declaring, "It is not too much to say that the profession of the law is more or less on trial."[10]

Politicians and reform spokesmen proposed various remedies, some seeking to reverse the decisions and some seeking to unseat the judges. There were proposals that Congress be given the authority to override Supreme Court decisions. There was a proposal that state court decisions be subject to recall by popular vote. This proposal was carried into law in Oregon (1908), California (1911), Arizona (1912), Colorado (1912), Nevada (1912), and Kansas (1914). There were proposals that federal judges, including the Supreme Court judges, be made elective and that their tenure in office be shortened.

---

[9] Roosevelt to Charles J. Bonaparte, December 23, 1907, quoted in Morton Keller, In Defense of Yesterday: James M. Beck and the Politics of Conservatism, 1861-1936 (New York, 1958), p. 86.

[10] Taft to Horace H. Lurton, May 22, 1909, quoted in Henry Pringle, The Life and Times of William Howard Taft 2 vols., (New York, 1939), 1:503; Taft, Ethics in Service (New Haven, 1915), p. 3; William C. Hook, "What the Public Criticizes in the Bench and Bar," Green Bag 25 (October 1913), 430-433 ably summarizes the themes in public criticism of the bench and bar in the progressive period.

Especially shocking to the bar elite was that a chief advocate of this latter measure was the Chief Justice of the North Carolina Supreme Court, Walter Clark. There were also proposals that state judges be made subject to removal by popular vote.[11]

The legal profession did not lack for responses to this flood of criticism and reform proposals. After 1905 the courts became less obstructionist to legislation, although there was no significant surrender of the doctrine devised in the 1890s. The state courts lagged behind the federal judiciary in softening their hostility to legislation.[12] The American Bar Association launched

---

[11] Judicial recall became a major political issue when Roosevelt championed it in 1912. Steidle, "Conservative Progressives," pp. 314-374 contains a full discussion of the judicial recall issue and the organized bar's campaign against it. For Walter Clark's proposals and the controversy they created, see Clark, "Law and Human Progress," American Law Review 37 (July-August 1903), 517-518; Clark, "The Election of the Federal Judges by the People," Albany Law Journal 67 (August 1905), 235-237; David J. Brewer, "Judiciary Immune to Corporate Influence," Albany Law Journal 66 (November 1904), 349-350; Frederick Bausman, "Election of Federal Judges," American Law Review 37 (November-December 1903), 886-891.

[12] Loren P. Beth, The Development of the American Constitution, 1877-1917 (New York, 1971), p. 84; Steidle, "Conservative Progressives," pp. 314-317.

a major public relations campaign, the largest in the Association's history to that date, against judicial recall proposals. A Minnesota attorney and conservative ideologue, Rome G. Brown, coordinated that campaign. Travelling throughout the country, he made speeches and stimulated state and local bar associations to conduct their own campaigns informing the public that the independence of the judiciary, the very bulwark of the rule of law, was at stake.[13]

---

[13]Steidle, "Conservative Progressives," pp. 330-374; Edson R. Sunderland, History of the American Bar Association and Its Work (n.p., 1953), pp. 155-157; M. Louise Rutherford, The Influence of the American Bar Association on Public Opinion and Legislation (Philadelphia, 1937), pp. 142-153; Hurst, Growth of American Law, pp. 139-140. For interesting dissents from the near hysteria among leading lawyers about judicial recall, see the altogether sensible remarks by J. Aspinwall Hodge of New York during the ABA's discussion of the issue, ABA, Reports 34 (1911), 59-60 and the remarks of Oregon lawyer Dunbar F. Carpenter, as reported by the American Judicature Society, Bulletin 3 (February 1914), 6. An example of Rome G. Brown's efforts is "Muckraking the Constitution," State Bar Association of Indiana, Report 18 (1914), 180-210. Elihu Root's 1911 peroration in the U.S. Senate against admitting Arizona as a state so long as judicial recall was included in its constitution is an example of the near demagogic language that issue inspired. He declared,

> "This provision, sir, is not progress, it is not reform; it is degeneracy. It is a movement backward to those days of misrule and unbridled power out of which the world has been slowly progressing under the leadership of those great men who established the Constitution of the United States. It is a move backward to those days when human passion and the rule of men obtained rather than the law and rule of principles; for it ignores, it sets at naught the great principle of government and of

But these were negative, defensive, and reactive responses. The bar required a more positive, complex, and long-term response. The needed response was worked out by bar leadership during the progressive period. Before examining that response, it will be useful to consider briefly a positive and comprehensive viewpoint that was never adopted, although it was never wholly rejected either. This was the view advanced by Roscoe Pound in a major address to the ABA in 1906.

****

Pound, then dean of the University of Nebraska Law School and not well known to the national bar, addressed the ABA's annual meeting in St. Paul on the topic "The Causes of Popular Dissatisfaction with the Administration of Justice." In his address Pound implicitly offered to the bar elite the law professoriate's emerging ideology as a key to understanding the problems that the bar and bench were facing. He began with

---

civilized society, the principle that justice is above majorities."
Root, <u>Addresses on Government and Citizenship</u>, ed. Robert Bacon and James Brown Scott (Cambridge, Mass., 1916) p. 402. The ABA campaign against judicial recall lasted from 1911 to 1916. Brown's special committee continued to function after 1916, taking on itself the duty of combatting all "anti-constitutional" and socialistic measures until the Executive Committee cut off its funds in 1919. See Rome G. Brown to George T. Page, September 4, 1919, copy in Roscoe Pound MSS, Paige Box 26, Harvard Law School Library.

an assertion no one cared to challenge: that although there always had been and always would be public criticism of the bench, bar, and courts, in 1906 "there is more than the normal amount of dissatisfaction with the present-day administration of justice in America."[14] This dissatisfaction focused on both the decisions of appellate courts and the speed and efficiency of lower courts. But the public's right to criticize did not imply its ability to devise workable remedies. In Pound's view, only members of the bar and bench had the necessary perspective to propose reforms that would simultaneously remedy abuses and preserve what was valuable in the common law tradition and in the historically derived organization of the bar and the courts. In developing this view, Pound carefully examined the reasons for public dissatisfaction, identifying those traceable to the nature of the Anglo-American legal system, those traceable to specific features of American judicial organization and procedure, and those traceable to

---

[14] Pound, "The Causes of Popular Dissatisfaction with the Administration of Justice," ABA, Reports 29 (1906), 396. Pound did not even feel it was necessary to include any evidence to convince his audience of this fact, and no one disputed it in the floor discussion which followed, although there was discussion and disagreement about whether such criticisms were justified or not.

environmental factors. Only lawyers, Pound argued, could determine which defects were endemic and had to be accepted in a necessarily imperfect world and which defects were remediable. Furthermore, only lawyers had the technical expertise to fashion reforms in those areas most open to reform--judicial organization and procedure.[15]

Leading lawyers could appreciate the elitism and professional-mindedness in Pound's analysis. Some keepers of the profession's lore have called Pound's 1906 address the seminal document in modern bar professionalism. The ABA placed a plaque at the site of the speech to commemorate it. John Wigmore, long-time dean of Northwestern University Law School, wrote in the 1930s that before the speech "there was universal complacent torpidity in the profession; the thermometer of conscious progressive and collective effort was at a freezing point." The speech was like a "surgeon's skilled diagnosis" by which "the broad underlying causes of the ailments in our justice [had been] made clear to all" and "the places and the possibilities for improvements had been designated . . . in a program for effort, a program rational, systematic and practical [and] ready for action." The speech provoked opposition from the complacent, but

---

[15]Ibid., pp. 395-417.

"the white flame of Progress was kindled."[16] In a similar, although even _more_ extravagant vein, Pound's biographer declared: "This address was . . . the most significant address ever delivered before the American Bar Association before or since."[17]

These claims are surely exaggerated. Pound's speech did act as a catalyst for an important group of young lawyers, both law professors and some recent graduates of elite law schools, who accepted the main thesis of Pound's address. In subsequent years these lawyers acted on his major thesis, which was that because of the increasing disjunction between a collectivist age and inherited substantive law and procedural rules appropriate to an individualistic age, comprehensive modernization and systematization of both legal doctrines and the administration of justice was required.[18] But

---

[16] Wigmore, "Roscoe Pound's St. Paul Address," _Journal of American Judicature Society_ 20 (February 1937), 177-178.

[17] Paul L. Sayre, _The Life of Roscoe Pound_ (Iowa City, 1948), p. 146.

[18] The American Judicature Society became an important organizational focus for these legal "progressives." Its history will be briefly sketched below. The legal progressives were also active within local, state, and national bar associations. They had an important influence, but they did not articulate the ideology or even the basic strategy of those associations.

the majority of the bar elite did not accept the
logical necessity of such sweeping changes, especially
when their theoretical and philosophical justification sounded very much like the justifications offered
for much progressive legislation. Bar leaders were
willing to accept changes, but only as a *strategic*
necessity.

Some of these differences between Pound's views
and those of the bar elite, as well as divisions within
the bar elite, were brought out in the discussion from
the floor which followed his address. There might have
been no discussion at all had not Everett P. Wheeler,
a long-time municipal reformer and leading lawyer from
New York, proposed printing 4,000 copies of Pound's
address for distribution within the profession and to
members of Congress. James D. Andrews, also of New York,
was instantly on his feet, declaring,

> I am willing in our assembled conferences that
> we should abuse each other if we see fit, that
> we find fault with existing conditions for their
> amelioration or amendment, that we find fault
> with our abilities, or our ethics or lack of
> ethics in order that they may be elevated; but
> I am opposed to sending out to the people at
> large such a discourse.[19]

---

[19] ABA, *Report* 29 (1906), 56.

The main reason for public dissatisfaction, concluded Andrews, was that speeches like Pound's aroused the public.

Two themes were expressed by Andrews and by other opponents of Wheeler's motion. One theme was that there was not really much wrong with the administration of justice. Andrews went so far as to call the system of procedure in the United States "the most refined and scientific system of procedure ever devised by the wit of man."[20] The other theme was that it was dangerous to excite popular doubts or concerns about the administration of justice and that the first priority of the organized bar should be to silence, not to encourage public debate.[21]

Of these two themes, the latter became dominant during the next few years as the organized bar discussed the administration of justice. Wheeler's motion was defeated in 1906, but a special committee, which included both Pound and Andrews, was appointed to examine the issues raised by Pound's address. The bar soon ceased to proclaim that there was nothing wrong with the administration of justice and began to promote many of the

---

[20] Ibid.

[21] Ibid., pp. 12, 55-65 contains the transcript of the floor discussion.

very changes Pound had recommended. Some of these changes had been actively promoted since the 1890s by some bar associations, often including the ABA. This was especially true in the areas of procedural reforms[22] and the selection of judges.[23] This fact calls into question the sincerity of those who protested in 1906

---

[22] For general discussions of nineteenth-century bar association concern about delays and uncertainties in the administration of justice, see Sunderland, History of ABA, pp. 65-67; Audra L. Prewitt, "Bar vs. Bench: New Fears in an Old Relationship," paper delivered at University of Texas at Arlington, in author's possession, pp. 1-10. For the early efforts of a major nineteenth-century bar leader to simplify procedural rules, see the discussion in Frederick H. Jackson, Simeon Eben Baldwin--Lawyer, Social Scientist, Statesman (New York, 1955), pp. 78-79. U.S. Supreme Court justices expressed concern and suggested remedies for delays in the 1890s. See H. B. Brown to James Bradley Thayer, March 29, 1897, Thayer MSS, Box 21, Harvard Law School Library; David J. Brewer, "A Better Education the Great Need of the Profession," ABA, Reports 18 (1895), 447-448. (Despite the title of the address, Brewer proposed a number of specific procedural reforms to make the disposal of cases speedier.) The ABA's early interest in federal court procedural reform can be traced in ABA, Reports 15 (1892), 313-315; 19 (1896), 44, 414-417, 424-432; 20 (1897), 54; 21 (1898), 454-465; 23 (1900), 35-36; 25 (1902), 25-26, 31-32. Lord Bryce reported that complaints about the law's delay were widespread among the legal elite he consulted in 1888. American Commonwealth, 2 vols. (New York, 1910, orig. pub. 1888), 2:682. However, none of these efforts was touched with the same sense of urgency that characterized similar efforts in the progressive period.

[23] For nineteenth-century bar association involvement in judicial selection, see Simon Fleischmann, "The Influence of the Bar in the Selection of Judges throughout the United States," American Law Review 29 (May-June 1905), 348-362; Hurst, Growth of American Law, pp. 129-134;

that such changes were not needed or would not work if they were needed. Perhaps the opponents were simply moved to hyperbole in their efforts to stifle further dissemination of dangerous criticisms.

Leading lawyers recognized that the point at issue was broader than technical concern about procedural rules in the civil and criminal courts or even the admittedly political question of the method to be used in selecting state and local judges. After 1906 increasing numbers of lawyers addressed themselves to the topic of public dissatisfaction with judicial decisions and the administration of justice and, especially, to the question of the lawyer's duty in meeting this crisis. Out of this collective soul-searching and these strategy sessions a coherent response emerged.

Richard A. Watson and Rondal G. Downing, The Politics of the Bench and the Bar; Judicial Selection Under the Missouri Nonpartisan Court Plan (New York, 1969), pp. 7-9. For New York City see George W. Martin, Causes and Conflicts: The Centennial History of the Association of the Bar of New York, 1870-1970 (Boston, 1970), pp. 107-109, 164-170; Richard S. Skolnik, "The Crystallization of Reform in New York City, 1890-1917" (Ph.D. dissertation, Yale University, 1964), pp. 147-148; Philip C. Jessup, Elihu Root, 2 vols. (New York, 1938), 1:200-201. For Chicago see: Herman Kogan, The First Century: The Chicago Bar Association, 1874-1974 (Chicago, 1974), pp. 110-114, 117-129; Chicago Bar Association, Summary of Activities (Chicago, 1965), passim; Hurst, Growth of American Law, pp. 132-133.

Elihu Root, who assumed the position of elder statesman and spokesman for the profession during the progressive period, succinctly summarized and articulated that response in a series of speeches. Addressing the New York State Bar Association in 1912, Root acknowledged that there were two kinds of public criticisms of the courts: one aimed at delays in the lower criminal and civil courts and sometimes at delays in appellate courts, the other aimed at laissez faire decisions by appellate courts. He argued that dissatisfaction with delays in the courts could be laid more at the feet of the bar than of the bench. He denied that the character of state or federal judges had deteriorated. He instead argued that "it is the bar that makes a great part of all our legislatures, and is responsible for the stupid and mischievous legislation regarding procedure which hampers the courts in their efforts to do justice."[24] He also castigated as irresponsible those

---

[24] Root, "Judicial Decisions and Public Feeling," Case and Comment 18 (April 1912), 667, also reprinted in Root, Government and Citizenship, pp. 447-460. Root made the same point in a 1915 address to the New York State Constitutional Convention, over which he presided. See Root, Government and Citizenship, p. 179. In making these criticisms of the legislature, Root had in mind the additions to the Field code which had expanded it from its original 393 sections in 1848 to 3,441 sections by 1900. See Hurst, Growth of American Law, pp. 91-92. During the 1890s alone, 804 sections had been added. See New York

members of the bar who exploited court procedure to
protect criminals from punishment.

Root recognized that the judges and the courts
themselves were under direct attack for decisions in
antitrust and constitutional law cases. He ascribed
these attacks mainly to ignorance and a misconception
of the role of the courts. But he admitted that to a
certain extent judges were basing their decisions on
social and economic conditions which were present
when they were in active practice but which were no
longer as salient in the age of industrial combinations.
Insofar as that was true, Root urged judges to inform
themselves more about changed conditions. He was convinced, however, that he had accurately identified the
main problem: the public did not understand that judges
were confined within narrow limits of reasonable interpretation and that their decisions were not political or

---

State Bar Association, Report 24 (1901), 296. The situation was similar in the twenty-eight other states which had codes of civil procedure based directly or indirectly on the Field code. Procedural reform tended not to be such a pressing issue in non-code states. However, nearly all states had codes for criminal procedure. See Roscoe Pound to W. C. Dunbar, May 7, 1917, Pound MSS, Paige Box 8.

based on a conservative ideology but were instead based on "some long-established limitation upon legislative or executive powers" or on "some crudely drawn statute [that] is inadequate to produce the effect that was expected of it."[25]

Root also emphasized that the public should respond to an unpopular decision by seeking to change the law, not by attacking the courts. Those who attacked the courts, he argued, were attacking some of the essential bulwarks of our system of government: separation of powers, protection of individuals, abstract and impersonal rules of conduct, and judicial review. Lawyers must educate the public about such matters.[26]

As he had declared to the Yale Law School graduating class in 1904, "to preserve and foster [the] living faith of the people in the supreme value of the great impersonal rules of right which underlie our system of law, is the highest and ever-present duty of the American lawyer."[27]

---

[25] Root, "Judicial Decisions," p. 667.

[26] Ibid., pp. 666-671.

[27] Root, "Some Duties of American Lawyers to American Law," in Root, Government and Citizenship, p. 419. Root was more doctrinaire than most in his defense of the inherited legal tradition. William Howard Taft expressed a more pragmatic view:
> "Now if the lawyers are educated to be rigid in their views of the maintenance of law as

By 1919 he was expressing the fear that public criticism was weakening the judiciary itself. "The Bench has been hammered so . . . that I think a good many judges are getting rather sensitive, and I do not think there is quite that sturdy independence in applying the Constitution that there was thirty or forty years ago."[28]

Lawyers had to understand, Root insisted, that whereas in the past they could safely concern themselves only with day-to-day obligations, they now lived in an era when "fundamental principles are questioned, doubted, discussed, possibly endangered."[29] "To-day all the old and tried institutions and traditions are questioned—some of them denied. . . . You will find a great number

---

it is, or as it has been, without understanding its elements, and without a knowledge of the science of jurisprudence, so that they can distinguish what is fundamental in it, with a view to its preservation for the good of society, and they oppose themselves to all sociological progress, they are going down, and we shall ultimately have such a result as they had in Athens and Rome. Therefore, we must look to the legal profession for this work of reconciliation and of preservation of what is valuable in the past, in order to make the proposed changes useful and not destructive."
Taft to Ezra R. Thayer, August 24, 1913, E. R. Thayer MSS, Box 2, Harvard Law School Library.

[28] Root, "Remarks to Judicial Section of American Bar Association," 1919, in Root, Men and Policies; Addresses (Cambridge, Mass., 1925), p. 188.

[29] Root, "Address to New York State Bar Association," 1916, in Root, Government and Citizenship, p. 512.

of people who think or feel that, after all, the best way is for men to do what seems to be right at the time, and that it is all wrong that we should be limited by so many constitutional provisions."[30] He was especially anxious that the bar counteract the influence of "the huge number of immigrants from countries which differ so fundamentally from the United States in conceptions of law and personal freedom," and that it counteract the university and law school professors who "believe they know better what the principles of government ought to be than the wisdom of the ages."[31]

Root recommended the following specific steps be taken to protect the legal system and its principles: (1) The quality of the bar should be improved. His target was the lower bar in large cities and lawyers in state legislatures. (2) Procedure in the courts should be simplified and returned to judicial control. "The true remedy is to sweep from our statute books the whole

---

[30] Root, "Address on Fiftieth Anniversary of The Association of the Bar of New York City," in Root, *Men and Policies*, pp. 115-116.

[31] Root, "Address to New York State Bar Association," 1916, p. 517. He was especially concerned that 15 percent of New York City lawyers were foreign-born and 50 percent were either foreign-born or of foreign-born parents. Native-born lawyers must teach them American institutions, he declared.

mass of detailed provisions and substitute a simple Practice Act containing only the necessary, fundamental rules of procedure, leaving all the rest to the rules of the Court. When that has been done the Legislature should leave our procedure alone."[32] Root also recommended greatly reducing the number of laws passed on all matters, since the mass of poorly drawn laws bred litigation.[33] (3) The bar should inform the public about the nature of the constitutional system and its importance.[34]

Root was urging the organized bar to take a more activist stance in the changed political context facing the profession. He was essentially suggesting that if the organized bar began to show a genuine concern for policing the weaknesses in the lower bench and bar, their professional-minded claims to expertise in defending appellate court judges would have greater political

---

[32] Root, "Reform of Procedure," New York State Bar Association, Report 34 (1911), 89.

[33] Root, "Address to American Bar Association," 1914, in Root, Government and Citizenship, pp. 485-491.

[34] Root, "Judicial Decisions," pp. 666-671; Root, "Address to the ABA," 1914, pp. 485-497.

credibility, especially if such judges became less doctrinaire in constructing and writing their decisions.[35] It was a marvelous strategic move for three reasons. First, it seemed to put lawyers more in step with the efficiency themes of professional-minded progressivism, without preventing them from defending conservative appellate court decisions. Second, the move allowed the bar elite to criticize and reform the elements in the profession they sympathized with least. Third, it provided an outlet for the anti-legislation sentiment so strong among the legal elite, because a common diagnosis attributed court delays to the cumbersome and even contradictory procedural rules that legislatures had passed piecemeal over the second half of the nineteenth century. In the view of critics like Root, the remedy was for the legislatures to surrender their rule-making authority to the courts.

---

[35] Another consideration, emphasized by William Howard Taft, was that the expense and delay in civil litigation worked to the advantage of the wealthy party as against the poorer party. Taft noted in 1908 that critics of private property and the existing distribution of wealth had not yet emphasized this particular inequity. He urged lawyers to correct the problem and thereby create the impression that the system could reform itself. "The Administration of Justice--Its Speeding and Cheapening," Virginia State Bar Association, Report 20 (1908), 233-244.

There was one matter that concerned many in the organized bar but did not trouble Elihu Root. This was the question of the quality of the lower court judiciary. Root believed it had not deteriorated. Some lawyers disagreed, often sharply. Everett V. Abbott and Charles A. Boston, for example, decried "the anomalous situation of a judiciary which does not command the intellectual respect of the bar which practices before it."[36] Bar

---

[36] Abbott and Boston, "The Judiciary and the Administration of Law," American Law Review 45 (July-August 1911), 487. Abbott and Boston were reporting on the results of a mail questionnaire they had conducted among leading lawyers and political scientists. The replies they received indicated significant dissatisfaction within local bars with procedure in courts, the jury system, low quality of the bar, and the judiciary. They received a long list of complaints about the judiciary, emphasizing poor legal ability, undue openness to political influence, and sometimes poor character or corruption. Adelbert Moot, an elite Buffalo attorney, conducted a survey of court congestion in 1911. He concluded that in upstate courts, congestion had been significantly reduced since a similar survey in 1903 because upstate judges had responded to publicity about congestion by working harder. This suggested to Moot that "the most important thing we can do to improve our Courts is to select able, independent, fearless, industrious, learned, and experienced lawyers of high character and courteous demeanor as Judges for them." New York State Bar Association, Report 34 (1911), 107-108, 115-125. Another elite New York City lawyer, Frederic R. Coudert, told the ABA in 1911 that the unpopularity and even disrepute into which the law and the administration of justice had fallen was "due primarily to incompetency both at the Bar and on the Bench." Coudert, "The Crisis of the Law and Professional Incompetency," ABA, Reports 34 (1911), 681. The list of similar statements could be extended by simply opening the pages of any bar association report or legal periodical from the progressive period.

association leaders preferred that they select the judges and therefore constantly attempted to use their influence in judicial elections. They also regularly urged that judicial selection be made appointive rather than elective or that elections be made non-partisan and separated from other elections and that state judges be given either life tenure or very long terms in office. Their success in both types of campaigns was very limited.[37]

---

[37] The most typical bar association activity was to rate candidates for judicial office, either in order of priority or as acceptable or not acceptable. The "bar primary," pioneered in Chicago in 1887, was one rating device; another was rating by a bar association committee. Bar associations rarely attempted to influence the nomination of candidates by political parties, since their influence within the parties was not very great. Judgeships were simply too important to political parties for them to surrender any of their power over the nomination process. See Wallace S. Sayre and Herbert Kaufman, Governing New York City (New York, 1960), pp. 538-543 for a good discussion of the importance of the judiciary to urban political parties. Joel Tarr, A Study in Boss Politics; William Lorimer of Chicago (Urbana, 1971), p. 126n lists many of the same factors in Chicago, with specific reference to the progressive period. There is no comprehensive study of bar associations and judicial selection, but see the report to the Conference of Bar Association Delegates in 1924 which presented data on the experience of New York, Cleveland, Detroit, Chicago, St. Louis, as well as other cities: American Bar Association Journal 10 (November 1924), 820-824. Bar associations occasionally mounted major campaigns, usually in conjunction with an elite urban reform organization or with the "out" political party, to elect its own special slate of judicial candidates. Such campaigns were only successful when especially flagrant abuses could be charged against the ruling political machine or its slate, as in the 1921 Chicago judicial election. See Chicago Bar Association Record 4 (June 1921), 1-2; Journal of American

Root's ideas and similar ones from other bar leaders were given careful consideration and often became the basis for local, state, and national bar association action. Committees were formed, conditions in the courts were documented, reform proposals were drawn up, and legislatures and the Congress were lobbied.[38] Many of the ideas

---

Judicature Society 5 (August 1921), 46-48; Kogan, Chicago Bar Association, pp. 132-135. For an unsuccessful effort by an elite group of New York City lawyers in 1906 and the lessons they learned from their defeat, see Charles C. Burlingham to E. M. Shepard, July 3, 1906, November 12, 1906, Shepard MSS, Miscellaneous Correspondence, Columbia University Library; Charles C. Burlingham, Oral Memoir, 1949, Columbia University, p. 9; comments by Frederic W. Hinrichs and the Report of the Committee on Judicial Nominations, New York State Bar Association, Report 30 (1907), 233-234, 258. Although an appointive judiciary long remained a favorite reform in the legal elite's mind, they rarely pressed the issue very hard, realizing its absolute lack of political appeal. See, e.g., Elihu Root to Eldon R. Brown, June 4, 1915, Root MSS, Box 129, Library of Congress.

[38] Roscoe Pound indicates the scope of these activities in a comprehensive bibliography on procedural reform and court reorganization, Illinois Law Review 11 (February 1917), 455-463. Illinois was a center of such efforts. In 1912 its state bar association called a conference on procedural reform, with delegates invited from every state. For other examples of efforts in Illinois, see Illinois State Bar Association, Report 31 (1907), 63-64, 151-157; Chicago Bar Association, Report (1910), pp. 3-4; Edgar B. Tolman to Roscoe Pound, January 28, 1915, Pound MSS, Paige Box 30. There was also much activity in the New York state and city associations. See, for example, the numerous reports prepared by the Committee on Law Reform for the Association of the Bar of the City of New York between 1910 and 1920; "Report of Committee on Law Reform," New York State Bar Association, Report 24 (1901), 287-293, 309-311; Adolph J. Rodenbeck, "The Reform of the Procedure in the Courts of the State of

were not actually new ones. As stated above, there had been a long-standing recognition of the problem of delay in the courts. What the reform program helped to stimulate was an increased activism and a new sense of urgency among the bar. By 1917 Roscoe Pound could report that his efforts in 1906 to stimulate activity were bearing fruit.[39] The strategy followed by the organized bar was the one Root had outlined: create a flurry of activity around the issue of delay and inefficiency in the lower

---

New York," ibid. 34 (1911), 354-466; "Report of the Committee to Examine the Practice Act," ibid. 43 (1920), 149-153; Elihu Root to Governor John A. Dix, March 15, 1912, copy in P. C. Jessup MSS, Box 253. The ABA was also active in securing federal court procedural reform. See Roscoe Pound's correspondence with Everett P. Wheeler, the Chairman of the ABA Committee on Law Reform, Pound MSS, Paige Box 30; Sunderland, History of ABA, pp. 128-134, 164-166; Steidle, "Conservative Progressives," pp. 379-380. Not all bar associations became active. The State Bar Association of Indiana steered clear of the issue, declaring that whatever problems existed were caused by individuals and not by the system. See "Report of the Committee on Judicial Administration and Remedial Procedure," State Bar Association of Indiana, Report 18 (1914), 88. Although bar associations in this period focused mainly on procedural reform, they also supported some efforts at court reorganization, such as the municipal court movement, and they continued their earlier efforts to raise bar admission standards.

[39] Pound to William G. Thompson, January 10, 1917; Pound to Herbert Harley, March 26, 1917, Pound MSS, Paige Box 8.

courts and unprofessional conduct among the bar, thereby defusing public and political criticism of the appellate courts' exercise of judicial review.[40]

****

Bar leaders recognized that if they were going to rely on organized bar activity to recapture a role of political authority for the profession, they would have to strengthen bar associations. This strengthening began at the local and state level after the turn of the century and was actively promoted in the ABA from 1912 on.

In 1902 the Chicago Bar Association, one of the most active local associations in the nation, established a special, large (forty-member) committee assigned the task of increasing the membership. In 1910 the current year's officers ran for re-election, declaring that discontinuity in leadership had hindered the Association's work in the past. In the same year the Association began publishing

---

[40] In 1919 Boston's Reginald Heber Smith discussed the narrowness of the bar elite's interest in law reform. Although progressive era reforms had done much to reduce the problem of delay in the courts, a wide variety of other abuses in the administration of justice which fell especially heavily on the poor--such as court costs and the expense of counsel--had been ignored by the bar elite. Smith judged the bar leaders as indifferent and insensitive to the human tragedy caused by the denial of justice to the poor. Smith, <u>Justice and the Poor</u> (New York, 1919), pp. 6-34.

a monthly journal, hoping thereby to stimulate activity among members and to publicize the Association among potential members and among citizens. After appearing irregularly for six issues, then suspending, the journal soon revived to become a permanent publication as the Chicago Bar Association Record. In 1920 the Chicago Bar Association, in a move to make bar activity more effective, began participating in joint meetings with other associations in the Seventh Superior Judicial District. Participating organizations included the Chicago Patent Lawyers Association, the Lawyers' Association of Illinois, the Women's Bar Association of Illinois, and county bar associations outside Cook County but within the judicial district.[41]

The Chicago pattern was to make the existing associations more inclusive by trying to add members from the middle strata of the bar, by better publicizing the association, and by federating informally with other bar associations, usually non-elite associations. This pattern was followed elsewhere throughout the eastern and north central states.

---

[41] Chicago Legal News, November 29, 1902, p. 128; June 11, 1910, p. 353; Kogan, Chicago Bar Association, pp. 121-122; Chicago Bar Association Record 4 (December 1920), 2.

A different pattern was followed in New York City. There the Association of the Bar of the City of New York was still under the control of its first generation of leaders, who were unwilling to see their organization lose its atmosphere of an exclusive social club. They were unwilling to relax their membership rules or in any other way expand their membership rolls. Their one concession to the new spirit of bar association activism was to expand the work of the ABCNY's grievance committee. The targets of the grievance committee's investigations were almost entirely lawyers from the lower bar who were not ABCNY members. The ABCNY's slow growth did not keep pace with the rapid expansion of the New York City bar. Younger elite and near-elite members of the profession in Greater New York found that they were either excluded from membership or from holding office in a local bar association just at a time when professional organizations elsewhere were expanding, becoming more activist, and often explicitly appealing to young lawyers. Therefore, in 1908 a new local body, the New York County Lawyers' Association, was formed. In contrast to the ABCNY, which had a policy of membership by invitation only, the new association was open to all lawyers admitted to practice in New York County. It was also more active, but its leaders and basic policies were cut from the same cloth as those of the ABCNY and other elite associations. The two associations did not compete. In fact, many ABCNY members joined the new organization, with the result that prominent lawyers commonly served as officers of both associations.[42]

Since most lobbying--for procedural reforms, increased bar admission standards, and court reorganization--and most policing of codes of ethics had to be carried out by local and state associations, it was natural that such associations would promote membership drives before the national association did so. However, there was a need for national leadership of the bar's efforts, a national reference point for the standards and the conceptions of the lawyer's duty which were emerging as the rationale for restoring the authority of the profession. The ABA had always sought to provide that national reference point, although its influence had been largely confined to the elite. The ABA had been slowly moving away from its social elitism, beginning with its abandonment of Saratoga Springs as a meeting site, its active involvement in the uniform laws movement, and, its passage in 1908 of a code of ethics designed to

---

[42] Martin, Causes and Conflicts, pp. 172-176, 181-184, 202; Benno Lewinson to Elihu Root, February 16, 1915, Root MSS, Box 133.

serve as a model for all other bar associations. But its membership base remained small; in 1910 its members constituted only 3.2 percent of the national bar.[43]

In 1903 the ABA took a first step toward increasing its membership by reducing from five to three the number of years after admission to the bar that a lawyer had to wait before being eligible for ABA membership. At the 1907 and 1908 meetings, there was much discussion from the floor about the need to increase membership, but the executive committee was not yet prepared to act on recommendations voted by the annual meetings. The issue of judicial recall, and the ABA's centralized direction of the campaign against it, proved to be the needed catalyst. In 1912, for the first time, a standing committee charged with increasing membership was appointed.

In the eight years that the committee functioned under Lucien Hugh Alexander of Philadelphia, it raised the percentage of the nation's lawyers who belonged to the ABA from 3.2 percent to 9.2 percent. In 1920 Alexander reported that 69 percent of the current members had been added to the rolls during the previous eight years. As a

---

[43] Corinne L. Gilb, Hidden Hierarchies: The Professions and Government (New York, 1966), p. 118.

consequence, the income collected by the ABA during those eight years was nearly twice the income collected during the preceding thirty-five years. Alexander's committee relied very heavily on the ABA vice-president and local ABA council in each state to solicit all eligible members. After 1921 a new national committee was selected, and a more centralized, but less intense, membership drive commenced. Besides constant exhortation, the national membership committee's main contribution was to prepare and send out "propagandic materials," as Alexander frankly labelled them. These materials made explicit comparisons between the American Bar Association and the American Medical Association, noting the latter's spectacular growth since about 1900. The materials included appeals by such prominent lawyers as Elihu Root, William Howard Taft, Simeon E. Baldwin, and Alton B. Parker. In his letter Root declared that the United States, indeed the whole world, had entered a period of re-examination and development of political and juridical systems. "In this juncture the highest duty of service to the country rests upon the Bar." But, he went on, "This duty cannot be effectively performed by lawyers acting singly each by himself." The age of individualism was coming to a close. "In modern times it is only by the power of association that the men of any occupation exercise their due influence in the community." Root acknowledged that there were many excellent state and local bar associations, "but the new questions are national, not local." As Root emphasized, the ABA was in the midst of creating a nationally-oriented sense of professionalism that would reach farther down into the bar than ever before.[44]

Besides the efforts of the membership committee, several other measures contributed to the ABA's early though still modest success in creating a broad-based sense of national identity. In 1915 the ABA began to publish a monthly journal, the American Bar Association Journal. Although not too impressive in its first years, consisting largely of reprints of articles and speeches, it soon became the most important single activity of the association and a major ingredient in the continuing

---

[44]"Special Communication in re The [ABA] Membership Situation," January 1, 1914, March 1915, copies in Charles J. Bonaparte MSS, Box 188, Library of Congress; Elihu Root to Members of the ABA, March 22, 1916, Bonaparte MSS, Box 188; Frederick E. Wadhams to Alton B. Parker, March 22, 1922, Parker MSS, Box 7, Library of Congress; ABA, Report 43 (1920), 299-303; Sunderland, History of ABA, pp. 85-92, 96-98; Alfred Z. Reed, Training for the Public Profession of the Law: Historical Development and Principal Contemporary Problems of Legal Education in the United States with Some Account of Conditions in England and Canada (New York, 1921), p. 215.

membership rise. The <u>Journal</u> filled a need in the profession for a non-technical publication that disseminated news and information from a national perspective.[45] Such a publication was especially important to a profession like law, which, unlike medicine, could not rely upon significant breakthroughs in knowledge and technique to promote national unity.

In 1916, while serving as ABA president, Root called a conference of state and local bar associations. The purpose of the conference was to help all bar associations coordinate their activities so that the associations could be more effective in influencing public decisions. The meeting was also an effort to make the ABA seem more representative, since the local and state associations included many lawyers who did not belong to the national body. The conference was repeated in 1917. In 1920 it became a section of the ABA, and finally in 1936 the ABA changed its structure to become a federation of state and local associations. During the twenty years before it, in essence, became the ABA, the local and state

---

[45] For an eloquent and forceful condemnation of the <u>Journal's</u> first few years of operation, see the letter from the ABA's outgoing membership chairman, Lucien Hugh Alexander to President William A. Bland and the Members of the Executive Committee, January 1, 1921, Pound MSS, Paige Box 10.

association body discussed and acted on all the crucial professionalism issues: legal ethics, selection of judges, legal education, removal of anachronisms in the law, legislative lobbying, judicial councils, and bar organization. It was through this body that the younger generation of lawyers who could change the ABA structure in the 1930s gained their professional organization experience and credentials.[46]

The movement to pass a code of ethics can also be interpreted as part of the membership drive. The ABA passed its code of ethics in 1908, at a time when only eleven state bar associations, primarily in non-industrial states, had such codes. The movement to establish these codes was usually described as a battle against the growing "commercialization" within the bar. "Commercialization" had several meanings, depending upon which stratum of the bar it was applied to. First and foremost, the term was applied to the growing segment of the urban bar which was socially and professionally shunned by the urban elite and which in turn did not identify itself with the elite's conception of professionalism.

---

[46] E. Smythe Gambrell to Elihu Root, July 2, 1936, copy in P. C. Jessup MSS, Box 253; Sunderland, History of ABA, pp. 85-92; James Grafton Rogers, "History of the American Bar Association," American Bar Association Journal 39 (August 1953), 661.

When elite lawyers thought about the "commercialization" of the lower bar, they conjured up images of "ambulance chasers," usually with an eastern or southern European background. Henry A. Forster of New York City expressed a generous version of the elite's perception. "Why should [Eastern Europeans] not be commercial? They do not believe in our ways and system, and, I think, do not perhaps altogether understand them. They work harder at what they regard as a profession than some of us do, and they are in their way, very successful, and we call them commercial." Elihu Root ticked off the traits which, in his nativist mind, characterized the commercialized lower bar. They took little interest in the public responsibilities of the profession; they were "in the lower grade as to attainment and cultivation;" they were not very familiar with the traditions of the profession; they had few clients, and these belonged to "that great class which seeks to prosper by doing injustice to others and uses the technicalities of the law to further that end;" their tools were knowledge of the code and skill in the obstructive use of its provisions.[47]

---

[47] Forster quote in New York State Bar Association, Report 46 (1923), 287; Root quote from 1914 address to ABA reprinted in Root, Government and Citizenship, p. 497.

But some bar association lawyers recognized a similarity between the ambulance chaser and the new breed of corporation lawyers. William F. Bundy of Centralia, Illinois told the Illinois Bar Association a story about hearing a corporation lawyer condemn an ambulance chaser for getting to the scene of a railroad accident immediately after the accident. The corporation lawyer also had sent one of his agents to the scene to try for a quick settlement. In his outrage at the tactics of the ambulance chaser, the corporation lawyer was totally unconscious of having acted in precisely the same way. Corporation lawyers were occasionally included in the attack on commercialization. In these attacks they were accused of being more concerned with the economic interests of their clients and their own firms than with the good name of the profession. Speaking of his fellow elite lawyers in New York City, Julius H. Cohen bitterly complained, "We are administering our discipline and our ethics committees upon the philosophy that the Bar is a profession, and we are conducting the practice of the law in large measure as though it were a business." In 1921 in a well-publicized case, the ABCNY grievance committee, which had just completed an active ten years prosecuting members of the lower bar, charged Thomas L. Chadbourne, a prominent Association member and Wall Street lawyer with an ethical violation. They accused him of conflict of interest in the settlement of a large estate. As the Association's historian notes, the case had symbolic importance because it "proved" to the public that the ABCNY was willing to tackle the rich and powerful as well as the poor and friendless.[48]

The emphasis on "commercialization" in the ABA's discussions leading up to the passing of the code of ethics in 1908 signalled that the major purpose of the code was to differentiate professional practice from purely business practice. This differentiation was intended to provide a way for the large middle stratum of the bar to identify with the bar elite's conception of professionalism.[49] The practice of law had always been both a business and a profession, and the tension

---

[48] Bundy quote in Illinois State Bar Association, Report 32 (1908), 84; Cohen, The Law: Business or Profession? (New York, 1916), p. 212; Martin, Causes and Conflicts, pp. 368-371. See also Henry W. Taft, "Some Responsibilities of the American Lawyer," New York State Bar Association, Report 43 (1920), 190-191 for a candid discussion of the commercialization of the corporation lawyer by a prominent member of the financial bar. In the original, the Cohen quote is italicized, indicating how strongly he felt.

[49] Joseph Katz, "The American Legal Profession, 1890-1915" (M. A. thesis, Columbia University, 1953), pp. 29-35 argues that the complaints about "commercialization" in the legal periodicals indicate the issue was of greatest concern to the average individual practitioners.

between the two tendencies was not unique to the twentieth century. It was the increasing stratification within the bar and the resultant decline in the elite's ability to define informally and enforce the "proper" balance between the two tendencies that produced the code of ethics movement. The more privileged strata of the profession were becoming insensitive to the economic pressures facing less privileged lawyers. Although the code ostensibly attacked the commercial aspects of law practice, it was actually very similar in spirit and in some specific provisions to the codes being enacted by trade associations in the business world, codes which "generally regarded a price cutter as a 'chisler' and price competition as immoral."[50] Elite lawyers preferred to limit competition to purely professional grounds. In a gentlemen's profession, they believed, open economic competition should be avoided. "Commercialism" seemed especially immoral at a time when the profession was

---

[50] For this characterization of trade association codes, see Ellis Hawley, The New Deal and the Problem of Monopoly (Princeton, 1966), p. 11. An explicit recognition of the parallels between the bar association and trade association movements by a proponent of both can be found in Cohen, Law: Business or Profession?, pp. 37-38, 302. Cohen, chairman of the New York County Lawyers' Association Committee on Unlawful Practice, considered advertising and solicitation, the contingent fee, fee-splitting, and the practice of law by corporations as the essence of his conception of unprofessional conduct (pp. 173-307). He declared that he would prefer to see fees abolished and the state pay all lawyers (p. 215).

attempting to win back public respect. The lower bar, and especially the ethnic bar, became the scapegoat both for the growing public criticism and for the erosion at all levels of gentlemanly qualities in the practice of law.

The bar's codes were not drawn up in a way that challenged the existing practices or sense of professionalism among average practitioners. The codes probably had very little effect on the practice of law. What they did was give sanction to bar association grievance committees which were actively harrassing "ambulance chasers" and others in the lower bar for about a fifteen-year period between 1905 and 1920. This harrassment and the codes themselves were deliberately calculated to improve the morale of the profession and to allay public criticism of the profession.[51] "Improving morale" clearly meant drawing the middle and

---

[51]"Report of Committee on Code of Professional Ethics," ABA, Reports 29 (1906), 600-604. For recent analyses demonstrating that bar codes of ethics are administered primarily to forestall public criticism of the profession and to preserve the stratified status quo in fees and allocation of legal services, see Jerome Carlin, Lawyers' Ethics: A Survey of the New York City Bar (New York, 1966), p. 170; Jethro K. Lieberman, The Tyranny of the Experts; How Professionals Are Closing the Open Society (New York, 1970), pp. 70-84, 96-101. For a state-level historical study which, more tentatively, comes to similar conclusions, see Corinne L. Gilb,

elite strata of the profession together, giving the impression that something was being done by bar associations to improve the declining status of the profession, and identifying the profession's problems with the practices and principles of the lower bar. The injection of an ethnic dimension into discussions of the "commercialization" of the lower bar aided greatly in unifying the middle and upper strata.

In addition to the very important aim of strengthening bar associations, the elite wanted to gain the support of the middle stratum because it supplied most of the lawyers who were in Congress and state legislatures. If the courts could not reduce the volume of legislation, perhaps the elite could appeal to the lawyer-legislators' sense of professionalism, by inducing them to identify with the institutions and concerns of the elite. There was hope, in the elite's view, since so many lawyer-legislators were relatively young, without a firmly established sense of professional identity.[52]

"Self-Governing Professions and the Public Welfare; A Case Study of the California State Bar," (Ph.D. dissertation, Radcliffe, 1956), chap. 4.

[52] Elihu Root, "Remarks to Judicial Section of ABA," 1919, in Root, *Men and Policies*, p. 137.

Bar association leaders did not rely entirely on the <u>American Bar Association Journal</u> and on appeals to professionalism to attract the middle stratum. They appealed to economic self-interest as well. A growing concern for such lawyers was the spread of lay agencies, which were encroaching on professional practice. These included trust companies, title insurance companies, insurance adjusters, collection agencies, and even the legal staffs of large industrial corporations. Lawyers lumped these together under the rubric "unauthorized practice of law" and sought to regulate and/or ban them, sometimes arguing that such lay competition provided the economic squeeze which forced lawyers into ambulance chasing.[53]

Bar association interest in the problem was roughly coterminous with local, state, and national membership drives. The New York County Lawyers' Association, like

---

[53]Katz, "American Legal Profession," pp. 24-28, 35-38; Francis M. Finch, "Presidential Address," New York State Bar Association, <u>Report</u> 24 (1901), 55. Part of the motivation behind efforts like procedural reform and court reorganization, which were designed to reduce the law's delay and uncertainty, was the belief that speedier and more certain justice would induce clients to forsake lay practice corporations and trade arbitrations and return to judicial proceedings and representation by lawyers. See comments by Chicago Bar Association President Edgar B. Tolman, Chicago Bar Association, <u>Report</u> (1912), p. 12.

other states and local associations, established a committee to work on the problem in 1913. In 1919 the issue was raised at the ABA Conference of Bar Association Delegates meeting, and in 1920 a special committee of the Conference presented a report defining practice of law and unauthorized practice. In subsequent years, that report became the basis for court contests and legislative lobbying in several localities. The ABA's Committee on Professional Ethics and Grievances issued opinions throughout the 1920s on what did and what did not constitute unauthorized practice. In 1928 the ABA added two new canons to the code of ethics, putting the organized bar's formal stamp of disapproval on lawyers who worked for lay competition corporations. Finally, in 1930 the ABA appointed a special committee, which became a standing committee in 1933, to focus only on the unauthorized practice of law issue.[54] The organized bar

---

[54] Sunderland, History of ABA, pp. 162-163; Rutherford, Influence of ABA, pp. 94-95; Gilb, "Self-Governing Professions," chap. 6; Martin, Causes and Conflicts, pp. 371-372. For general commentaries on the lay competition issue and the organized bar's response, see Charles E. Clark and William O. Douglas, "Law and Legal Institutions," in Recent Social Trends in the United States; Report of the President's Research Committee on Social Trends (New York, 1933), p. 1482; Wilbert E. Moore, The Professions: Roles and Rules (New York, 1970), p. 177.

never devoted as much energy and manpower to opposing unauthorized practice as it did to combatting judicial recall or to promoting procedural reforms or even higher bar admission standards. But its record was sufficient to demonstrate a commitment to the economic concerns of the middle stratum.

The local, state, and national association membership drives during the 1910s greatly enlarged the rolls of the organized bar and increased the potential effectiveness of the bar association movement. But these drives did not bring even a majority of lawyers into the fold, and the political effectiveness of bar associations remained much less than bar activists desired.[55] As Henry W. Taft complained to the New York state bar meeting in 1924, "The Bar of this State and the bar at large does not exercise an influence in the affairs of State and the Nation which is commensurate with its proper professional functions. Now, one reason for that is that the bar is not organized so as to give expression to its views."[56]

---

[55] Alfred Z. Reed estimated just before 1920 that 25-30 percent of all lawyers were in some kind of bar association. Training, p. 216.

[56] New York State Bar Association, Report 47 (1924), 173-174.

A bar organization strategy increasingly favored by bar leaders after 1920 was to make state bar association membership compulsory for all lawyers. This came to be called the "integrated bar" movement. The idea seems to have originated around 1913 in the American Judicature Society, and in 1918 the Society devised a model statute for an integrated bar. The ABA endorsed the idea in 1920 after its Conference of Bar Association Delegates had revised the Society's model statute. By 1923 state bar associations in ten states, mainly in the South and West, but including Michigan, had voted in favor of the integrated bar. North Dakota, Alabama, Idaho, and New Mexico were the first states to establish compulsory bar associations. The Conference of Bar Association Delegates discussed the issue at length in an August 1926 special meeting presided over by Charles Evans Hughes, indicating that the issue had now become a live one in the industrial states. The breakthrough for the movement came in 1927, when California became the first large industrial state to create an integrated bar. The California legislature had actually passed the act in 1925, but had seen it vetoed.[57]

---

[57] "Report Submitted by Delegates from Association of the Bar of New York City to the Conference of Bar Association Delegates Special Meeting April 28, 1926,"

In northeastern states, the integrated bar idea became a major source of controversy among the bar elite. In New York the two sides were led by Hughes, who favored the idea, and William D. Guthrie, who opposed it. These two men had only recently led opposing factions in the conflict within the ABCNY over whether, and in what way, to respond to the state legislature's decision to oust its five Socialist members. The forces led by Hughes won that first battle, thereby giving a significant boost to the city association's membership rolls. But Guthrie's more conservative faction prevailed in the second battle, after protracted discussions among the state's lawyers between 1922 and 1928.[58]

Newton D. Baker MSS, Box 63, Library of Congress; Gilb, "Self-Governing Professions," chap. 2; New York State Bar Association, Report 50 (1927), 124.

[58] The New York County Lawyers' Association voted in favor of the integrated bar in 1922, and the New York State Bar Association approved it in principle in 1924 and 1925 before the opposing forces mobilized. In 1926 the ABCNY voted against the proposal, the county association reversed itself, and a conference of bar associations from upstate New York refused to support the integrated bar although they favored the principle of a more complete organization of the bar of the state. The state bar association voted at its 1927 meeting to table the question and to empower its Committee on Organization of the Bar of the State to study the results of the operations of the integrated bar in other states. That committee reported in 1930. New York State Bar Association, Report 50 (1927), 120-126; "Report of the Committee on the Organization of the Bar and Cooperation between State and Local Bar Associations

The issue provides a measure of the nativist sentiments of New York's organized bar. The opponents of the integrated bar did not oppose it on the grounds it would violate the historic individualistic ethos of the profession. Instead they expressed fears that first- and second-generation immigrant lawyers with "alien principles" would take over the bar association. Henry A. Forster of New York City expressed the feelings of the nativist majority in the state association.

> There are in this country and coming here in the last thirty years, a great multitude of very intelligent men and women from the three great empires in Eastern Europe. . . . The majority of them believe sincerely in an empire to control the country as a whole, and a bureaucracy to control the locality. If you are going to admit a much larger number who honestly believe that an empire is the thing in national affairs, and a bureaucracy the thing in local affairs, you will have some fun, both in the local and general meetings of your state organization.[59]

---

to 53rd Annual Meeting of New York State Bar Association, January 17 and 18, 1930," copy in Baker MSS, Box 63; Martin, Causes and Conflicts, pp. 210-213, 221-222. The Baker MSS, Box 179 contain letters and pamphlets relating the deliberations of Ohio lawyers about the integrated bar.

[59] New York State Bar Association, Report 46 (1923), 287. William D. Guthrie did argue that the compulsory bar was "an oppressive and unconstitutional interference with the individual liberty and independence of lawyers," but Guthrie's views were always extreme and even he did not press that argument very strongly. See "Report Submitted by Delegates from ABCNY," Baker MSS, Box 63. Proponents of the integrated bar in New York were able

Forster was also concerned about the radicals among immigrant lawyers. He recognized that only a minority were radicals, but they constituted a minority "large enough to swamp one of our ordinary meetings, and I tell you gentlemen, they will attend meetings. . . . and you may find it difficult to uphold Republican ideals."[60] Apparently Forster feared a coalition of monarchists and socialists, united in hostility to native American republicanism.

Proponents of the integrated bar argued that although a voluntary association could accomplish something, it could not accomplish as much as the entire bar could if the entire bar belonged to one association.[61] But the proponents were not able, or even very willing, to speak to the fears of men like Forster. In fact, the proponents accepted, at least privately, the opponents'

---

to counter Guthrie with the legal opinion submitted by Elihu Root that nothing in the statutes or traditions of the state or the profession prohibited compulsory bar organization. Root to Julius H. Cohen, February 25, 1925, copy in P. C. Jessup MSS, Box 253.

[60] New York State Bar Association, Report 46 (1923), 287.

[61] Ibid. 47 (1924), 165 for remarks by Martin Conboy of New York City.

image of the immigrant lawyer. For example, although bar activist H. R. Medina argued that only by achieving organizational solidarity could the entire bar be improved, at the same time he sympathetically described the barriers to such solidarity: "One element of our Bar, for reasons which are easy to understand, simply will have nothing to do with another element of our Bar. It instinctively dislikes the element in question, has no respect for it, and would as leave avoid even standing alongside of one of its members in the subway."[62]

****

By the 1920s the modern pattern of bar organization had been established. Membership drives had reduced the exclusiveness and social elitism of bar associations.[63] In many states the movement to increase membership had gone so far as to make state bar association membership compulsory for all lawyers. The stage was set for a

---

[62] H. R. Medina to Philip J. Wickser, November 18, 1930, quoted by Wickser, "Law Schools and the Law," Association of American Law Schools, Proceedings 28 (1930), 90. Medina was chairman of the New York County Lawyers' Association Committee on Bar Admission. Wickser was probably the leading upstate New York bar activist in the late 1920s and 1930s.

[63] Wickser estimated in 1930 that approximately 50 percent of all lawyers were members of some bar association. Ibid.

more organizational-minded and rationalized approach to the bar and its problems. This change of emphasis did occur. Yet, bar associations continued to serve the purposes envisioned for them by the conservative elite at the time membership drives began: to achieve self-regulation for the profession as a means of forestalling public criticism of the bench and bar and to restore the profession's prestige and historic conservative political role.

CHAPTER 8

"A BAR WITHIN THE BAR:" THE LAW PROFESSORS'
IDEOLOGY, 1870-1900

During the 1890s full-time law teaching emerged as a specialty. By the turn of the century a self-conscious group of law professors in the leading schools had constructed their own distinctive professional ideology and were organizing a national professional association to spread their ideas about legal education and law reform. Indeed, these law professors formulated the fullest and most coherent conception of professionalism found among the bar in the 1890-1930 period, a development which can be ascribed partially to the fact that they were a new professional group and partially to the fact that they were participating in the general trend toward professionalization in the academy.

The history of the emergence of this distinctive group among the law professoriate can be divided into two stages. Prior to 1900 the emphasis was on establishing the principle that a majority of the faculty in "respectable" university law schools ought to be full-time. For reasons that will be explored below, the professors committed to the Harvard case method tended to be the leaders of that movement. After 1900 and until about 1920, this small nucleus of first-generation full-time professors sought to extend their conception of legal education to non-elite but non-proprietary law schools and sought, by their writings, expert testimony, and influence on students, to affect both legal doctrines and the administration of justice. Speaking of the professoriate collectively, Alfred Z. Reed declared, "Its primary interest is not with the law as it is, but with the law as it may become."[1] These aims signalled that the first generation had come of age and that its conception of professionalism had matured. As Harlan F. Stone explained, the professors saw themselves as constituting

> a bar within the bar, composed of men with liberal and professional education who are preserving the best traditions of the profession, setting their own standards of professional attainment and right conduct,

---

[1] Alfred Z. Reed, Training for the Public Profession of the Law: Historical Development and Principal Contemporary Problems of Legal Education in the United States with Some Account of Conditions in England and Canada (New York, 1921), p. 291.

> believing and acting on the belief that law
> is a profession worthy of the most rigorous
> and exacting training and that it demands
> the loyal adherence to those intellectual
> and ethical standards of excellence which
> are essential to the well-being and effective
> service of any profession.[2]

Although their activities made the professors "reformers," their commitment to reform was "professional-minded" and their conception of professionalism very narrow. The limited nature of their reform commitment was revealed clearly in the 1920s. During that decade, the bar elite, often for very conservative reasons, began to accept and act on many of the professors' ideas. At the same time, a new generation of law professors, who had a broader although still very guild-minded conception of their professional mandate, emerged to challenge the orthodoxy of the first generation.

Although the professors were important in their own right, their broader significance for this study is that they were trying to gain a position of influence within the legal profession that law teachers, as a group, had not had before. They were seeking to join the legal

---

[2] Harlan F. Stone, "Address of the President," Association of American Law Schools, Proceedings 17 (1919), 102-103. (Hereafter referred to AALS, Proceedings).

elite. Until about 1915 the most that can be said is that they were attracting an increasing amount of attention. After 1915 they began to gain a measurable degree of influence, primarily because the practitioner elite was beginning to appreciate the advantages of the rationalization theme the professors had been promoting in the areas of doctrine, training, and the administration of justice.

Yet the interests and outlooks of the professors and practitioners never wholly converged. The elite practitioners had political, economic, and cultural identities which were broader than their strict professional role. In contrast, the professors, whose socioeconomic backgrounds and political loyalties were not greatly different from those of the practitioner elite, cherished a more abstracted conception of the law and their professional role. The nature of academic life undoubtedly contributed to that difference, as did the different experiences the two groups had during the crucial 1890-1915 period. The practitioners, as we have seen, were defensive and suspicious of innovations during this period. The professors, on the other hand, were assertive and optimistic, as befitted an emerging elite.

Three converging trends were responsible for the emergence of a small cadre of full-time law professors, largely loyal to the case method, in the 1890s. The first trend was that during the 1890s bar leaders became increasingly positive about the case method and the conception of legal education its advocates had attached to it. A second important trend was the change in the structure and ideology of higher education in general, which saw the demise of the nineteenth-century college and the emergence of the modern university. Finally, and probably most importantly, the increasing trend toward law school as the preferred method of preparation for the bar came to floodtide in the 1890s, creating a demand for a new corps of law school teachers.

****

The origin of the case method can be unambiguously traced to President Charles W. Eliot's appointment of Christopher Columbus Langdell as dean of the Harvard Law School in 1870. With Eliot's backing, Langdell changed legal education at Harvard by introducing his new system of law teaching, by raising entrance and graduation requirements, and, as soon as possible, by making changes in the faculty. His most audacious appointment was his first, James Barr Ames in 1873; then a young man one year out of law school, Ames had no experience in practice and was committed to the still largely untested case method of instruction.[3]

But the case method did not spread immediately, or even rapidly, to other law schools. Indeed, proponents of the case method met considerable opposition, not only in the wider law school world and legal profession, but also in the Harvard community. In fact, it was not until the mid-1880s that the case method was fully established even at Harvard. In the first place, Langdell's appointment was almost blocked in the Board of Overseers because his ideas were novel and because the Overseers saw no need to tamper with a school that was already financially successful. This opposition faded only when several prominent New York City lawyers, especially James C. Carter, strongly endorsed Langdell. The students were harder to convince. Only a small handful, stigmatized as "Langdell's freshmen," attended his classes during his first year, and for several years after that the students were divided into Langdellians and anti-Langdellians.

---

[3]Arthur E. Sutherland, The Law at Harvard: A History of Ideas and Men, 1817-1967 (Cambridge, Mass., 1967), pp. 183-191.

Established members of the bar were equally hard to convince, although here also there was a handful of supporters. Especially notable were Carter in New York and the editor of the American Law Review, who greeted favorably the casebooks published by Langdell and Ames during the 1870s. More characteristic, however, was the reaction of the reviewer for the Southern Law Review, who opined in 1879 after reading the second edition of Langdell's Cases on Contracts that "there is just as much sense in endeavoring to instruct students in the principles of law by the exclusive reading of cases as there would be in endeavoring to instruct the students of the West Point Military Academy in the art of war by compelling them to read the official reports of all the leading battles which have been fought in the world's history." This same attitude inspired the founding in 1872 of a rival and more practical law school, the Boston University Law School. As Ames reported, "hardly one of the Boston lawyers had any faith in [the case method]."[4]

This lack of faith extended even to the second and third faculty members Langdell selected, James Bradley Thayer and John Chipman Gray. They were both lecture-method professors and, in striking contrast to Ames, had

---

[4] Charles Warren, History of the Harvard Law School, 2 vols. (New York, 1908), 2:362, 501-503; James Barr Ames, "C. C. Langdell," in Ames, Lectures on Legal History and Miscellaneous Legal Essays (Cambridge, Mass., 1913), p. 479.

many years of practical experience at the bar. Gray, in fact, remained in practice in Boston after his appointment as a full-time professor to the faculty, the only full-time law professor after 1870 to do so at Harvard.[5]

Although both Gray and Thayer eventually produced important casebooks, it was not until the late 1880s that they could be counted among the supporters of the case method.[6] Gray complained to President Eliot, in reference to the tendency of Langdell's reforms, that a law school "where the majority of the professors shuns and despises the contact with actual facts has got the seeds of ruin in it and will go and ought to go to the devil."[7] Gray's letter was probably prompted by the appointment of William A. Keener, a young and relatively

---

[5] Sutherland, Law at Harvard, pp. 183-191.

[6] Gray published the first of his six-volume Select Cases and Other Authorities on the Law of Property in 1888. He had been appointed to the faculty in 1875. Thayer published his first casebook, Select Cases on Evidence at Common Law in 1892. He had been appointed Royall Professor in 1874.

[7] Gray to Eliot, January 3, 1883, quoted in Hugh Hawkins, Between Harvard and America; The Educational Leadership of Charles W. Eliot (New York, 1972), p. 205.

inexperienced lawyer, to replace the departing Oliver Wendell Holmes, Jr. as the Weld Professor. That appointment prompted a complaint in a similar vein from Epraim W. Gurney, dean of the faculty of Harvard College, which reveals that even academicians opposed an overly academic approach to professional education.

> [Langdell's] ideal is to breed professors of law, not practitioners. . . . The whole tendency of the [Langdell] system would be to build up a great school of law as an exact science, and divorce it more and more from its actual administration. One hardly needs more evidence of this tendency than the contemptuous way which both Langdell and Ames have of speaking of Courts and Judges. . . . The trouble in their mind with those judges is that they did not treat this or that question as a philosophical professor, building up a coherent system would have done, but as the judges before whom the young men are going to practice will do.[8]

In large part, the early opposition to the case method can be attributed to the tendency of a conservative profession to treat any striking innovation warily. It

---

[8] Gurney to Eliot, 1883, quoted in Sutherland, Law at Harvard, p. 188. More direct testimony of the tenor of Ames' and Langdell's criticisms of the judiciary comes from Louis D. Brandeis, while a student at Harvard Law School. "Last year it seemed to be Ames' great aim and object to convince us that nine-tenths of the judges who have sat on the English Bench and about ninety-nine-hundredths of the American judges 'did not know what they were talking about'--that the great majority of the Judges were illogical, inconsistent and unreasonable." Brandeis to Otto A. Wehle, November 12, 1876, Brandeis, Letters of Louis D. Brandeis; Urban Reformer, 1870-1907, ed. Melvin I. Urofsky and David W. Levy (Albany, N. Y., 1971), p. 10.

also seems to be traceable to the newness of the inductive method itself in university instruction generally in the 1870s and 1880s, to say nothing of its newness in professional instruction. Because the inductive method was so new, there were few in the university community willing to support the case method on pedagogic grounds. The newness of the inductive method might also be what led Langdell and Ames to excesses of overstatement and formalism in developing the case method.

Langdell declared his formalistic and positivistic credo in the preface to his first casebook, Selected Cases on Contracts, published in 1871: law is a science. The number of fundamental legal doctrines discoverable in the vast corpus of the law was, he declared, fewer in number than was commonly supposed.

> It seemed to me, therefore, to be possible to take such a branch of the law as Contracts, for example, and, without exceeding comparatively moderate limits, to select, classify, and arrange all the cases which had contributed in any important degree to the growth, development, or establishment of any of its essential doctrines; and that such a work could not fail to be of material service to all who desire to study that branch of law systematically and in its original sources.[9]

---

[9] Quoted in Lawrence M. Friedman, A History of American Law (New York, 1973), p. 532.

The principles of law were to be discovered by the law professor just as the principles of science were to be discovered by the chemist or physicist. As Learned Hand sardonically remarked,

> Langdell had arrived at the case-system because he thought of law as a set of principles to be derived from the reports by the process of induction; he appealed to the analogy of the physical sciences. . . . It often led him altogether to disregard the judges' reasons, and to substitute, in justification of their results, explanations entirely foreign to anything that had been in their minds.[10]

Hand thought Ames fell victim to the same tendency.

> Ames was a great legal historian, who had traced many doctrines from their seeds to fruition; he was given to finding the leaf and flower more perfect in the bud than was always obvious to others. In practice, the law which he taught had an esoteric flavor somewhat like Langdell's. Both were great men; but both were disposed to search for, and find, underlying syntheses that were at times authentic with them.[11]

Oliver Wendell Holmes, Jr. was, characteristically, more pithy in making the same point about Langdell. Langdell, Holmes thought, "was somewhat wanting in horse sense."[12]

---

[10] Learned Hand, "Foreword," in Samuel Williston, Life and Law (Boston, 1941), p. vii.

[11] Ibid.

[12] Holmes to Sir Frederick Pollock, July 6, 1908, Mark De Wolfe Howe, ed., Holmes-Pollock Letters: The Correspondence of Mr. Justice Holmes and Sir Frederick Pollock, 1874-1932, 2 vols. (Cambridge, Mass., 1961), 1: 140, quoted in David Wigdor, Roscoe Pound: Philosopher of Law (Westport, Conn., 1974), p. 35.

By the 1890s, when the case method began to spread, its ideology had undergone a subtle but important change. The basic message was still the same, as was indicated by William Keener, who carried the case method from Harvard to Columbia. In 1894 Keener remarked, "If law is a science--and if it is not a science it has no place in the curriculum of a university--all will agree that the most scientific method should be adopted in teaching law."[13] But Langdell's positivist optimism that the law could be reduced to a few principles was abandoned, to be replaced by a recognition that the law was exceedingly complex, often inconsistent, and constantly growing. No longer was it believed that students could learn all the fundamental legal doctrines during their years in law school. Instead, by the 1890s it was argued that the main value of law school instruction, especially via the case method, was the development of the future lawyer's powers of legal analysis and synthesis. The case-method schools endeavored to teach their students "to think clearly and accurately in terms of settled legal

---

[13] William A. Keener, "The Inductive Method in Legal Education," ABA, *Reports* 17 (1894), 475.

principles, to analyze, test and weigh precedents under the fierce light of reason, and trained them in the art of applying old principles to new states of fact."[14]

The case method undoubtedly was well adapted to training the new generation of counselors. When men trained by the case method sought positions with major firms in Boston or New York, they found a welcome, at least after the senior practitioners discovered that such men were well prepared, with a sound grounding in the principles of the law, an ability to think in a "lawyerly" way, and an ability to research points of law.[15] There was a negative side as well. Moorfield Storey complained,

> I should say that the gentlemen who are the products of the case system . . . brought into the office some more of intellect, somewhat greater confidence in their opinion, somewhat greater imperviousness to advice and suggestion than the products of the old system. I find students coming to me and laying down with confidence doctrines of the law for which I can find no authority in cases, and which are wholly unknown to some of the leaders of our bar.[16]

---

[14] Columbia University Foundation for Research in Legal History, A History of the School of Law: Columbia University, ed. Julius Goebel (New York, 1955), pp. 140-141; Reed, Training, pp. 371-379; William R. Vance, "The Ultimate Function of the Teacher of Law," AALS, Proceedings 11 (1911), 33.

[15] Williston, Life and Law, p. 206.

[16] ABA, Reports 17 (1894), 379.

But Storey hired them nonetheless. So, too, did Walter S. Carter, the key figure in the growth of large firms in New York City. He maintained close contacts with Ames and solicited his advice on hiring recent Harvard graduates. Yale Law School, which resisted the new method, found, especially in the 1890s, that it was unable to attract even its own undergraduates, as there was, to quote the Governing Board of the Law School, an "increasing annual exodus of Yale graduates to Harvard Law School."[17] Presumably, they anticipated greater career advantages from a Harvard than from a Yale law degree.

On the other hand, graduates of Columbia, where the case system had not made any inroads in the 1880s, were also well received in major firms throughout that decade. Walter S. Carter was as willing to hire Columbia men as Harvard men. Similarly, in the Midwest the University of Michigan Law School rose to prominence as a national, or at least a regional, law school of the first rank before it adopted the case method. Yale's problems in the East

---

[17] Otto E. Koegel, *Walter S. Carter; Collector of Young Masters; or, The Progenitor of Many Law Firms* (New York, 1953), p. 11n; Yale statement of June 21, 1898 quoted in Frederick C. Hicks, *Yale Law School: 1895-1915* (New Haven, 1938), p. 40.

were at least partially traceable to its location and
to certain peculiarities in its educational philosophy
and not merely to its failure to adopt the case method.
Practitioner approval, we may conclude, was important
in providing sanction for the case method, but practitioner
pressure on the law schools did not significantly contribute to its spread.[18]

In gaining practitioner sanction, it was not only
important that the case method turned out well-trained
young lawyers. It was also significant that the case
method contributed to the development of a truly national
law. With so many jurisdictions, each drawing on the
other for precedents, it was often hard to know what
principles should be applied in the interstate commercial
transactions that were becoming more and more important
in the late nineteenth century. The case method promised
to discover these principles and to relate them to the
facts of the modern world, and in a safe way.[19] In its

---

[18] Elizabeth G. Brown, Legal Education at Michigan, 1859-1959 (Ann Arbor, 1959), pp. 694-696; Frederick C. Hicks, Yale Law School: 1869-1894 (New Haven, 1937), p. 18. Within five years of its founding in 1859, 60 to 70 per-cent of Michigan's students were from out of state, a figure that was not affected by the creation of many new law schools in the Midwest, some of which adopted the case method before Michigan did.

[19] See Alfred Mack to Thayer, November 8, 1892 and Henry P. Kaufman to Thayer, August 29, 1892, J. B. Thayer MSS, Box 21, Harvard Law School Library, for early

early years, the case method confined itself rigorously to private law; by separating private law from public law and by treating it as a science, the case method implicitly protected private law from the claims of political control. The professors were quite capable of severely criticizing particular judicial decisions; but their criticisms were made in the spirit of modernizing and strengthening the common law and the historic role of the judiciary, although their purpose was not always appreciated.

Of course, textbooks could, and to a certain extent did, serve the same nationalizing function as the case method. But the textbooks ultimately were not thought

---

expressions of practitioner use of casebooks in their practice. The plethora of jurisdictions and the resulting confusion over legal doctrine help explain why, as Robert Stevens has noted, American academic lawyers have a position more like those in Germany than like those in Great Britain, despite the shared common tradition. Stevens, "Two Cheers for 1870: The American Law School," Perspectives in American History 5 (1971), 469. In England, as Edwin A. Jaggard reminded the ABA, the bar tended to search for truth in law books and to have a controlling regard for precedents as the embodiment of law, whereas "American lawyers, confronted by vastly more numerous and often inconsistent opinions of different jurisdictions, are driven . . . to justifying decisions by principle. American law schools are therefore sound in theory in teaching that the law is not merely what judges, with their localized knowledge and restricted intelligences, have held to be law, but that the law is a progressive science." ABA, Reports 29 (1906), 6.

to be as authoritative as casebooks, a circumstance which seems traceable to the special role universities were coming to play in American life. By the early 1900s it was understood in the university world, that, with a few exceptions, the case system and all it implied, was the university system, whereas textbooks, and all they implied, were the proprietary school system.[20]

An important reason for this identification between the case method and the university was the similarity between that method and the dominant trend in that part of the university world closest to the law school: the social sciences. As one student has commented, "The history of the social sciences in this period can best be understood as the story of the implementation of the inductive ideal in the methodology of the specific disciplines; and much of the fragmentation of the conceptions of man and society can be attributed . . . to

---

[20] Like all norms, this identification of the case system with the university and the textbook system with proprietary schools describes a consensus rather than an absolute existential fact. As will be shown below, an important function of the Association of American Law Schools from 1900 to 1920 was to stimulate the adoption in non-elite universities of all the features associated with the case system: full-time professors, adequate library, three-year curriculum, and some collegiate pre-legal training.

the diverse forms this implementation took." In addition, "the student no longer received a defined body of social principles; instead he was taught to find such principles for himself." In other words, the inductive ideal led the social sciences both to a more open-ended and less positivistic conception of social knowledge and to a narrower professionalism.[21]

The contrast between Harvard and Yale Law Schools helps make the difference between old and new trends concrete. Yale adhered to the older pedagogy and conception of law. Yale professors like Simeon E. Baldwin believed that the principles of the law were known and that the students should learn them directly from those who had already mastered them and not be asked to ferret them out from a collection of cases that would necessarily be incomplete. Students would learn best by a combination of textbook reading and recitation in class. After

---

[21] Paul Buck, "Introduction," in Buck, ed., Social Sciences at Harvard, 1860-1920: From Inculcation to the Open Mind (Cambridge, Mass., 1965), pp. 3-4. The same point about the parallels between the case method and contemporary intellectual trends is made by Richard Hofstadter and C. Dewitt Hardy, The Development and Scope of Higher Education in the United States (New York, 1952), pp. 74-77.

mastering the principles, students might profitably be led to compilations of cases for advanced study. Baldwin even prepared a casebook, Cases on Railroad Law, in 1896, with this use in mind.[22]

The Yale system clearly was based on the conceptions of knowledge and pedagogy that had characterized the nineteenth-century American college before the advent of the university, conceptions that were being cast aside by educational reformers in the late nineteenth century. However, it would be wrong to suggest that the contrast was simply one between misguided positivism and enlightened pragmatism, as in-house Whig interpretations have usually portrayed it. It should also be remembered that the "Yale System" included a broader and more liberal conception of professionalism and of the functions of a professional school than the case system

---

[22] Simeon E. Baldwin, "Teaching Law by Cases," Harvard Law Review 14 (December 1900), 258-261; Baldwin, "The Study of Elementary Law, The Proper Beginnings of a Legal Education," Yale Law Journal 13 (October 1903), 1-15; Baldwin, "Education for the Bar in the United States," American Political Science Review 9 (August 1915), 437-448; Hicks, Yale Law School: 1869-1894, pp. 32-35; Hicks, Yale Law School: 1895-1915, pp. 76-78; Frederick H. Jackson, Simeon Eben Baldwin--Lawyer, Social Scientist, Statesman (New York, 1955), pp. 106-107.

envisaged. As Brainerd Currie has pointed out in his study of the realist movement of the 1920s and 1930s, it was entirely appropriate that Yale would be a stronghold of that movement since its interdisciplinary aims and conceptions of professionalism were very similar to those that dominated the Yale Law School in the 1870s, 1880s, and 1890s.[23] This broad conception of professionalism was formalized by Yale President Theodore D. Woolsey in 1874 at the Law School's fiftieth anniversary.

> Let the school, then, be regarded no longer as simply the place for training men to plead causes, to give advice to clients, to defend criminals, but let it be regarded as the place of instruction in all sound learning relating to the foundations of justice, the history of law, the doctrine of government, to all those branches of knowledge which the most finished statesman and legislator ought to know.[24]

Yale carried out this ideal by including in its curriculum lecturers from elsewhere in the university who offered instruction in such subjects as medical jurisprudence, forensic elocution, Roman law, and international law. Also, in 1876 Yale created a two-year

---

[23] Brainerd Currie, "The Materials of Law Study," Journal of Legal Education 3 (Spring 1951), 381-383.

[24] Quoted in Jackson, Simeon E. Baldwin, p. 92.

graduate program leading to a D.C.L. degree. That degree was explicitly established to allow students to pursue studies in public law, Roman law, comparative jurisprudence, style in oratory and composition, constitutional history, and political science--courses of study which, in the main, were not to become available to students in case-method schools until after 1915.[25] Yale professors like Baldwin and Francis Wayland expressed this broader conceptualization of professionalism in their own lives, becoming active in a wide range of social science and genteel reform associations.[26] But their various activities smacked too much of the gentleman amateur scholar and not enough of the professional scholar to suit the modernizing temper of universities in the 1890s.

The support of university administrators was often crucial to the spread of the Harvard rather than the Yale conception of the law professor's vocation. The key role of Eliot at Harvard has been mentioned. At Columbia, President Seth Low fulfilled a similar function. In 1890

---

[25] Hicks, Yale Law School: 1864-1894, pp. 9-10, 24-26; Jackson, Simeon E. Baldwin, pp. 93-94.

[26] Hicks, Yale Law School: 1895-1915, pp. 18-19; Jackson, Simeon E. Baldwin, pp. 70, 113-138.

the newly appointed Low was seeking a way to rejuvenate the Law School; he looked to Harvard as the "most vigorous alternative" and was able to hire away William Keener, who was then engaged in a salary dispute with Eliot.[27]

Several other schools attempted to draw away Harvard faculty during the 1890s. For example, Samuel Williston received offers of deanship from three law schools between 1890 and 1895. If a Harvard professor were not available, then perhaps a Harvard-trained man with experience elsewhere could be obtained. That was the thinking at Western Reserve University in 1892 when it invited Eugene Wambaugh to become the dean of its new law school, which was being constructed along Harvard lines, with a three-year course, instruction chiefly by casebooks, and full-time professors. Wambaugh, who had introduced a modified version of the case method to the State University of Iowa in 1889, declined Western Reserve's offer and returned to Harvard.[28]

---

[27] Columbia University, History of the School of Law, pp. 118-119.

[28] Williston, Life and Law, p. 140; Reed, Training, p. 380; Wambaugh to Thayer, February 17, 1892, J. B. Thayer MSS, Box 24.

In 1902, when William Rainey Harper was creating the Law School at the University of Chicago, he explicitly attempted to create a "Harvard of the West." He obtained Joseph H. Beale from Harvard on a one-and-a-half-year leave of absence to set up the new law school on the Harvard model. In addition, he hired Julian W. Mack and Blewett Lee, both of whom held Harvard LL.B. degrees, away from Northwestern University School of Law. By the end of the first academic year, the regular Chicago faculty of eight included five with Harvard law degrees. At the State University of Iowa, Dean Emlin McClain expressed the hope in 1892 that he could secure another Harvard man, "for a few matters in which I take especial interest will not, I fear, be developed sympathetically by anyone not educated at Harvard." At the same time, McClain had to acknowledge that to please the Regents, he needed someone who had been in practice for several years.[29]

---

[29] Williston, Life and Law, pp. 129-130; Sutherland, Law at Harvard, p. 215; Chicago Legal News, April 19, 1902, p. 276; Richard J. Storr, Harper's University (Chicago, 1966), pp. 292-296; Reed, Training, p. 380; Wambaugh to Thayer, February 17, 1892, McClain to Thayer, December 23, 1891, May 12, 1892, J. B. Thayer MSS, Box 24. McClain was not entirely sold on the case method because he thought it took too much time if used alone. He preferred a modified system: cases in the first year to teach elementary principles, lecture and textbook (with cases as

When the University of Cincinnati opened its law department in 1896, it called on five local practitioners and judges who were known to be sympathetic to the Harvard system. The five included William Howard Taft and two Harvard graduates, Gustavus H. Wald and J. B. Brannan. Wald and Taft quickly got in touch with Ames and Thayer at Harvard, asking for advice. "We should not have ventured to trouble you gentlemen of Harvard at all, if we had not felt that you were greatly interested in promoting the cause of legal education throughout the country," Taft explained.[30]

However, the university administrators did not always fully share the case method advocates' conception of legal education. The cases of both Columbia and Chicago show that. Both Low and Harper had broader conceptions of what a professional school should do than

---

illustrative material) thereafter to teach the branches of law that merely applied elementary doctrines. See McClain to ABA Committee on Legal Education, March 9, 1892 in ABA, Reports 15 (1892), 373-374; McClain, "The Best Method of Using Cases in Teaching Law," ibid., 16 (1893), 407-408.

[30]Taft to Thayer, May 4, 1896, May 15, 1896, J. B. Thayer MSS, Box 21; ABA, Reports 25 (1902), 787. In 1904 James Barr Ames reported there were 70 Harvard Law School graduates teaching in other law schools. As late as 1927 Roscoe Pound reported that 143 of the 604 law school teachers in the nation were Harvard men. Harvard Law School Association, Report 18 (1904), 71; Paul Lombard Sayre, The Life of Roscoe Pound (Iowa City, 1948), p. 211.

did the Harvard men to whom they turned. In each
case, the president sought, with some success, to include
public law in the law school curriculum. Ames and Beale,
dissenting, presented the Harvard viewpoint to Harper.
Ames declared, "We believe the success of our School is
due in no small degree to the solidarity of our faculty
and to its concentration upon the work of teaching the
law pure and simple." Beale pointed out that at Columbia
"the curriculum . . . includes a few non-legal electives
from the School of Political Science. These facts have
been suggested as accountable for the striking failure
of the school to take the position to which her location,
her wealth, and the ability of her faculty seem to en-
title her."[31]

Significantly, the strongest advocate of the public
law curriculum at Chicago was Ernst Freund, a relative
outsider to the law professors' world. The son of middle-
class German Jewish parents and the possessor of a law

---

[31] Ames to Harper, March 31, 1902; Beale to Harper, April 2, 1902, quoted in "Ernst Freund--Pioneer of Administrative Law," University of Chicago Law Review 29 (Summer 1962), 764, 766-767. The originals are in the University of Chicago Archives.

degree from the University of Heidelberg, Freund had come to the United States in 1884, practiced law in New York City, taught public law at Columbia, and been a member of the University of Chicago's political science faculty for eight years before joining the new law school. He maintained his dual professional identity, helping to found the American Political Science Association in 1903 and serving as its president in 1916. Freund's major contribution to legal education was to initiate the study of administrative law, along with another relative outsider to the law school world, Felix Frankfurter, and Columbia political scientist Frank J. Goodnow.[32]

Although Low and Harper were able to "dilute" the curriculum (from the Harvard viewpoint), the fact that they actively supported the introduction of the case method and hired faculty trained in it or sympathetic to it was ultimately more significant in shaping the professional identity of the law faculty at both Columbia and Chicago.

---

[32] Oscar Kraines, The World and Ideas of Ernst Freund: The Search for General Principles of Legislation and Administrative Law (University, Ala., 1974), p. 2.

At other institutions, where the administration wanted to hire young full-time professors but only nominally supported the introduction of the case system, the dedication to the system that a Harvard training could instill was useful in its spread. Northwestern University School of Law was a case in point.[33] Three Harvard products--John H. Wigmore, Julian W. Mack, and Blewett Lee--were hired in the early 1890s to rejuvenate the school. They were members of the remarkable Harvard class of 1887 which had founded the Harvard Law Review. They had all been on the editorial board of the Review in its founding year, as was future Harvard professor Joseph Beale.[34] Not surprisingly, they kept in close contact with their Harvard mentors, especially Thayer, about developments at Northwestern.

When the enrollment increased from 127 to 181 after his first year, Wigmore reported to his former professor,

---

[33] By 1908 Beale was able to list twenty-two law schools, mainly in the Midwest and Far West, which "have come to the Harvard Law School for teachers to such an extent that their policy may be said to be largely influenced by the case method." Warren, History Harvard Law School 2:511-512. Also, as will be shown below, a number of schools were influenced indirectly by Harvard and adopted the case method.

[34] Warren, History Harvard Law School 2:440; Harry Barnard, The Forging of an American Jew: The Life and Times of Judge Julian W. Mack (New York, 1974), pp. 25-26; J. A. Rahl and K. Schwerin, "Northwestern University School of Law: A Short History," Northwestern University

> The President is now quite convinced--you will understand me--which way the wind blows; and he already refers to "the <u>old</u> method." In short, heterodoxy has now become orthodoxy; and the President is ready and anxious to complete the entrenchment of our 'doxy by replacing two local practitioners, who give a part of their time, by one man who will give all his time.³⁵

Six months earlier, Wigmore had drawn on the metaphors of warfare to describe his situation. He was optimistic that the faculty was united. "Domestic happiness and unity is an important prerequisite for successful external warfare." At first, he battled mainly with the students, especially with the "class having the traditions of laziness and text-books. But there was a general assault on the part of us all with the case-method as the year went on, and it has practically carried the day."³⁶ Blewett Lee reported in the same vein. "At

---

Law Review 55 (May-June 1960), 138-143.

³⁵Wigmore to Thayer, November 30, 1894, J. B. Thayer MSS, Box 21. The "President" was Henry Wade Rogers, chairman of the ABA's Section of Legal Education, former dean of the University of Michigan Law School (which did not use the case method), and future dean at Yale, where he presided over a faculty split between the Yale system and the case method. Although Rogers was known as progressive in educational administration, he taught by the textbook and recitation method and was one of the last at Yale to adopt the case method. His opposition to American imperialism in the Philippines probably forced his resignation from Northwestern. Hicks, <u>Yale Law School: 1895-1915</u>, p. 60; Richard Hofstadter and Walter P. Metzger, <u>Development of Academic Freedom in the United States</u> (New York, 1955), pp. 421-422.

³⁶Wigmore to Thayer, May 6, 1894, J. B. Thayer MSS, Box 21.

Harvard you can hardly appreciate the difficulties under which we labor in introducing teaching by cases in this place--we have 'friction' with the powers that be on this subject ever and anon. . . . If we only had a three years course, we could do great things out here."[37] A two-year course allowed insufficient time for all the subjects Wigmore and Lee thought necessary; consequently the students were pushed very hard, which undoubtedly contributed to their discontent. In addition, the expense of casebooks was a problem. "Every new Harvard textbook [sic] that we introduce here is met by a chorus of growls from the impecunious."[38]

The attitude of the "powers that be" was revealed by Northwestern Trustee James H. Raymond, a Chicago practitioner. Raymond did not believe the case method

---

[37] Lee to Thayer, March 21, 1894, ibid., Box 20. For Lee's even more frustrating experiences trying to introduce the case method at a private law school in Atlanta in 1892, see Lee to Thayer, May 14, May 30, August 16, and August 28, 1892, ibid., Box 21.

[38] Lee to Thayer, January 30, 1894, ibid., Box 20. For additional evidence that the cost of casebooks to the students was a barrier to their acceptance, see Maulsby Kimball (Buffalo Law School) to Thayer, September 17, 1898 and Arthur L. Hubbard (Notre Dame) to Thayer, September 30, 1899, ibid., Box 20.

should be the basis for legal education, but he based his opposition on the same arguments that the case-method advocates used to support their position.

> The power of everyman's mind is the power of original thought, induction and deduction. . . . You cannot educate a lawyer without educating him to think for himself, and, by so much as you put into him the power of original thought, which must be by inductive methods in my opinion, by just so much do you make of him a lawyer instead of a machine.[39]

Reporting to Thayer in the spring of 1895, Wigmore lamented that not only were the two part-time faculty not to be dismissed, but "we are struggling with the trustees for the very principle of case-study itself."[40]

At other institutions, where non-Harvard men introduced or helped spread the case method, the very struggle to master the method instilled a commitment to it. These were men, already full-time professors, who decided (for reasons that are not well documented) to teach themselves the case method. For example, the first

---

[39] ABA, Reports 17 (1894), 375.

[40] Wigmore to Thayer, March 4, 1895, June 1, 1895, J. B. Thayer MSS, Box 21. An instructive contrast to the struggles of Wigmore, Lee, and Mack is the relative ease that another Harvard man, Roscoe Pound, had in introducing the case method ten years later in his first year as dean at the Nebraska College of Law (University of Nebraska). For details see Wigdor, Roscoe Pound, pp. 36, 108-110.

three professors hired at Columbia to help Keener introduce the case method were self-taught: Francis M. Burdick, George W. Kirchwey, and George M. Cummings. Burdick, who was hired away from Cornell, where he had been one of the three original members of the law faculty in 1887, was a scholar-practitioner who adopted a modified version of the case method, using a casebook and textbook together. Along with Keener, whose casebook on quasi-contracts was published in 1888, Burdick compiled one of the first casebooks not put together by Ames or Langdell. His <u>Cases on Torts</u> was used at Columbia during the 1891-1892 school year. Kirchwey was hired away from the Albany Law School, where he had been dean for two years. Although not trained in the case method, he had adopted it in his classes because he was impressed by the claims of its advocates at Harvard. At Columbia he taught courses for which there were no casebooks, daily assigning five to eight cases for the students to look up before the next class. As soon as James Bradley Thayer's <u>Cases on Evidence</u> was published, Kirchwey adopted it.[41]

---

[41] Columbia University, <u>History of the School of Law</u>, pp. 162-163, 165; Keener to Charles Power, January 22, 1892, Keener MSS, Columbia University Libraries; Kirchwey to Thayer, October 5, 1893, J. B. Thayer MSS, Box 21. These appointments established that Columbia was not going to be a carbon copy of Harvard. Once this had been established, the next four appointments went to Harvard LL.B.'s:

Cummings' story was similar, as were those of Dean William Draper Lewis and Professors Pepper, Milell, and Bohlen at the University of Pennsylvania, of Austin Abbott at New York University, of Charles Noble Gregory at the University of Wisconsin, and of others at such widely diverse places as Trinity in North Carolina, Dickinson University in Pennsylvania, the University of Texas, and, eventually, the University of Michigan.[42]

Henry P. Starbuck, George F. Canfield, Henry W. Hardon, and John W. Houston.

[42] Warren, History Harvard Law School, 2:512; Merle Curti and Vernon Carstensen, The University of Wisconsin, 2 vols. (Madison, 1949), 2:430. As important as the dedication of these men was to the spread of the case method, the availability of usable casebooks was nearly as important. Until the 1890s the available casebooks did not cover the range of topics a law school might want to give, and they were designed more with their use at Harvard in mind than for a wider audience. In the 1890s a plethora of casebooks appeared, stimulated no doubt by the booming law school enrollments of that decade. Thayer brought out his tremendously influential Select Cases on Evidence (1892) and Cases on Constitutional Law (1895). He personally supervised their sale and distribution, sent complimentary copies to law school professors and practitioners throughout the nation, and personally answered the queries that came back about using the casebooks in the classroom. Other casebooks produced by Harvard professors in the 1890s made the list truly impressive: Gray's six volumes on property (1888-1892), designed to cover three years of course work; Ames' casebooks on torts (1873, revised and expanded 1893), pleading (1875), bills and notes (1881), trusts (1881-1882), and partnerships (1894); Langdell's casebooks on contracts (1871), sales (1872), equity pleading (1875-1876), and equity jurisdiction (1879); and casebooks by Herman W. Chaplin (1891), Jeremiah Smith (1897, 1898, 1899), Eugene Wambaugh (1896, 1899-1900), and Samuel Williston (two in 1894). But non-Harvard men were also producing casebooks which were

One other name might have been added to that list, that of Charles Evans Hughes, Jr. of Cornell. Compulsive worker and perfectionist that he was, he decided when he went to Cornell in 1891 that if he were going to become a law professor he should teach himself the case method. This he did while at the same time teaching

---

widely used. Keener's 1888 casebook on quasi-contracts was joined in the 1890s by a casebook on equity jurisdiction. Emlin McClain and Eugene Wambaugh at Iowa, Francis M. Burdick at Columbia, and Floyd R. Mechem, Harry Hutchins, Horace Wilgus, and Elias Johnson at Michigan, among others, produced casebooks in the 1890s. The Michigan casebooks were especially useful at schools which had not completely switched to the case method, as they were "illustrative material" casebooks, to be used with textbooks and/or lectures. Wambaugh also produced a handy volume entitled Study of Cases, which attempted to teach the manner in which cases should be studied. By 1908, of the eighty-three casebooks advertised in the Harvard Law Review, only twenty-seven had been prepared by Harvard professors; the rest were the work of professors at fourteen other law schools. See Frederick N. Judson (St. Louis Law School) to J. B. Thayer, October 5, 1893, Box 21; Arthur L. Hubbard (Notre Dame) to Thayer, September 30, 1899, Box 20; Lucius W. Hoyt (University of Denver) to Thayer, September 11, 1899, Box 20; George E. Gardner (University of Maine and University of Illinois) to Thayer, September 1, 1898, Box 20; Charles A. Rhetts (University of Indiana) to Thayer, November 24, 1896, Box 20; William A. Maury to Thayer, June 28, 1901, Box 20; Henry A. Morrill (University of Cincinnati) to Thayer, July 6, 1897, Box 20; John R. Taylor (University of Cincinnati) to Thayer, July 15, 1898, Box 20; Maulsby Kimball (Buffalo Law School) to Thayer, September 17, 1898, Box 20; Cuthbert W. Pound (Cornell) to Thayer, March 31, 1896; Eugene Wambaugh to Thayer, February 17, 1892, Box 24, all in J. B. Thayer MSS; William A. Keener to Christopher G. Tiedeman (University of Missouri), February 6, 1892, Keener MSS; ABA, Reports 17 (1894), 419-420; Brown, Legal Education at Michigan, pp. 196-209; Warren, History Harvard Law School, 2:512; Warren, A History of the American Bar (Boston, 1911), pp. 556-557.

fifteen hours per week, holding moot courts, and advising graduate students. As he remembered in his Autobiography, "My life was one of constant toil; in truth, I was about as busy with my courses as I had been with my practice in New York." But Hughes did not stay at Cornell. The $10,000 differential between his Cornell salary and what he had been earning in his New York law practice proved to be too much to give up.[43]

Although Hughes developed a reputation as a lawyer of principle, a statesman-lawyer above the narrow materialism of much of the profession, he lacked the emotional distance from the competitive and materialistic-centered life that seems to have been important in leading men into the law professoriate. Samuel Williston, for example, reported that he believed his best chance for success was "in the bookish side of the law."

---

[43] Charles Evans Hughes, The Autobiographical Notes of Charles Evans Hughes, ed. David J. Danelski and Joseph S. Tulchin (Cambridge, Mass., 1973), p. 96; Merlo J. Pusey, Charles Evans Hughes, 2 vols. (New York, 1951), 1:100-101. In his last year of practice before going to Cornell, Hughes earned $13,500; at Cornell he dropped to a salary of $3,000--which was actually very good for a law professor at the time. A survey conducted in 1897 revealed that the average compensation for full-time professors was $2,564.12. Harvard, one of the highest paying, paid assistant professors $2,250. Most other major schools paid full professors $2,500-3,000 and deans $3,500-4,000. Charles Noble Gregory, "The Wages of Law Teachers, ABA, Reports 20 (1897), 512-518.

> I was not well fitted for cajoling or dominating hostile witnesses in order to confute them; and the bargaining, negotiating, and compromising that form a large part of lawyers' dealings with one another were not suited to my talents. Especially too, in the art of attracting clients, I felt that I should not be a success.

Roscoe Pound found in the 1890s that he was dissatisfied with active practice although he was very successful. His biographer summarizes, "First, he didn't like the pretense of virtue, combined with rather shady methods which he sometimes found at the bar; and second, he didn't want to spend his whole life in quarrels over other people's money." In later years, Felix Frankfurter expressed the same sentiment. "To introduce the atmosphere and methods of a business arrangement in the world of science is, as you know, extremely distasteful to me. I left the practice of law and came to the Law School, I suppose, fundamentally because I did not want to be a trader and preferred the life of scholarship."[44]

Reinforcing these inclinations toward full-time academic life was the fact that in the smaller towns where many state universities were located, law professors found

---

[44] Williston, Life and Law, p. 140; Sayre, Roscoe Pound, p. 87; Frankfurter to Sheldon Glueck, November 21, 1928, Frankfurter MSS, Box 139, Library of Congress.

that even if they wanted to combine practice and teaching, there was little legal business available. In addition, the case method was quite demanding of time and effort, not only because it was less dogmatic, but also because it encouraged the students to prepare thoroughly before class and to "demand the reason why."[45] Law teachers came to believe, with Thayer, that "the main secret of teaching law, as of all teaching, is what Socrates declared to be the secret of eloquence, understanding your subject; and that requires, as regards any one of the great heads of our law, in the present stage of the science, an enormous and absorbing amount of labor."[46]

****

As their numbers grew and as the legitimacy of their methods came to be affirmed, full-time professors began to think of the influence they could have beyond their immediate campuses. Austin Abbott, who had come to the deanship of New York University Law School at the

---

[45] Vance, "The Ultimate Function of the Teacher of Law," pp. 31-34 has a useful discussion of the reasons why full-time professorships in law emerged in the late nineteenth century.

[46] James Bradley Thayer, "Presidential Address," Section of Legal Education, ABA, Reports 18 (1895), 416.

age of sixty, wrote earnestly to Thayer asking him to join in a movement to make "the learning and skill spent in selecting cases for students . . . useful to the profession at large." He expressed the growing feeling of many professors "that in this direction lies the greatest opportunity for increasing the usefulness and influence of the schools, and promoting the infusion of sound law into the vast conglomeration of 'judicial' minds composing the courts of this great country and leveling up the law toward the standards of the higher."[47] The fundamental work of preparing casebooks was largely done. From the mid-1890s on, the main job was to prepare articles and monographs that would restate and systematize the law in an ongoing process.[48]

---

[47] Abbott to Thayer, January 29, 1895, J. B. Thayer MSS, Box 24. Abbott was a recent convert. He had introduced the case method into New York University Law School in 1892, but in 1893 had declared to the ABA's Section of Legal Education that "there is no best way of teaching law" and that the main benefit of the case method was that it introduced the colloquy into the law school. He applauded this as a step toward a more practical education, since the colloquy approximated the way established lawyers discussed the law. Abbott, "Existing Questions of Legal Education," ABA, Reports 16 (1893), 385. See also his April 27, 1892 letter to the Committee on Legal Education, reprinted in ABA, Reports 15 (1892), 375-377. See also L. J. Tompkins, New York University Law School, Past and Present (New York, 1904), p. 34.

[48] See the remarks of James Barr Ames to the 1904 Harvard Law School Association dinner, Harvard Law School Association, Report 18 (1904), 71-72; for a similar statement see Floyd R. Mechem (Univerisity of Chicago), "The

An integral part of this increasing sense of professionalism among law faculties was the creation of law reviews. Harvard's, established in 1887, was the first, although it was inspired by the short-lived Columbia Jurist, established in 1885. Iowa and Yale established their periodicals in 1891. Michigan, Northwestern, New York University, and Cornell all established reviews between 1892 and 1894, but none survived past 1898. The founding of the Dickinson Law Review in 1897 and the Columbia Law Review in 1901 marked the period when viable law reviews began to be created at all law schools aspiring to national status. These reviews served as major vehicles for the research that the new law professoriate was beginning to engage in.[49]

In his presidential address to the Section of Legal Education of the ABA in 1895, James Bradley Thayer outlined the steps he believed had to be taken to make the law schools that were then adopting the case method into true centers for the scientific study of law. The

---

Opportunities and Responsibilities of American Law Schools," ABA, Reports 29 (1906), 180-182.

[49] Frederick C. Hicks, Materials and Methods of Legal Research (Rochester, 1942), p. 207.

workload of each instructor should be limited to three subjects at most. If an instructor were to prepare in more than one subject, the subjects should be closely related. The aim of an instructor's work should be publication in his specialty. Instructors should give, substantially, their whole time and strength to their work. "In mastering their material and qualifying themselves for their task, they have in hand, say for the next two generations, much formidable labor in exploring the history and chronological development of our law in all its parts." Furthermore, the students should be full-time, to insure that the school have a serious atmosphere and because no one could properly learn law unless he devoted his entire time to the task. In sum, Thayer concluded, "It is the simple truth that you cannot have thorough and first rate training in law, any more than in physical science, unless you have a body of learned teachers; and you cannot have a learned faculty of law unless, like other faculties, they give their lives to their work."[50]

Thayer's presidential address represented the opening of the breach between the professors' and the practitioners' conception of the professors' functions.

---

[50] Thayer, "Presidential Address," (1895), pp. 416, 426-427.

John Wigmore of Northwestern underscored this. He congratulated Thayer on the "exalted tone" and the "high standards" expressed in his speech and lamented that no one else at the ABA meetings ever seemed to take such a high stand. "I remember very well the hopeless feeling I had--a year ago at Saratoga--as I listened to the conversation about me and found what mediocre standards were looked up to as the best, and how desperately Philistine on all points (of legal education) the majority seemed."[51]

Examining the discussions that the Section of Legal Education had during the 1890s on legal education issues confirms Wigmore's assessment of the majority viewpoint. There was great interest in finding and promoting the proper pedagogical method, but very little interest in the role law professors might play in modernizing or systematizing the law. The contrast between the Section's discussions in the 1890s and the Association of American Law Schools' discussions in the 1900-1920 period is

---

[51] Wigmore to Thayer, November 3, 1895, J. B. Thayer MSS, Box 20. Thayer's address was reprinted in the Harvard Law Review, November 1895. He received letters of praise from many law professors, from university administrators, such as Wisconsin's President Charles R. Adams, and from some practitioners, such as long-time Harvard supporter and leader of the New York City bar, James C. Carter.

striking in this regard. In the 1890s there was some hostility to the case method in the Section, especially the representatives of institutions which used other methods and those practitioners who feared the method would turn out mere "case lawyers" unfamiliar with the principles of the law. The position of spokesmen for places like Yale and Boston University was that it was wiser, especially for beginning students, "to make the lecture the main thing and the cases the additional thing, rather than to make the cases the main thing and the lecture the additional thing." The argument was that students would be confused unless they were first given explicit instruction in the fundamental principles of law. But the general tone of the meetings was one of curiosity and sympathetic support. By 1900 there was a positive consensus among the legal elite about the use of full-time professors and the case method in education.[52]

---

[52] For examples of the opposition from non-case-method schools, see ABA, Reports 15 (1892), 367-368; 17 (1894), 376-377. For examples of practitioner questioning, see ibid. 17 (1894), 467-468; 19 (1896), 600-601. For examples of support for the legal education standards being urged by the full-time professors, see ibid. 19 (1896), 450-461; 20 (1897), 31-34.

By 1900 the case method was no longer an issue of major controversy in the elite law school world either. The last major holdouts among elite law schools, Yale and Michigan, were slowly converting and by 1912 could be classified as predominantly case-method schools.[53]

Despite Yale's holdout status, Simeon E. Baldwin of Yale, who also sat on the Connecticut Supreme Court, was elected the third president of the AALS. In his presidential address at the 1903 meeting, which was held in conjunction with the ABA meeting at Hot Springs, Virginia, Baldwin predictably defended Yale's approach. After making the usual philosophical arguments about the inapplicability of the inductive method to law, he informed his fellow professors that as a judge, "no argument now impresses me from the Bar more than one proceeding from settled principles, with no reference to reported cases." What is significant is that Baldwin's speech provoked no excited reply from the advocates of the case

---

[53] Charles P. Sherman, Academic Adventures (New Haven, 1944), pp. 191-193; Hicks, Yale Law School: 1895-1915, pp. 43-45; Brown, Legal Education at Michigan, pp. 70-82, 196-209. Yale's attempt to hire Roscoe Pound in 1909 suggests how much sympathy to the Harvard system had grown by then. Henry Wade Rogers to Pound, April 20, 1909, Pound MSS, Paige Box 29.

system, as it surely would have ten years previously. James Barr Ames responded, "I do not wish to engage in any discussion on the merits of the case system of teaching. . . . The battle is fought. It is a mere question now how quickly it will make its way all over the country." William P. Rogers of the Cincinnati Law School noted that fourteen schools, including his, had unreservedly adopted the case method. "These schools, it seems to me, do not particularly care whether the others adopt and teach the case sytem or not."[54]

---

[54] Simeon E. Baldwin, "The Study of Elementary Law, A Necessary Stage in Legal Education," AALS, Proceedings 3 (1903), 33, 36; Ames quote, ibid., p. 12; Rogers' quote, ibid., p. 10. In 1902 Ernest W. Huffcut of Cornell reported that his examination of catalogs revealed that 12 schools relied exclusively on the case system, 34 relied exclusively on textbook or textbook and lecture, 15 announced regular use of both texts and cases, and 33 announced they combined the best features of the case, textbook, and lecture systems. ABA, Reports 25 (1902), 541. In 1908 the Committee on Legal Education of the Illinois State Bar Association reported that the case method was used exclusively at Harvard, Columbia, University of Cincinnati, New York University, University of Chicago, Fordham, Stanford, Franklin T. Backus Law School, University of California, and University of Nebraska. In addition, the case method was used chiefly but not exclusively at 19 schools, including Northwestern, Cornell, University of Illinois, University of Indiana, University of Minnesota, and University of Wisconsin. Finally, the Committee reported it found "large use of the textbook system, free use of the case system, and limited use of the lecture system" at Yale, University of Michigan, Chicago-Kent Law School, Chicago Law School, and John Marshall Law School. "Report of Committee on Legal Education," Illinois State Bar Association, Proceedings 32 (1908), pt. 1, p. 112.

What now concerned men like Ames and Rogers was spelled out by Ames in a 1901 address entitled "The Vocation of the Law Professor." He stated many of the same themes Thayer had six years previously and advanced a step beyond. In Ames' view, the law professor had three roles: teacher, writer, and expert counselor in legislation. The role of teacher was well understood. The chief contribution of the professor as writer would be to correct the "principal defect" Ames perceived in "the generally admirable work of the judges." "Too often the just expectations of men are thwarted by the action of the courts, a result largely due to taking a partial view of the subject, or to a failure to grasp the original development and true significance of the rule which is made the basis of the decision." Judges could not be expected to become specialists in the kind of legal research needed to remedy this defect; but they ought "to have the benefit of the conclusions of specialists or professors, whose writings represent years of study and reflection, and are illuminated by the light of history, analysis, and the comparison of the laws of different countries." Professors could serve a similar function with respect to legislation. "No one will be so rash as to regard the law professor as a panacea against the evils of unwise legislation. But I know of no better safeguard against such evils than the existence of a permanent body of teachers devoting themselves year after year to the mastery of their respective subjects." In order to fulfill all of these roles, law professors had to be full-time, have an adequate library, and have sufficient time to research and write.[55]

---

[55]Ames, "Vocation of the Law School Professor," in Ames, Lectures on Legal History, pp. 366-368.

CHAPTER 9

"A BAR WITHIN THE BAR:" THE LAW PROFESSORS'
IDEOLOGY, 1900-1920

The unique role that James Barr Ames had sketched out for law professors in 1901--as the systematizers of the law and the instructors, not only of law students, but of judges and laymen as well--was insisted on again and again by law professors in the progressive period.[1] Roscoe Pound placed the elite professors' self-image in a historical context. He asserted in 1912 that the nation was at the beginning of a new period in the making over of the common law. Just as an infusion of morals in the sixteenth and seventeenth centuries, of mercantile custom in the eighteenth century, and of Bentham's ideas via legislation in the nineteenth century had made over the common law, so in the twentieth century an infusion of

---

[1]See Henry M. Bates, "The Strategic Position of the Law Teacher and the Law School," AALS, Proceedings 13 (1913), 29-31; William R. Vance, "The Ultimate Function of the Teacher of Law," ibid. 11 (1911), 36-43; Floyd Mechem, "The Opportunities and Responsibilities of American Law Schools," ABA, Reports 29 (1906), 180-182; Eugene A. Gilmore, "The Relation of the University to Professional Instruction in Law," ibid., pp. 56-57; Harlan Fiske Stone, Law and Its Administration, (New York,

new economics and new social science via both judicial decisions and legislation would make over the common law once again. But, he asked, who would provide this infusion? Certainly not the courts or the legislatures. In America they were not centralized enough to exert such influence on the common law. "The law teacher and the law writer--and I take it they will be one--must be our chief reliance."[2] More specifically, as Michigan's dean, Henry M. Bates, saw it, there were two great changes through which American jurisprudence seemed destined to pass in the near future: "change of emphasis from extreme individualism to a broader social policy . . . [and] reduction of our whole body of law to a real system."[3] Pound had made the same points. The law teachers must make the common law both more national and more systematic, and they should teach more about the social consequences of law.

1915), pp. 222-223; Alfred Z. Reed, Training for the Public Profession of the Law: Historical Development and Principal Contemporary Problems of Legal Education in the United States with Some Account of Conditions in England and Canada (New York, 1921), pp. 34-35.

[2] Pound, "Taught Law," AALS, Proceedings 12 (1912), 55-76.

[3] Bates, "The Strategic Position of the Law Teacher and the Law School," pp. 29-31.

Typically, scholars place this activity by law school professors during the progressive period within the context of the emergence of the liberal creed of sociological jurisprudence to challenge the formalistic and mechanical jurisprudence which the conservative bench and bar steadfastly adhered to in their opposition to social legislation. But to place the law school professors unambiguously in the progressive and liberal camp is to misread what they were doing. They _were_ self-conscious reformers; but their conception of reform was very narrow and excessively professional-minded. They were not working primarily to provide a more equitable distribution of legal services, and only in a limited sense were they trying to open the door for the public to take a greater role in decision-making on legal matters. In fact, they wanted to close many of the doors that progressives were trying to open. At the most, law professors were willing to recognize the claims of new groups of experts, non-lawyers, to play a role in the modernization of the law and the administration of justice. But even this willingness was less typical of the first generation of professors, in the 1895-1920 period, than of the second generation, in the 1920s.

This difference is illustrated by the contrast between Roscoe Pound, who was one of the most advanced of the first generation, and Felix Frankfurter on the question of administrative tribunals taking over some of the work formerly confined to the courts. Pound was concerned that such tribunals typically followed "the layman's mode of deciding cases. A practising lawyer soon learns that arbitrators, instead of trying to refer their decision to some principle, try to find the line of least resistance by way of compromise and satisfy no one."[4] Frankfurter agreed, but only up to a point: "Undoubtedly Pound fairly summarized the general characteristics of industrial and international arbitrations to date. I think, however, a lot of other considerations besides the lawyer's and the layman's way of deciding things come into play." Frankfurter was convinced that when such bodies became permanent rather than ad hoc, there would be called into play "a deep rule of psychology" affecting laymen and lawyers alike "to decide according to, or at least in the light of, prior similar cases."[5]

---

[4] Pound to Morris R. Cohen, May 1, 1914, copy in Felix Frankfurter MSS, Box 45, Library of Congress.

[5] Frankfurter to Cohen, May 17, 1914, ibid.

Frankfurter, like Pound, wanted the lawyer's way of deciding issues to prevail; but unlike Pound, Frankfurter was confident that lay experts could think and act in legalistic fashion.

We can better understand what the professors thought they were trying to accomplish by taking seriously their oft-repeated insistence that if the profession heeded their advice, it could restore its prestige and power. They saw themselves as possessing a broader conception of the law than the rest of the profession had, a conception more in keeping with the spirit of the times. "The lawyer," Columbia Law School Dean George W. Kirchwey reminded the American Bar Association in 1904, "has largely lost the social and intellectual pre-eminence which was generally conceded to him in the period preceding the Civil War."[6] Kirchwey recognized that the causes for this decline were many and varied. He conceded that some of them lay beyond the control of the bar, citing as examples the growing importance of wealth and industrial leadership and the rise of a new type of political leadership, which was based on compassion and

---

[6] George W. Kirchwey, "The Education of the American Lawyer," ABA, Reports 27 (1904), 518.

a knowledge of human nature but which was too often at war with the administration of justice. He thought, however, that the main cause of the bar's decline was that the "lawyer has abdicated [his] high function of leadership in secular affairs" by not keeping up with changed conditions.[7]

Perceiving the profession in general as passive, the victim of inadequate legal education in the past and submerged in commercialism and traditional conservatism, the professors saw themselves as in step with the march of progress. They rejoiced at the public mood of the late progressive period, when they saw the public coming to believe strongly "in expertness, in specialization, and in sound thinking," to cite Henry M. Bates' summary. "The long-sneered-at scholar is coming into his own," Bates declared triumphantly.[8]

But it was the technocratic and elitist, not the democratic, spirit of the progressive period that Bates and other professors welcomed and identified with. They were distressed by the tendency of some progressives to propose drastic remedies, such as judicial recall, to

---

[7] Ibid., p. 520.

[8] Bates, "The Strategic Position of the Law Teacher and the Law School," pp. 29-31.

deficiencies in the courts and in the administration of justice. The professors often agreed that some reforms were needed, that judicial decisions were often based on principles that were excessively formalistic and had become indefensible, and that the administration of justice was burdened by unnecessary delays.[9] But they proposed remedies different from those that appealed to progressives, and they insisted that the legal profession should retain control of legal doctrines, judicial appointments, and the details of the administration of justice. The trouble with the critics of the legal profession, Pound declared, was that they were too often "zealots" who were "eager to readjust without any well-defined new standards."[10]

---

[9] Ibid., pp. 36-46; Roscoe Pound, "Enforcement of Law," Illinois State Bar Association, Proceedings 32 (1908), pt. 2, 84; Edson R. Sunderland, "Teaching Practice," AALS, Proceedings 13 (1913), 49-62; Walter W. Cook, "A Council on Legal Education," ibid. 16 (1916), 114; Harry S. Richards remarks, ibid. 11 (1911), 6; letter protesting Ives decision sent by 14 university professors, including such law professors as Ernst Freund, Frank Goodnow, and Roscoe Pound, to The Outlook 98 (July 29, 1911), 709-711, cited in Barbara C. Steidle, "Conservative Progressives: A Study of the Attitudes and Role of Bar and Bench, 1905-1912" (Ph.D. dissertation, Rutgers University), 1969, pp. 216-218.

[10] Pound to Oliver Wendell Holmes, Jr., February 22, 1913, quoted in Paul L. Sayre, The Life of Roscoe Pound (Iowa City, 1948), p. 270.

As we have seen, the professors were prepared to take upon themselves the task of defining those standards in their writing and teaching. But they increasingly recognized that it would not be sufficient to confine themselves to those traditional activities. They found they had to engage in what Barry Dean Karl has called the "politics of ideas."[11] To do this, they developed a comprehensive analysis of the reasons for the decline in power and prestige of the bench and bar, an analysis which stressed the parochialism, commercialism, and lack of professional spirit in much of the bar. With this analysis in mind, they devised a list of remedies, emphasizing the need to suppress commercial schools, raise bar admission standards, and in other ways reorient the bar to take a more professional conception of itself. They lobbied with the public and especially with the practitioners to convince them that this analysis and these remedies were correct. As an important part of this strategy, they attempted to

---

[11] Barry Dean Karl, "The Power of Intellect and the Politics of Ideas," Daedalus 97 (Summer 1968), 1005. Karl defines the "politics of ideas" as "the activity that takes place when men committed to the development of certain ideological positions which they seek to establish within the intellectual community achieve sufficient influence over the professional mechanisms of that community to assure their own continued research and production, the

use their professional association, the Association of American Law Schools, to improve the standards of non-elite law schools so that a corps of several hundred full-time professors, created in the image of the elite professors, could be placed in the fifty or so "respectable," or potentially respectable, law schools. Such a large corps would better insure that the necessary scholarly writing could be accomplished; it would also directly spread the influence of the elite professors' viewpoint to practitioners and to law students throughout the nation.

****

The Association of American Law Schools was born in 1900 at the instigation of the American Bar Association's Section of Legal Education. In 1899 the Section passed without discussion a resolution introduced by Henry Wade Rogers, creating a committee of three to consider what action, if any, should be taken to bring "the reputable law schools of the country" into closer relations with each other and with the Section. That

---

growth of a community engaged in the development of related interests, and the dissemination of the results of that work to the largest potentially interested public."

committee, consisting of Rogers, John Chipman Gray of Harvard, and Judge George M. Sharp of Baltimore, the long-time secretary of the Section, issued a call for such law schools to meet in conference with the Section at the 1900 ABA meeting at Saratoga Springs, New York.[12] At that meeting the AALS was created, enrolling thirty-two of the 102 law schools then in existence.

During its first thirteen years the AALS met each year in late August in conjunction with the ABA, its attendance fluctuating, like the ABA's, with the attractiveness and accessibility of the meeting site, reaching a low of twenty-three in Seattle in 1908. In 1914 the Association moved its meetings to the Christmas break, a more convenient time for the professors, and chose Chicago as the permanent meeting site because of its central location. Attendance increased markedly. The shift away from the joint meetings with the ABA symbolized the sense of autonomy the law teachers developed as their professional association matured. This shift also reflected the estrangement between the academic and practitioner wings of the legal profession that developed during the progressive years.

---

[12] ABA, Reports 22 (1899), 565-566.

The Association was clearly controlled by the elite university law schools. Of its first twenty-eight presidents (1901-1930), fourteen were from Ivy League schools and ten from major Midwestern universities. Yale led the list with five, Harvard supplied four, and Columbia, Michigan, and Iowa three each.

Surveying the record of the first decade of the Association's work, Charles Noble Gregory declared, "though not merely that, ours is largely a bureau of standards."[13] The membership requirements of the Association were the most closely attended to items at the annual meetings. The requirements were raised just fast enough to encourage the "respectable" but marginal schools to raise their own standards and gain or maintain membership. The requirements were stringent enough that seventeen of the thirty-five schools enrolled at the 1901 inaugural meeting dropped out by 1909. At the same time, eighteen new schools qualified for membership, so that the Association had thirty-six members by 1909.[14] During its first twenty years of existence, the Association

---

[13] Charles Noble Gregory, "The Past and Present of the Association of American Law Schools," AALS, Proceedings 9 (1909), 43.

[14] Ibid., p. 41.

found itself enrolling a steadily decreasing percentage of all the law schools in the nation. That is, the total number of law schools was increasing at a more rapid pace than the Association's membership. Midway through the period, in 1909, John Wigmore estimated that nearly 40 percent of law school students and about 25 percent of bar admittees were from AALS schools, the discrepancy being accounted for by the 20 percent of the admittees with office training and the longer course of study in AALS schools.[15]

The Association's original membership requirements seem modest enough. Membership was by school rather than by individual professors. Schools had to require law degree candidates to have completed "a high school course of study, or its equivalent." The course of study for the law degree had to be "at least two years of thirty weeks per year with an average of at least ten hours' required classroom work each week for each student." It was also declared that this standard would go up to three years after 1905. Degrees could not be conferred

---

[15] Jerold S. Auerbach, "Enmity and Amity: Law Teachers and Practitioners, 1900-1922," *Perspectives in American History* 5 (1971), 565n; AALS, *Proceedings* 9 (1909), 10-11.

unless students had passed examinations. Students had to have access to a library with the U.S. reports and the local state reports.

No substantial changes were made in the requirements until 1909, although several "constructions" had to be placed on the existing rules because of special practices in several schools. In 1905 and again in 1916, the "high school course of study" rule was clarified to mean that the course of study had to be completed before the student entered the law school; the requirement was also tightened in 1905 to read "four years' high school course."[16] In 1907 the three-year course rule was clarified to mean three years of actual law study. This construction was devised because at least three member schools permitted bright or advanced students to take the three-year course in two years. The AALS decided this was not a good precedent and gave such schools two years to bring themselves into compliance with the new construction. Boston University Law School and New York University Law School resigned in 1908; the University of Maine followed suit in 1909 for the same reason.[17]

---

[16] AALS, Proceedings 5 (1905), 9, 11; 16 (1916), 81.

[17] Ibid. 7 (1907), 23-47.

The Association recognized that undue haste in raising requirements would drive away aspiring new members because compliance would render such schools unable to compete with proprietary schools. Nonetheless, in 1908 the AALS was moved to pass a pious resolution.

> The Association deems it highly advisable that the requirements for admission to the Law Schools which are members of this Association shall be advanced as rapidly as the conditions, under which the work of the several schools is carried on will permit, and strongly commends the action of those schools which have already advanced their requirements so as to require one or more years of work at college as a prerequisite to admission to the Law School and expresses the earnest hope that this advancement may continue until all of the members of the Association shall ultimately require at least two years of college work as preliminary to the study of law.[18]

It was hoped that this resolution would put trustees and presidents on notice and would encourage them to raise the standards of their schools.

In 1909 the possibility of raising the AALS membership requirements to two years of prelegal college work or even to a college degree was debated at length, following speeches by John H. Wigmore and Harry Pratt Judson (of the University of Chicago). Wigmore presented statistics compiled at Northwestern which tended to show

---

[18] Ibid. 8 (1908), 4-5.

college-educated men did not do better in law school than high-school graduates. Objections were raised to Wigmore's interpretation, and the clear consensus of the discussion was that college men did better. Judson presented the ideological justification for the standard-raisers. He argued that AALS schools did not merely prepare students for the state bar examination, but also prepared them to be professional men of value to the community. The university law school ought to look more to quality than to quantity, he argued, as was done "in medicine and chemistry and economics, making specialists of the small number of highly trained rather than of the large number with less training." Although there was general agreement with Judson's ambition for AALS schools, the discussion revealed concern that instituting a college education requirement would not serve that purpose but rather would merely encourage students to go to lesser schools where the requirements were lower, thereby lowering the standard of the bar. In the end, no decision was reached and the question was held over until the next meeting. The debate made clear the limits of AALS action. Unless bar admission requirements could be raised in the states, AALS action could be self-defeating. The meeting did produce one significant action, however. For the first time the Association distinguished between schools with day classes and full-time students and schools with night classes and part-time students, requiring the latter to have a four-year course of study if they wished AALS membership.[19]

Reflecting this concern about undue haste, the Association's Executive Committee proposed in March 1910 that AALS membership requirements should not be raised and that for the immediate future, the general AALS policy should be to focus on increasing membership and extending the influence of member schools. Rather than proposing membership requirements, the addresses to the annual meeting would focus on some topic of importance concerning the functioning of the law school. The annual meeting in August 1910 endorsed this policy.[20] One result of this policy was that the speeches and discussions at

---

[19] John H. Wigmore and Frederic B. Crossley, "A Statistical Comparison of College and High School Education as a Preparation for Legal Scholarship," ibid. 9 (1909), 112-136; Harry Pratt Judson, "Education Preparatory to a University Law School Course," ibid., pp. 137-140, quote on p. 139; the debate reported on pp. 9-31, the decision on night schools on pp. 34-36.

[20] Ibid. 12 (1912), 40-41.

the 1910 meeting were fairly boring, focusing on the organizational problems of running a law school and on whether the honor system was effective in law schools. The list of delegates attending the meeting (held in Chattanooga, Tennessee) was short and less distinguished than previously.

The Association decided on a slightly more vigorous policy in its 1912 meeting at Milwaukee. It agreed that membership applications would no longer be accepted from schools that offered courses at night parallel to courses in the day, on the grounds that such a policy "tends inevitably to lower educational standards." The library requirement was made more explicit. Member schools had to maintain a library of at least 5,000 volumes. No longer would mere access to an adequate library be sufficient.[21]

Like the 1914 decision to meet separately from the ABA, these changes in requirements were symptomatic of a more restless spirit in the law school world. So too was the 1915 presidential address by Harry S. Richards of Wisconsin, in which he expressed his concern that some schools were not complying with the requirements. In

---

[21] Ibid. 12 (1912), 45, 37-40.

response to Richards' address, the 1915 meeting voted to send investigators to member schools about which questions had been raised; to cover the costs of investigators, the annual assessment to member schools was raised from ten dollars to twenty dollars.[22]

In 1916 a proposal to require members to maintain at least three full-time instructors was heatedly debated and then passed. Since twelve of the forty-seven member schools were not then in compliance, a three-year grace period was included in the resolution. Franz C. Eschweiler of Marquette pleaded, "We want to ask and urge upon all here whether it is the purpose to make this an exclusive Association of those who have ample funds, or whether it is the purpose to let those who are striving to the same ends that you all are have a chance to carry out their method of reaching the same end." He was joined by representatives from Syracuse University and the University of Pittsburgh, who eloquently extolled the virtues and the dedication of their large part-time faculties. Dudley O. McGovney of the University of Iowa replied,

---

[22] Ibid. 15 (1915), 49-50; Richards, "A Survey of the Progress in Legal Education," ibid., p. 70.

> It seems to me, when this resolution came out in the mails that we were for the first time getting a substantial requirement for admission to the Association and continuance in it. It has been apparent to us all that we have been proceeding with the utmost conservatism, that we have never set up a high standard, and the standard now proposed by the committee will be a very moderate one for a first-rate or an acceptable American law school.

Besides, he concluded, the resolution would provide the teachers in the smaller schools with the ammunition they needed to convince their trustees that permanent faculty members had to be appointed. Walter W. Cook of Yale provided what may have been the coup de grâce when he pointed out that many of the twelve law schools not then in compliance belonged to universities whose medical schools complied with the requirements of the Council on Medical Education for Class A schools, which stipulated six permanent instructors. He was sure that with a little pressure from the AALS, the non-complying schools could get three full-time law professors.[23]

There were other symptoms of this new spirit. Harlan Stone of Columbia became involved in a controversy over bar examination questions with the State Board of Bar Examiners in New York. Professors lobbied for a

---

[23] Ibid. 16 (1916), 69-80; Eschweiler quote p. 69; McGovney quote p. 70.

Council of Legal Education within the ABA, to serve the same functions as the Council of Medical Education within the AMA and to replace the moribund Section of Legal Education.[24] These activities were carried out in a combative spirit, reflected in Bates' opinion that "the A.B.A. has come to be only a husk. Its journal is a joke, its principal activity is the annual meeting with its pompous banquet and days devoted mostly to guff. It is utterly failing to have the influence in law that the Medical Association is having in its field."[25]

---

[24] For a good summary of the professors' approaches to the ABA between 1915 and 1922, see Preble Stolz, "Training for the Public Profession of the Law (1921): A Contemporary Review," in Herbert Packer and Thomas Ehrlich, New Directions in Legal Education (New York, 1972), pp. 235-241. See also Auerbach, "Law Teachers and Practitioners," pp. 564-601 for an incisive analysis of the practitioners' perspective on legal education issues in these years. The bar examination issue is best followed in the private papers of those involved: Ezra Thayer MSS, Boxes 1, 2, and 3, Harvard Law School Library; Roscoe Pound MSS, Paige Boxes 28 and 29; Harlan F. Stone MSS, Miscellaneous Correspondence, Columbia University Libraries. For explicit appeals to the professors to exert pressure on and seek allies among individual members of the bar, judges, bar associations, and boards of bar examiners, see Richards, "A Survey of the Progress in Legal Education," p. 76; Vance, "The Ultimate Function of the Law Teacher," p. 32; Harlan F. Stone, "Address of the President," AALS, Proceedings 17 (1919), 106.

[25] Bates to Pound, March 16, 1916, Pound MSS, Paige Box 26.

This new spirit of activity among the elite professors indicated that in their minds the "bureau of standards" phase of professionalization was coming to a close and more direct efforts to affect legal education and the administration of justice should be pursued. It is significant that by the 1920s the interest of elite professors in their law school association had greatly diminished. They attended the meetings and continued to hold the offices. But for them, the AALS had already served its basic purpose and was now a more or less routine academic professional association. Henry M. Bates of Michigan expressed the new attitude in the 1920s. "I confess I have reached a state where only the presence of friends lends much attraction to these meetings. Some good and worthwhile things are said and done at the meeting, but there is an immense amount of mere talk."[26]

****

The AALS, after all, had merely been a staging area; it had not dealt with the substantive reforms the professors believed were important. The substantive reform the professors were most interested in, as has been

---

[26] Bates to Stone, January 15, 1921, Stone MSS, Miscellaneous Correspondence.

suggested above, was the acceptance by the bench and bar of the restated and systematized national law they were creating in the various specialties they had carved out within the common law tradition. There were, of course, variations among the professors. Some, probably the majority, saw themselves as rather strictly carrying on the traditions of Langdell, Ames, and Thayer. Others, including Pound, began an oblique attack on one assumption of the Langdellian case method--the asuumption that the study of the common law could be hermetically sealed off from non-legal factors which might influence its growth. In Pound's view, principles from the new economics and other social sciences, which were increasingly influencing legislation, would have to be incorporated into the common law in the form of a new theory of interests, so that courts would not mechanically invalidate social legislation and thereby increase needlessly the mounting conflict between the courts and the people. "What we need is . . . a real ministry of justice charged with studying the needs of the community and the defects in the administration of justice not a priori but in the light of actual experience and working out a definite, consistent and lawyer-like programme of improvement." A few others went beyond Pound, by urging curricular reforms which seemed to be the logical corollary of his sociological jurisprudence, but which he resisted, and by conducting research in such novel areas as administrative law and the functional ways that the law was shaped and used.[27]

But there were barriers to the acceptance of the professors' work by the bench and bar. Analyzing the barriers and the reasons behind them, the professors concluded that they were dealing with the same factors that explained the bar's apparent decline in public esteem and influence. The professors discerned two main problems: (1) the continuing hold that outmoded conceptions of law had on the bench and bar; (2) the commercial rather than the professional spirit among large numbers of the bar and the resultant lack of corporate spirit and organizational strength. Roscoe Pound, in advising William Howard Taft on a speech he was to give about the importance of legal education to the bar,

---

[27] David Wigdor, Roscoe Pound: Philosopher of Law (Westport, Conn., 1974), pp. 161-162; Columbia University Foundation for Research in Legal History, A History of the School of Law: Columbia University, ed. Julius Goebel (New York, 1955), pp. 218-230; Samuel Williston, Life and Law (Boston, 1941), pp. 189-190; William Twining, Karl Llewellyn and the Realist Movement (London, 1973), pp. 33-36; Oscar Kraines, The World and Ideas of Ernst Freund:

summed up the general line of the professors' analysis.

> It is generally felt by those who have studied the matter that the legal profession is far behind the medical profession in organization and training and that it is largely because of this that it has lost the confidence of the public and has not the influence as to matters upon which it is competent to speak which it ought to have. . . . public attention ought to be directed to this subject because here and not in a further pulling down of our judicial establishment may be found in large part a remedy for matters of which the public justly complain.[28]

However, the complaint about outmoded conceptions of law often fell on deaf ears, not only because of the bar's conservative resistance, but also because the complaints were so often theoretical and philosophical rather than practical. As William Twining, the historian of the realist movement, has commented about the work of the foremost advocate of sociological jurisprudence, "Pound's theories were not in such a form that they could be <u>used</u> in reforming the law or legal education or legal research or by judges or practitioners in their

---

The Search for General Principles of Legislation and Administrative Law (University, Ala., 1974), pp. 10-11, 76-77; A. A. Berle, Jr., "The Expansion of American Administrative Law," Harvard Law Review 30 (March 1917), 430-448; Pound quote is from Pound to Charles A. Boston, January 24, 1917, Pound MSS, Paige Box 8.

[28] Pound to Taft, n.d. [1913?] copy in Ezra Thayer MSS, Box 2.

daily work."[29] Insofar as the professors' critique touched ground during the progressive years, it did so most frequently in relation to procedural reform.

Law professors were attracted to procedural reform, but not because they considered procedure an intrinsically interesting subject. In fact, they rarely included procedure in their curriculum. One of the few critics of this practice, William Draper Lewis of the University of Pennsylvania Law School, complained that there was no course in elite schools from which the student learned anything more about the administration of justice than how to advise a client. "The faculty [of university law schools] have one and only one conception of their duty towards their students, and that is to turn them out able to answer any legal question likely to be put to them by private clients."[30] Ironically,

---

[29]Twining, *Karl Llewellyn*, p. 24.

[30]William Draper Lewis, "Legal Education and the Failure of the Bar to Perform Its Public Duties," ABA, *Reports* 29 (1906), 46-47, quote on p. 47. See also the comment by Wisconsin Law School Dean Harry S. Richards, AALS, *Proceedings* 11 (1911), 5. His school's treatment of practice and pleading was more extensive than many other schools, but it was an on-again, off-again matter. See Merle Curti and Vernon Carstensen, *The University of Wisconsin*, 2 vols. (Madison, 1949), 2:437-439. Lewis had a reputation among practitioners as one of the most liberal of law professors, especially after he supported the judicial recall movement. William Howard Taft

Lewis was speaking at the same meeting of the American Bar Association in St. Paul where Pound made his famous speech on "The Causes of Public Dissatisfaction with the Administration of Justice," a speech which he later credited as the beginning of sociological jurisprudence.[31] When Pound called the bar elite's attention to problems in the administration of justice, he was not speaking from experience in teaching the subject at the University of Nebraska, where he then was, nor had he urged its teaching on his fellow professors in the AALS. Yet during the subsequent four-year period, when he was making his reputation and moving rapidly from the University of Nebraska to Northwestern to the University of Chicago and to Harvard, Pound's main interest was procedural reform.[32]

---

considered the possibility that Woodrow Wilson might appoint Lewis to the Supreme Court one of the most compelling reasons that Charles Evans Hughes, as the Republican Party's strongest candidate, should give up his Supreme Court seat to run against Wilson in 1916. See Taft to Hughes, April 13, 1916, Hughes MSS, Box 3B, Library of Congress.

[31] Pound to Paul L. Sayre, September 14, 1945, Pound MSS, Paige Box 13.

[32] Wigdor, Roscoe Pound, pp. 147-155. This fact is significant since it reveals that Pound's clear strategy was to focus attention on defects in the lower courts rather than in the appellate courts; that is, he hoped to rally the organized bar to reform the unorganized element in the profession, hoping that lessons learned in that effort would stimulate reform at higher levels.

Pound and the other professors who emphasized procedural reform were trying to achieve a dual objective. They wanted to make the administration of justice more efficient and they wanted to discredit formalistic legal thinking. The professors believed that the tendency in the bar to emphasize inherited procedural rules and forms for their own sake--as the essence of the law, as ends rather than as means--was not only one of the major barriers to the efficient administration of justice but was also the ultimate ideological bulwark of outmoded thinking in the profession. Formalistic procedural rules encouraged lawyers to engage in the delaying tactics which evoked public criticism of the civil and criminal courts. This was serious enough and in itself sufficient grounds for reform. But what finally propelled the professors into the alien world of pleading and practice was their conviction that the emphasis on inherited procedural rules discouraged lawyers from considering the professors' more pragmatic view of what the law really was. Related to this, since procedural rules were different from one jurisdiction to another, the emphasis on procedure gave "unreasonable permanence to local peculiarities in the law," fostering "local anomalies of practice as though they had some intrinsic importance in the administration of justice" and (here was the rub) also fostering "a similar notion with respect to anomalies of substantive law"---just at the time when the elite professors were trying to construct a national law and trying to reshape non-elite law schools into nationally-oriented law schools.[33]

The professors traced this reverence for inherited procedural rules to two segments of the bench and bar, which they defined characteristically in terms of the legal training they had received. The two segments

---

[33] Pound to Taft, n.d. [1913?], copy in Ezra Thayer MSS, Box 2. The question of a national versus a local law orientation was an especially sensitive one to professors like Pound because it was a live issue within the AALS and one of the major barriers to creating a law professoriate entirely in their own image. Professors in middle-level law schools, aware that the overwhelming majority of their students would practice locally and do relatively routine work, insisted on the importance of teaching local peculiarities of substantive law and local procedural rules. Albert M. Kales of Northwestern, where the relationship with local practitioners was closer than in most elite schools, was a leading spokesman for this viewpoint, urging the preparation of casebooks that would meet this need. See the illuminating discussion at the 1907 meeting of the AALS, where Kales brought the issue into the open: AALS, Proceedings 7 (1907), 3-16, 82-110. Even Harvard gave token recognition of the need, at the urging of students and alumni like Brandeis, who observed as a result of his experience as a bar examiner that Boston University students were better prepared for the Suffolk bar exam than were Harvard students. Brandeis to Langdell December 30, 1889, August 10, 1893 in Brandeis, Letters of Louis D. Brandeis; Urban Reformer, 1870-1907, ed. Melvin I. Urofsky and David W. Levy (Albany, N. Y., 1971), pp. 84-86, 113-115; Reed, Training, p. 293.

were the older generation of office-trained lawyers and the younger generation of "box-office-law-school"-trained lawyers.[34] The older generation was significant because from it came both the judges and at least some of the leadership and inertia in bar associations, the judiciary and the bar associations being the two sources from which the professors believed genuine lobbying for law reform would have to come. The younger lawyers were the main offenders in producing delays in the courtrooms of the large cities; in addition, they threatened to become a commercially-minded majority of the profession, thereby further retarding bar association development and law reform--or at least so the law professors believed.

With this critique of the profession in mind, Harlan Stone prescribed the remedy: "more exacting requirements for admission to the bar which conform to sound educational standards, and the stimulation and preservation in every possible way of the professional spirit and corporate feeling of the bar."[35] The latter was an essential prerequisite to achieving procedural reforms and to insuring a greater reliance on professional

---

[34] The phrase was Pound's.

[35] Stone, *Law and Its Administration*, p. 177.

criteria in the selection of judges. In turn, higher admission requirements were an essential prerequisite to elevating the professional spirit and corporate feeling of the bar and to ending the yearly infusion into the profession of men "imbued with the notion that the license to practice law is a privilege to play a game in technicalities at the expense of their clients."[36] Or, again, at least so the professors believed.

In linking the promotion of professional feeling in the bar to higher admission requirements, the professors revealed a strain of nativism. They usually expressed this nativism indirectly, through veiled references to the need to get "the wrong sort" out of the profession. But Wisconsin Law School Dean Harry S. Richards said it quite plainly in his 1915 presidential address to the AALS. He pointed out the "very large

---

[36] Ibid., pp. 165-189, quote on p. 195. Stone reiterated these views and also stated his opinion to Pound that "there is no very great disagreement between us. I certainly recognize the need of just the work you are doing." Stone to Pound, November 22, 1915, Pound MSS, Paige Box 29. Insofar as there was a difference in emphasis between the Columbia and Harvard deans, Stone placed less stock in procedural reforms and greater stock in improving the quality of the bench and bar.

proportion of foreign names" on the class rolls of urban night law schools. For them, he asserted,

> admission to the bar is sought, not because of any desire to practice, or with any sense of the responsibilities and duties of a lawyer, but because such admission is regarded as an asset, a sort of privateering commission. . . . The result is a host of shrewd young men, imperfectly educated, crammed with the philosophy of getting on, but viewing the Code of Ethics with uncomprehending eyes.[37]

The professors recognized, at least by 1915, that their efforts in the AALS were not affecting the proprietary schools. Therefore, they turned to activities which would have the effect of raising bar admission standards and undercutting the commercial law schools. Stone attempted to make the New York State Board of Bar Examiners write bar examinations which would test legal-thinking ability rather than memorization. The AALS leadership attempted to make the ABA, and through it the state bar associations, take a stronger stand in urging higher admission standards on the courts and legislatures of the various states. Among other reforms, the professors promoted prelegal education requirements, designed to make law a learned profession, and standards for law

---

[37] Richards, "A Survey of the Progress in Legal Education," p. 63.

schools similar to those of the AALS, designed to dissuade the purely commercial-minded from studying law and to drive the more blatant commercial law schools out of business.

The professors never attempted to use the AALS and rarely used their own teaching or scholarly writing as instruments for procedural reform.[38] They "went public" earlier in this area. Indeed, they joined an ongoing movement among practitioners and laymen, giving it greater coherence and unity and, not incidentally, linking it to their own movement to reform legal education. The main procedural reforms they urged would replace the multitude of statutory provisions governing procedure with a general practice act, give trial court judges more power and discretion in procedural matters, restrict legislatures in the number and types of amendments they could make to rules of procedure, shift the selection of judges from political to professional criteria, and reorganize lower courts along the municipal court model so that case loads could be shifted by the chief judge in the interests of efficiency. Other often heard proposals included narrowing the categories of

---

[38] Stone, "Address of the President," p. 106.

reversible error so that substantive rather than procedural questions would be argued before appellate courts, confining the granting of re-trials to the specific questions decided wrongly rather than to the entire cause, encouraging measures like workmen's compensation to reduce the volume of accident litigation initiated by contingent-fee lawyers, and speeding jury selection by fixing the number of preemptory challenges. The message was clear: take the control of the administration of justice away from the legislature and ambulance-chasing attorneys, and give it to responsible members of the bench and bar so that justice can be swifter and, hence, more efficient.[39]

As might have been expected, some elite members of the bar responded positively to the professors' reform program. These "legal progressives" responded most favorably to reforms that were specific and that called attention to the inadequacies of the non-elite segments of the profession. Procedural reform and the

---

[39] Stone, Law and Its Administration, pp. 198-210; Henry M. Bates, "Defects in Our Legal System," Michigan Law Review 12 (January 1914), 167-184; "Law Schools and Reform in Procedure," Illinois State Bar Association, Proceedings 38 (1914), 399-412. Pound's ideas are summarized in Wigdor, Roscoe Pound, pp. 147-155.

promotion of higher bar admission and legal education standards were examples.[40] Throughout the progressive period, however, the majority of the bar elite was suspicious of, and at times openly hostile toward, the law professors. Since the professors' reforms were conservative in the sense that they were designed to preserve the common law, restore the profession's social-political prestige and power, and transfer control over the administration of justice from politicans to the bar and bench, it would seem that a harmonious relationship between the professors and practitioners should have emerged. Hence, there is a temptation to interpret the bar elite's hostility as evidence of a hopelessly blind reactionary spirit.

But this view overlooks factors which lend rationality to the hesitant practitioners' viewpoint. One such factor is that the breach between practitioner and professor is a structural feature of any profession. The practitioner comes to see the professor as overly theoretical, and the professor comes to see the practitioner as overly practical. The professors' credo was,

---

[40] Wigdor, Roscoe Pound, pp. 136, 139-140, 157-158.

in the words of Henry M. Bates, that "the Law School should [not] rest content with merely teaching the law as it is, uncritically and dogmatically, for such teaching would amount to little more than mere training, as for a trade." Practitioners, believing in the value of mere training which emphasized information and practical expertness, were inclined to display toward the professors, at best, "the kindly tolerance and sympathetic approval that the mere school teacher is apt to receive from vigorous men of affairs," to quote Alfred Z. Reed. John Wigmore summed up the situation by observing that "lack of progressiveness is the most characteristic feature of the legal profession in general. Among practitioners, however, it is not a fault; it is only a trait. But among law school teachers it is a fault."[41]

This structural division was intensified in the 1900-1920 period because always lurking in the background of specific and "reasonable" reforms were the philosophical and theoretical explanations that Pound and a few others provided for what they were doing. That these explanations remained vague and confined to the

---

[41] Bates quoted in Brown, *Legal Education at Michigan*, p. 25; Reed, *Training*, pp. 235-236, 260, 408; Wigmore quote, AALS, *Proceedings* 19 (1921), 38.

"impractical" realm of jurisprudence did not make them appear any less threatening. Indeed, the vagueness and impracticality of these explanations heightened the resemblance nervous practitioners were likely to see between progressives and professors.

The professors' criticism of the judiciary was especially troubling to the practitioners because it gave the imprimatur of the expert to the rumblings of dissatisfaction coming from less well-informed laymen. That the aim of the professors was to salvage the role of the courts vis-à-vis administrative bodies and legislatures did not seem very important if their criticisms gave ammunition to those apparently intent on weakening the power of courts in American life. In this respect, the fact that the law professors' criticisms occurred at a time when the reform impulse was at floodtide and when it seemed especially aimed at the judiciary, greatly influenced the way practitioners saw the criticisms, especially when the criticisms themselves were often general or philosophical in nature and hence pointed to open-ended solutions.[42]

---

[42] For a private expression of these concerns, see William D. Guthrie to Harlan F. Stone, January 14, 1915, Stone MSS, Miscellaneous Correspondence. For an impassioned public expression of these concerns, see the two articles by Judge Robert Ludlow Fowler, "The New

In addition, individual professors allied themselves from time to time with particular progressive reform movements and occasionally adopted the terminology of the progressives. They betrayed what Zechariah Chafee, in speaking of himself, described as an "instinct to reform something or other," which did not find a sufficient outlet in law teaching itself. Sometimes the alternative outlet was primarily rhetoric. Consider how Michigan Dean Henry M. Bates used the code term "social justice" in his 1913 presidential address to the AALS: "Law teachers of today occupy a strategic position, and are fortunate . . . in the possession of opportunity for conspicuous service in the cause of social justice." The professors possess "strategic strength for helping to direct social movements toward a more nearly perfect justice." Or consider the rhetoric the University of Chicago's Floyd Mechem used to analyze the reasons that the public had come to see law as a commercialized profession. The public developed this view, he explained, because "the best effort and ability of the profession are constantly retained by the greatest

---

Philosophies of Law," Harvard Law Review 27 (June 1914), 718-731; "The Future of the Common Law," Columbia Law Review 13 (November 1913), 595-611.

enemies of our people, the huge, soulless, monopolistic combinations of capital and labor, standing to exact toll at every gateway of commerce, at every vantage ground of opportunity, at every storehouse of natural wealth which should be common." Mechem hastened to say that he was not judging how much truth and how much slander there was in the popular view. He only wanted to make the point that the view existed and that it was the duty of the law schools more than anyone else to promote professionalism over commercialism. They should instill in the minds of their students "such notions of the dignity of their calling, of their relations to the law and to the public, and of their duty to truth and honor and right conduct as will enable them to withstand the temptation, if it does come, to prostitute their talents to ignoble ends and to sell their birthright for a mess of pottage."[43]

The rhetoric had a special meaning in the progressive period even though neither Bates nor Mechem were prominent in progressive reform movements. However,

---

[43] Chafee to Pound, August 17, 1921, Chafee MSS, Box 2, Harvard Law School Library; Bates, "The Strategic Position of the Law Teacher and the Law School," p. 29; Mechem, "The Opportunities and Responsibilities of American Law Schools," pp. 185-186.

several professors were. Ernst Freund was very active in the American Association for Labor Legislation and in the Immigrants' Protective League; William Draper Lewis was a leading strategist in the eastern wing of the Progressive Party; Felix Frankfurter established close ties with The Survey social justice group. The list could be extended somewhat--but not very far unless the definition of progressivism were broadened to include the civic reform efforts that the elite lawyers themselves were often involved in.[44]

Harlan Stone undoubtedly spoke for many professors when he described the progressive period as "characterized by fantastic political theories and by vague and impractical aspirations for sudden social reform," and expressed his satisfaction in 1915 that it appeared

---

[44] Kraines, Ernst Freund, pp. 4-6; Harold L. Ickes to William Draper Lewis, January 31, 1917, Lewis to Ickes, February 10, 1917, copies in James R. Garfield MSS, Box 115, Library of Congress; Clarke A. Chambers, Seedtime of Reform: American Social Service and Social Action, 1918-1933 (Minneapolis, 1963), pp. 68-75. For citations on civic reform activities, see Columbia University, History of the School of Law, p. 173; Curti and Carstensen, University of Wisconsin, 2:430. For evidence of university administration pressures to curb liberal law professors or to limit their numbers, see ibid. 2:429; Nicholas Murray Butler to Stone, February 1, 1915, Stone MSS, Miscellaneous Correspondence; Pound to Frankfurter, December 30, 1918, April 4, 1919, May 17, 1919, Frankfurter MSS, Box 90.

to be drawing to a close. The views of law professors on Brandeis' Supreme Court nomination are not well documented; but Columbia's Munroe Smith surely was not alone when he opposed it on the grounds of personal evidence from a Boston lawyer that Brandeis had placed personal morality above professional ethics in advising a client. "A judge," Smith declared, "should not have too subtle a mind. Brandeis should be a professor of philosophy or of sociology."[45]

Roscoe Pound, who had the reputation of being one of the most advanced among the professors, provides evidence on the limits of their progressivism. He lent his support to many liberal measures. Like most law school professors, he considered commercialism one of the greatest foes of the advancement of professionalism. Therefore, he did not bow to the sacred cows of business-oriented lawyers. He supported the child labor law and argued the case for it in the courts. He had sympathy, if not great enthusiasm, for the cause of labor. He courageously supported Brandeis' nomination to the Supreme Court at a time when his own appointment to the deanship

---

[45]Stone, Law and Its Administration, p. 191; Munroe Smith to Stone, February 4, 1916, Stone MSS, Miscellaneous Correspondence.

was not yet confirmed and President Lowell was active in the anti-Brandeis movement. He denied that Sacco and Vanzetti had had a free trial. His students reported that he often debunked the cant about rugged individualism. He often gave up to 20 percent of his income to what he considered deserving reform causes. For all of these activities, he aroused the grave suspicions of powerful conservatives. "Many zealous alumni think that all my writing is a cover for socialism," he reported to Oliver Wendell Holmes during one particularly bad time.[46]

But, as he went on to assure Holmes, "I need not tell you I never have been in any degree a technical socialist--even when socialism was academically fashionable."[47] As his biographer has summarized: "You never found Pound in any 'Reform Movement' of any kind. He was for particular reforms in administration, but he had his eye on the reform itself rather than the substituting of one pack of selfish politicians for another."

---

[46]Sayre, Roscoe Pound, pp. 91, 313-314; Pound to Albion Small, June 4, 1917; Pound to Owen R. Lovejoy, July 25, 1917, Pound MSS, Paige Box 8; Pound to Oliver Wendell Holmes, July 24, 1919 quoted in Sayre, Roscoe Pound, p. 273; Wigdor, Roscoe Pound, pp. 193-198; Florence Kelley to Pound, October 17, 1923, Pound to Kelley, October 22, 1923, Pound MSS, Paige Box 29.

[47]Sayre, Roscoe Pound, p. 273.

He was a life-long Republican and voted for Taft in 1912, which might be considered a litmus test election.[48]

A good indication of the limits of Pound's liberalism and commitment to egalitarianism was his attitude toward the admission of women to Harvard Law School. He was against it.

> I am convinced from many years of teaching classes of both men and women that the methods of instruction required are radically different. With a class of men you have got to grab each man individually, wrestle with him and compel him to understand the subject more or less against his will. This process which alone makes lawyers cannot be used with the best women students. They, on the other hand, get hold of the subject by perceiving quickly what the teacher has on his mind and developing it thoroughly. . . . The teaching which is adapted to one is not to the other. Harvard Law School has set out to do a relatively small thing as thoroughly as possible. I should be sorry to see it interfere with its usefulness by trying to do something else. Besides the morale of the student body is the great thing here. If we begin to introduce social stunts and all the inevitable accompaniments of co-education I suspect our efficiency will fall off markedly.[49]

---

[48]Ibid., p. 91.

[49]Pound to Stone, March 29, 1917, Pound MSS, Paige Box 8. Pound and Stone, who found the idea of admitting women "personally distasteful," worked closely on the issue. Their position appears especially rigid since most other law schools did admit women by this time. Three times during the late progressive years, the Harvard Law School faculty voted to admit women, only to see the Harvard Corporation overrule them. Yale's faculty voted to admit in 1918 and managed to gain corporation approval. Columbia's faculty was divided. Columbia finally admitted

Although there was a strong element of pure prejudice in Pound's position on admitting women, it is significant that he felt most comfortable using the jargon of professionalism to defend his views. His writings and correspondence reveal that his characteristic approach to most issues was to translate them into legalistic concepts.[50] The same, as we have seen, can be said of the approach of most other members of the law professoriate.

---

women in 1927, but Harvard did not until 1950. See Felix Frankfurter to Thomas Reed Powell, November 16, 1915, Frankfurter MSS, Box 91; Stone to Virginia C. Gildersleeve, November 10, 1914, Stone Memo "To All Members of the Faculty of Law," June 17, 1915, George W. Kirchwey to Stone, July 22, 1915, Munroe Smith to Stone, July 1915, Henry S. Redfield to Stone, July 1915, Nathan Abbott to Stone, July 1915, J. B. Moore to Stone, July 1915, all in Stone MSS, Miscellaneous Correspondence; Stone to Pound, March 27, 1917, Pound MSS, Paige Box 29; Columbia University, History of the School of Law, p. 291; Arthur E. Sutherland, The Law at Harvard: A History of Ideas and Men, 1817-1967 (Cambridge, Mass., 1967), p. 319; Frederick C. Hicks, Yale Law School: 1895-1915 (New Haven, 1938), pp. 75-76.

[50] Pound to Oliver Prescott, October 2, 1917, Pound MSS, Paige Box 8 is a good example of his legalistic approach to the child labor issue.

CHAPTER 10

SURVEYS, SYSTEMATIZATION, AND CONSERVATIVE
REFORM, 1920-1930

During the 1920s statements and activities by bar leaders took on a new tone. Gone was the siege mentality that had characterized the progressive years, the belief that the legal system was under sustained attack and was suffering from a loss of middle-class support. Radicals and organized labor were still understood to be hostile to the purposes of the bar elite, and public respect for law and for the legal profession was still dangerously low; but the crisis of the progressive years had passed. In this new atmosphere, leading lawyers were more open to bureaucratic and bureaucratic-minded law reforms than they had been previously.

As has been indicated, the trend toward specialization and bureaucratization in the profession was well under way before the 1920s; but in that decade the trend intensified markedly. Large law firms grew dramatically in number and size, increasing the de facto specialization in elite law practices.[1] This experience no doubt sensitized lawyers, in a way few other developments could have, to the possibilities of using specialized expertise for law reform. At the same time, because public criticism of the courts and the legal profession had declined and because the actions of government regulatory agencies showed the elite that these agencies could serve conservative purposes, the bar elite felt less fearful about innovations designed to rationalize and systematize substantive law, the administration of justice, and the organization and control of the profession.[2]

---

[1] See chap. 5 above for a full discussion of the emergence of large law firms.

[2] G. Cullom Davis, "Transformation of the Federal Trade Commission, 1914-1929," Mississippi Valley Historical Review 49 (December 1962), 437-455 summarizes the conservative capture of the FTC by the early 1920s. Leading lawyers had recognized the inadequacy of a purely judicial solution to the trust issue, but had been apprehensive about the FTC. For evidence see the following: William D. Kerr, "The Trade Commission and the Courts," Illinois Law Review 9 (December 1914), 338-344; Michael F. Gallagher, "The Federal Trade Commission," Illinois Law Review 10 (May 1915), 31-42; Thomas M. Lillard, "The New Federal Anti-Trust Legislation," Bar Association of the State of Kansas, Annual Meeting 32 (1915), 81-90; Alexander G. Barrett, "The Federal Trade Commission," Central Law Journal 81 (September 3, 1915),

Hence, in the 1920s the elite sponsored or supported such innovations as judicial councils, the American Law Institute, crime surveys and crime commissions, the integrated bar, and higher and more nationally uniform bar admission standards.[3] Through their bar associations, elite lawyers organized support for many of these innovations. Increasingly, however,

---

166-171, (September 10, 1915), 183-189, (September 17, 1915), 201-207; Gilbert H. Montague, "The Federal Trade Commission and the Clayton Act," in Francis Lynde Stetson et al., Some Legal Phases of Corporate Financing, Reorganization, and Regulation (New York, 1917), pp. 275-326; George Sutherland, "Private Rights and Government Control," Central Law Journal 85 (September 7, 1917), 169-172. By the 1920s the elite was no longer so apprehensive, thanks to court-imposed limitations on the FTC and to the demonstrated accuracy of George W. Wickersham's prescient comment of 1914: "On commissions, the practice of overlapping terms and reappointment of incumbents is the recognition and application of an essentially aristocratical principle, exhibiting a paradoxical result which contrasts strangely with the prevailing current of Democracy." Wickersham, "Government by Administrative Commission, A Democratic Paradox," Pennsylvania Bar Association, Report 20 (1914), 267. For evidence on the 1920s, see Edgar Watkins, "Courts versus Commissions," Central Law Journal 94 (April 28, 1922), 297-302; Gilbert H. Montague, "Present Tendencies in the Anti-Trust Laws," New York State Bar Association, Report 50 (1927), 311-337; William D. Guthrie, "Presidential Address," ibid. 46 (1923), 169-189. Experience with administrative agencies during the First World War had also influenced the legal elite. See Wayne C. Williams, "The War and the State," Case and Comment 24 (March 1918), 771-774.

[3]See Charles E. Clark and William O. Douglas, "Law and Legal Institutions," in Recent Social Trends in the United States; Report of the President's Research Committee on Social Trends (New York, 1933), pp. 1462-1466 for

they looked to experts and specialized agencies for new ideas and for the detailed development of those ideas. These agencies often drew on lay financial and political support and on the services of experts about whom the legal elite had earlier had grave suspicions--experts outside the profession and those inside the profession, such as law professors.[4]

It should be emphasized, however, that this openness to bureaucratic or bureaucratic-minded innovations did not signal a change in the legal elite's professional ideology. That is, there was no discernible shift in the elite lawyers' conception of their goals or the goals of the legal system. They did, however, change their views about the source of major threats to social stability and to the rule of law. Misguided

---

a summary treatment of major trends in and agencies of law reform in the 1920s.

[4]Symbolic of this new conception of lay input into professional matters, the ABA began in 1919 to hold three-day meetings in New York City, at which trade organizations, railroads, women's clubs, and all business interests could appear and testify about legislation they believed the ABA should support. The list of groups consulted was not very inclusive, but it was a departure from the past. Corinne L. Gilb, <u>Hidden Hierarchies: The Professions and Government</u> (New York, 1966), p. 216.

middle-class reformism no longer appeared to be a serious threat to what the legal elite most believed in. Instead, the elite saw the dangers as coming from three other sources: (1) those within the profession who, the elite was convinced, did not respect the profession's historic heritage and who were commercializing the practice of law; (2) impersonal social forces accompanying increasing urbanization which were spreading disrespect for law; (3) impersonal forces of inertia and tradition which were making certain areas of the substantive law and of the administration of justice anachronistic and increasingly inefficient. All of these dangers had been perceived by leading lawyers before the 1920s. But these dangers had not been emphasized to the extent that they were in the twenties. Increasingly, the elite tended to conceive of problems and solutions in terms of a system rather than of bad men. However, this was only a tendency, and elite lawyers were still fully capable of personalizing an issue.

The emphases on system and efficiency rather than on individuals were precisely what law school professors and legal progressives had been urging on the elite for nearly twenty years. It is not at all surprising, therefore, that these two groups gained increasing influence during the 1920s. They were the groups in the profession with ideas and programs relevant to what now seemed to be the major problems and challenges facing the profession. Furthermore, the structural division between the elite professors and the elite practitioners was being overridden by their growing functional interdependence. This functional interdependence is difficult to document; the antagonisms between the teaching and practicing wings of the profession were more likely to receive public expression or notice than were the various ways in which they served each other's interests.

The crucial function binding the two groups was that the elite law schools trained the men who moved into the elite firms. This had several implications. First, by the 1920s a significant proportion of junior and senior partners in elite firms were men who not only had attended an elite law school but also had learned law according to the case method and been exposed to professors imbued with a pragmatic conception of the law. Second, as large law firms grew in size and number, they became increasingly dependent upon the law schools. They developed the habit of recruiting associates every year from the elite schools' graduating classes, and they came to rely more and more on the law faculties' grading system and letters of recommendation as a screening device. Third, the elite practitioners' reliance on elite law schools led them to take an active interest in the governance of those schools and therefore to take on willingly the duties of serving on visiting committees and boards of trustees. The ties created by this informal patronage system that professors and practitioners participated in were strengthened by the sense of loyalty that practitioners felt for their undergraduate and law school alma maters. This sense of loyalty was easily generalized to other institutions of the same standing, creating a shared sense of culture and social position not only among elite practitioners but between these practitioners and the law professors. Moreover, a sense of common professional identity, which had always existed to some extent, grew stronger as legal briefs and judicial decisions increasingly came to use ideas expressed by the professors in law review articles.

However, a significant gulf remained between, on the one hand, the perceptions and ideology of the professors and legal progressives and, on the other hand, those of most lawyers. An examination of the major projects in the 1920s on which the bar elite worked with professors or legal progressives or both will demonstrate both the similarities and dissimilarities in the two groups' evolving adjustment to the organizational society.

****

The first signs of rapprochment between elite practitioners and law school professors appeared when they cooperated on the issue of raising bar admission standards. In 1921 the American Bar Association for the first time declared firmly and clearly its support of the elite law professors' long-standing desire for national standards of bar admission and therefore for national standards of legal education. At the annual meeting in Cincinnati that year, the ABA passed, on the recommendation of the Section of Legal Education, a resolution declaring that all candidates for admission to the bar should have two years of prelegal college work and a law degree from a three-year day law school or an equivalent period of study in a night school. The resolution also established a Council of Legal Education to develop a classification scheme for law schools, similar to the American Medical Association's classification of medical schools. In 1922 a special meeting of the Conference of State Bar Association Delegates was held in Washington, D.C., to stimulate local lobbying for the ABA resolution in the various states, few of which were then in compliance. The resolution and the conference action were significant steps for the ABA.

But progress in raising bar admission standards to the new ABA level was slow until the 1930s, when state legislatures and courts acted in response to the depression-induced "overcrowded bar" issue.[5]

As Jerold S. Auerbach has demonstrated, revived nativist sentiment among the bar elite was an important motivating factor behind the ABA's action.[6] Leading lawyers were alarmed at the increasing numbers of first- and second-generation eastern and southern European immigrants who were gaining admission to the bar. The bar elite was convinced that such lawyers neither appreciated nor understood American institutions and values, that they did not respect the professional status of the bar, and that therefore they would commercialize and degrade the practice of law. The elite hoped that the two-year prelegal requirement would discourage many immigrants from even considering the law

---

[5] Preble Stolz, "Training for the Public Profession of the Law (1921): A Contemporary Review," in Herbert Packer and Thomas Ehrlich, New Directions in Legal Education (New York, 1972), pp. 233-242; Jerold S. Auerbach, "Enmity and Amity: Law Teachers and Practitioners, 1900-1922," Perspectives in American History 5 (1971), 593-600; Robert Stevens, "Two Cheers for 1870: The American Law School," ibid. pp. 494-504; Edson R. Sunderland, History of the American Bar Association and Its Work (n.p., 1953), pp. 140-147.

[6] Auerbach, "Law Teachers and Practitioners," pp. 574-601.

as a career and that college would teach the rest to respect American conceptions of the rule of law and traditions of professionalism.

Nativism supplied the bar elite with a compelling counter-image to the long-standing, cherished professional self-image personified by Abraham Lincoln, the earnest, hard-working, but poor boy, for whom the openness of the legal profession both stimulated and allowed upward social mobility and public service. Nativism provided leading lawyers with the image of the sharp immigrant lawyer, who was often Jewish, more interested in money than service, indifferent to the professional standards of the bar's leaders, and willing to resort to questionable, even unethical practices. Leading lawyers convinced themselves that this latter image was more real than the Lincoln image; so they became willing to work more actively than ever before for high admission standards. At the same time, they felt compelled to explain that the new proposed standards were not elitist and were fully in keeping with the democratic traditions of the profession. They argued that any truly dedicated young man could obtain two years of college education, no matter how poor he was. They also pointed out that the proposed admission standards would not eliminate part-time study at night law schools, although it might reduce the number of such schools.[7]

Besides demonstrating the bar elite's nativism, the 1921 resolution and the 1922 bar association delegates' conference reflected the new organizational strength of the bar association movement, and especially of the ABA. In 1919 the ABA had reorganized itself under a new constitution, which permitted a more expeditious movement of resolutions from the sections to the main body at the annual meeting. This new procedure was important because opponents of higher standards had been able to use stalling tactics to keep the ABA as a body from acting on recommendations made by the Section of Legal Education.

The 1919 reorganization plan was also significant because it energized the law professors to take a more active role within the ABA. The plan had this effect because it eliminated the Council on Legal Education,

---

[7] For example, these two images dominated debate at the 1924 New York State Bar Association meeting. Report 47 (1924), 242-285. See also, Joseph T. Tinnelly, Part-Time Legal Education: A Study of the Problems of Evening Law Schools (Brooklyn, 1957), pp. 5-17; Robert McMurdy to Elihu Root, August 13, 1921, Root to McMurdy, August 23, 1921, Root MSS, Box 139, Library of Congress; Arthur L. Corbin, "Democracy and Education for the Bar," AALS, Proceedings 19 (1921), 143-156.

a recently created body dominated by the elite professors. They lost the fight to retain the Council at the 1919 meeting; they then resolved to capture the Section of Legal Education. With that object in mind, they held a special meeting of the Association of American Law Schools at the time of the 1920 ABA meeting. By that time, however, they had learned to exercise their influence more subtly and to draw on practitioner cooperation.

William Draper Lewis, dean of the University of Pennsylvania Law School, engineered the strategy, which was to support Elihu Root as chairman of the Section in 1920 and to pass an innocuous-sounding resolution setting up a special committee of the Section. This committee, to be chaired by Root, was to determine what the Section could do to "strengthen the character and improve the efficiency of those admitted to the practice of law." As Lewis guessed, Root was very amenable to suggestions that the ABA endorse higher bar admission standards. He had advocated higher standards even in the progressive years, when he was deeply suspicious of law school professors, especially Lewis. But the World War stood between those earlier years and 1920, and Root's focus of concern had shifted from combatting progressivism to supporting national unity, protecting historic American traditions and institutions, and combatting alien influences. Hence, he was glad to lend his name and prestige to the movement to raise bar admission standards, although he actually did very little of the work involved in preparing the special committee's recommendation. He was preoccupied during 1921 with the Permanent Court of International Justice and with the Conference on Limitation of Armament, for which he served as an American delegate.[8]

---

[8] Stolz, "Training," pp. 233-238 provides the best summary of the law professors' role. For evidence of elite law school control of the Council, see Roscoe Pound to Henry M. Bates, November 27, 1916, Pound MSS, Paige Box 8, Harvard Law School Library; Walter Wheeler Cook to Harlan F. Stone, October 5, 1917, George Whitelock to Stone, October 24, 1917, Stone to Cook, May 21, 1918, Stone MSS, Miscellaneous Correspondence, Columbia University Libraries. On the 1919 reorganization of the ABA and the professors' reaction to it, see resolution addressed to the Executive Committee of the ABA from Deans of American Law Schools, n.d. [1919], Pound MSS, Paige Box 29; Stone, "Address of the President," AALS, Proceedings 17 (1919), 101-102; floor discussion, ibid., pp. 33-42. For the Root committee, which included five eminent practitioners in addition to Root and William Draper Lewis, see Lewis' report to the AALS, Proceedings 19 (1921), 73-79; Lewis to Pound, June 10, 1920, June 23, 1920, Pound MSS, Paige Box 10; Arthur L. Corbin to Stone, June 1, 1921, Stone MSS, Miscellaneous Correspondence. As a quid pro quo, the AALS relaxed its previous ban on admitting night schools. The move was a self-conscious effort to make the AALS appear fair and thereby to help move the ABA's recommended admission standards through the state legislatures. AALS, Proceedings 20 (1922), 83-104. At least one law school dean, Roscoe Pound,

The rapprochment established between law school professors and elite practitioners as a result of the 1921 ABA resolution reached full fruition in 1923 with the creation of the American Law Institute. Once again William Draper Lewis and Elihu Root played the key liaison roles. Lewis did the organizational work and became the executive secretary of the Institute. Root served as honorary president and was instrumental in obtaining crucial money from the Carnegie Corporation to finance the Institute.[9]

The task of the American Law Institute was to prepare authoritative restatements of the law in such areas as trusts, property, agency, contracts, conflict of laws, torts, and criminal procedure, all of which were in a state of great uncertainty because of the growing mass of reported cases and of statutory law. Root dramatized the situation as one in which the law was becoming

---

was outraged. He contemplated taking Harvard out of the AALS, bellowing, "Why should you [Columbia] and I be used to give respectability to the Youngstown Y.M.C.A. Law School and institutions of that sort?" Pound to Stone, January 2, 1923, Pound MSS, Manuscript Box 33.

[9] AALS, Proceedings 20 (1922), 37-39; Philip C. Jessup, Elihu Root, 2 vols. (New York, 1938), 2:470-471; Samuel Williston, Life and Law (Boston, 1941), pp. 309-313.

guesswork; without some organization like the Institute, he declared, "Our law, as a system, would have sunk below the horizon, and the basis of our institutions would have disappeared."[10] The Institute proved to be a durable and extremely elitist organization characterized by a careful and precise but conservative approach to law restatement. Typically, the restatements were drafted by law professors, then circulated among other law professors and elite practitioners, then rewritten and submitted for ratification to the Institute's membership, which remained small and exclusive. The American Law Institute allowed law professors to exercise significant influence through the highly technical law writing they were especially skilled in; but it provided no scope for new ideas and conceptions.[11]

The most exciting new ideas in the law school world were being developed by younger professors, such as

---

[10] Elihu Root, Address as Chairman of Bench and Bar Meeting to Organize American Law Institute, 1923, in Root, Men and Policies; Addresses (Cambridge, 1925), p. 160.

[11] The attitude of the men with the new ideas, the legal realists, was stated by Felix Cohen: "The 'Restatement of the Law' by the American Law Institute is the last long-drawn-out gasp of a dying tradition. The more intelligent of our younger law teachers and students are not interested in 'restating' the dogmas of legal theology." The Legal Conscience: Selected Papers of Felix S. Cohen, ed. Lucy Kramer Cohen (New Haven, 1960), pp. 59-60, quoted in Wilfrid E. Rumble, Jr., American Legal Realism; Skepticism, Reform, and the Judicial Process (Ithaca, N. Y., 1968), p. 156.

Karl Llewellyn, William O. Douglas, Hessel Yntema, and Herman Oliphant, and a few older professors, such as Walter Wheeler Cook and William Underhill Moore. They all were the leaders of the realist movement, which was concentrated at Columbia, Yale, and the new Johns Hopkins Institute of Law, but which had wide influence and generated a significant new outlook in other national law schools. In contrast to those professors and practitioners who supported the American Law Institute, the realists believed that confusion in substantive law was due to the persistence of the formalistic view of law, not merely to the proliferation of case law. The realists called for an entirely new conception of the relationship between law and society, for an abandonment of the formalistic categories of law inherited from the past, and for their replacement by more functional categories. As Oliphant told the Association of American Law Schools, law professors should focus the scientific study of law on the way judges actually decide cases, not on the vague and shifting rationalizations judges give for their decisions. However, the realist movement remained more potentiality than actuality in the 1920s, insofar as its influence on law reform or legal institutions was concerned.[12]

Less interesting intellectually, but more productive of immediate law reforms, was the work of professors and practitioners involved in efficiency-minded reforms and in the crime survey and crime commission movements. The major organizational expression of those legal progressives who favored efficiency-minded reforms such as judicial councils and unified court systems was the American Judicature Society.[13]

---

[12] Major studies of the realist movement include the following: Rumble, <u>American Legal Realism</u>; William Twining, <u>Karl Llewellyn and the Realist Movement</u> (London, 1973); Edward A. Purcell, Jr., "American Jurisprudence Between the Wars: Legal Realism and the Crisis of Democratic Theory," <u>American Historical Review</u> 75 (December 1969), 424-446. For Oliphant's views, see "A Return to Stare Decisis," AALS, <u>Proceedings</u> 25 (1927), 67-83. The older generation of law professors, for the most part, resisted the new trend, arguing that introducing new categories and terminology would block the path to greater communication among professors, lawyers, and judges and would improperly prepare future lawyers. See Joseph H. Beale, ibid. 25 (1927), 89, 26 (1928), 53; Harry S. Richards, ibid. 26 (1928), 50. Pound and Stone anticipated the new departure and vowed to oppose it, as they did. Pound to Stone, March 26, 1917, Pound MSS, Paige Box 8; Stone to Pound, March 27, 1917, ibid., Paige Box 29.

[13] Several other organizations also advocated law reform stressing the efficiency theme. The National Economic League, a largely Boston-based organization issued a major report jointly authored by Charles W. Eliot, Moorfield Storey, Louis D. Brandeis, Roscoe Pound, and Adolph J. Rodenback (from New York) on efficiency in the administration of justice after that topic had been voted on by the League's 1600-member Council in 1913 as the

The chief figure in the Society was Herbert Harley, a lawyer-newspaperman from Manistee, Michigan, who secured the financial backing of local philanthropist Charles F. Ruggles and then moved in 1912 to Chicago, which seemed at the time to be the most advanced city in the law reform movement. There Harley established the Society in 1913. In its first decade, the Society was almost wholly a Chicago enterprise, although it built up a nation-wide mailing list for its Journal and secured the advice of several outside experts, the most prominent of whom was Roscoe Pound.[14]

---

subject of greatest importance for consideration by the country. The report stressed the same points that the American Judicature Society came to champion in the next few years. The National Civic Federation, which was a leading advocate for bureaucratic regulation as a way of defusing the politically volatile trust issue, established a Department of Reform in Legal Procedure in 1912. A copy of the results of the National Economic League's 1913 poll can be found in James R. Garfield MSS, Box 147, Library of Congress. The report is summarized in Green Bag 26 (November 1914), 502-503.

[14]Harley to Pound, February 6, 1912, Pound MSS, Paige Box 27. Harry Olson, the Chief Judge of the Chicago Municipal Court, served as chairman of the board of the Judicature Society from 1913 to 1929. Several Northwestern University faculty members, especially Albert M. Kales and John H. Wigmore, were very active in the Society's ventures. Harley was given an office and a faculty position at Northwestern and also served on Judge Olson's Municipal Court staff. Several elite Chicago lawyers were placed on the board of directors, "to dress the window and obtain bar confidence." Harley to Newton D. Baker, April 20, 1931, Baker MSS, Box 27,

From the beginning the American Judicature Society, whose main activity was the publication of its journal and the dissemination of its various model acts of law reform legislation, preached the message of efficiency. The slogan on its letterhead was "To Promote the Efficient Administration of Justice." The Society's governing idea was that the court system should be run like any modern bureaucratic institution. The courts in each state should all be under one executive head, who could control the flow of cases, the allocation of judges, the procedural rules, and other such details. Politics should play no part in these decisions. Judges should be selected just as any other executives in bureaucratic agencies were selected, according to criteria of expertise, competence, and responsibility. The Chicago Municipal Court was advanced as a model of rationalized court organization, although the fact that it remained imbedded in an old-style state court system was considered a major

---

Library of Congress. The Society published fourteen issues of a Bulletin between 1914 and 1917 and thereafter published a bi-monthly Journal. For details of the Society-Northwestern connection, see J. A. Rahl and K. Schwerin, "Northwestern University School of Law: A Short History," Northwestern University Law Review 55 (May-June 1960), 151. See also Wigmore to Baker, April 15, 1931, Baker MSS, Box 27.

defect. The judicial council movement of the 1920s was a more encompassing, though still partial, realization of the Society's court reorganization ideas. Higher bar admission standards and the integrated bar were other reforms sponsored by the Society, especially in the 1920s.[15]

The efficiency movement developed increasing support among the bar elite after 1920, as leading lawyers came to appreciate its conservative potential. Whenever an efficiency-minded reform was considered, the American Judicature Society's model acts were an important source of ideas. Despite the growing influence of its proposals, the Society itself limped along in a financially precarious state, especially after Ruggles withdrew his support in 1926. Unlike the American Law Institute, the Society lacked an activist membership

---

[15] American Judicature Society, Bulletin, 1914-1917, passim; Journal of American Judicature Society, 1917-1930, passim; see also Emmet O'Neal, "Reorganization of the Judical Administration of Justice," Central Law Journal 86 (June 7, 1918), 406-415 for an AJS-influenced call by the Governor of Alabama for a unified state court system as the number-one law reform priority. The Society's original thinking on court reorganization, which was strongly influenced by Judge Olson and Albert Kales, relied very heavily on the Chicago Municipal Court model. Roscoe Pound encouraged a more comprehensive view, looking to state-level court reorganization. Pound to Clinton Rogers Woodruff, January 15, 1917, Pound MSS, Paige Box 8;

base or permanent foundation support, and its reputation as an organization for "progressive lawyers" kept the elite at arms length, even when they approved many of its specific recommendations.[16]

The bar elite responded even more positively to the crime survey movement of the 1920s than it had to the efficiency movement. Therefore, the crime survey movement illustrates especially well the pattern of law professionalism established by that decade. The movement was stimulated, as was so much in the history of the profession, by public awareness of a problem in the administration of justice. In this case, the problem was the much-discussed "crime wave" of the 1920s. Whether there was indeed a crime wave during the decade is still open to scholarly dispute, crime statistics being the

---

Kales to Zechariah Chafee, December 31, 1917, Chafee MSS, Box 60, Harvard Law School Library. Kales, "Methods of Selecting Judges," Central Law Journal 85 (December 14, 1917), 425-429 explains the reasoning behind the judicial selection plan adopted by the Society in 1921.

[16] Harley to Baker, April 20, 1931, Baker MSS, Box 27, contains details of the Society's financial problems in the 1920s. See Rome G. Brown to Pound, March 13, 18, and 31, 1915, Pound MSS, Paige Box 26, for an example of a conservative lawyer's suspicions about the "soundness" of the Society. Brown believed certain provisions in an early draft of the Society's model Judicature Act were too much of a concession to the judicial recall principle.

uncertain measures that they are. But the objective fact was not nearly so important in the history of the profession as was the public belief that a serious problem existed.

Bar leaders responded to the problem by searching for a remedy which, like the procedural reform and court reorganization efforts of the progressive period, would both relieve the source of complaint and provide convincing evidence of bar self-regulation. The response chosen--the crime survey--represented several significant new departures by bar leaders. The decision to delay concrete suggestions until the survey results were in could be interpreted as a stalling tactic, as a strategy to create a satisfying illusion of activism. Such an interpretation would not be entirely wrong; urban crime was such an intractable problem that the bar elite really had few effective solutions, which many leading lawyers recognized.

However, the crime surveys were more than merely smoke screens. By calling in outside experts and including laymen on the administrative boards of the surveys, the bar elite was admitting that the problem could not be solved merely by applying the age-old principles of the law and the lawyer's professional expertise. In addition, the widespread publicizing of the surveys, which the bar elite encouraged, implied that the public had a role to play in formulating solutions to the crime problem. Admittedly, the role was a passive one, since the lawyers thought of the public primarily as ratifiers. But the bar was "going public" to a greater extent than ever before. It was also significant that the experts they chose to rely on were frequently drawn from the law schools and from the social sciences, two communities which had seemed suspect to the bar elite during the 1890-1920 period. Law professors, however, did not dominate the surveys. The surveys were truly interdisciplinary studies, paralleling the general turn to interdisciplinarity in the social sciences in the 1920s.

There were, of course, many elements of continuity with the past in the crime survey movement. The most direct continuity was with the American Institute of Criminal Law and Criminology, formed in 1909. The Institute was an interdisciplinary, professional-minded body dedicated to reforming not only the criminal justice system but also to alleviating the urban social and economic conditions thought to be causes of crime. Lawyers and law professors did not dominate the Institute, but they played a very important role in its work.

John H. Wigmore and Roscoe Pound played key roles in planning the June 1909 conference which led to formation of the Institute, and Wigmore served as its first president. The Institute's proceedings were published in the ABA Reports between 1910 and 1919. Despite the professional tone of the Institute, it did not sponsor basic research into the administration of the criminal justice system or into the causes of crime.[17]

The crime survey movement also recalled the elitist crime study commissions of the progressive period. Chicago, New York, and other major cities had formed such commissions as part of the civic reform movement. These early commissions did not emanate from the organized bar, although they typically included a few bar leaders. The progressive period crime commissions were in the gentleman-amateur tradition of urban reform. The crime surveys of the 1920s were more professionalized in tone and in personnel. But both focused on technical points in the administration of justice. Both also shared an assumption that the criminal population was not being adequately punished and deterred by the criminal justice system.

---

[17] David Wigdor, Roscoe Pound: Philosopher of Law (Westport, Conn., 1974), pp. 142-146; Sunderland, History of ABA, p. 121.

Along with this assumption and its accompanying confidence in structural changes, went a basic failure to understand either the motives for crime or the nature of the criminal underworld.[18] Neither the crime commissions nor the crime survey movement was much concerned about how the quality of justice affected the civil rights of defendants. The chief concern was the disruption of public order and the threat to the security of property permitted by the inefficient administration of justice.[19]

---

[18] Felix Frankfurter, who was very caught up in the crime survey movement of the 1920s, later expressed disenchantment with that movement's focus on "mechanical tinkering iwth the machinery of the law. . . . to speak of the law in terms of machinery is to employ a dangerous metaphor. The problems raised by crime go far deeper than what is ordinarily implied by proper standards in the administration of criminal law. . . . Does punishment deter? Do we deal with criminals on proper principles?" Frankfurter, "Foreword" in Sheldon and Eleanor Glueck, "After-Conduct of Discharged Offenders," (published under the auspices of the Department of Criminal Science of the Faculty of Law in the University of Cambridge, 1945), copy in Frankfurter MSS, Box 133, Library of Congress. See also Mark H. Haller, "Urban Crime and Criminal Justice: The Chicago Case," Journal of American History 57 (December 1970), 619-635.

[19] Despite his pioneering work in the crime survey movement, Roscoe Pound recognized the dangers to civil liberties in the national attitudes which made the surveys possible. "There is really great danger that the movement for tightening up our administration of criminal justice will lead to making it still more difficult for the obscure and friendless to make a proper defence, while at the same time not detracting from the power of those with means to escape," Pound to Forrest Bailey,

The crime survey movement of the 1920s tended to see such inefficiencies in terms of a system which had to be overhauled and reformed rather than in terms of occasional corrupt or incompetent individuals whose replacement would set things right. The focus on system rather than on bad men was more common, however, among the academic experts than among their lawyer sponsors. When judicial elections rolled around or when a particularly flagrant failure in the administration of justice seemed evident, a conflict often developed between the elite lawyers and the academics. The lawyers wanted to use the influence of the survey to sponsor a particular slate of judges or a change in police or other personnel. The academics, however, usually resisted endorsing the extravagant claims made for the changes, claims which the lawyers thought were politically necessary.

December 7, 1925, Pound MSS, Paige Box 12. See also, Pound to Harlan F. Stone, October 27, 1924, Pound MSS, Manuscript Box 33. Learned Hand's viewpoint was more typical. He declared: "We must in some way learn to deal more directly and effectively with the commission of crime if we are to check the lawlessness which is our curse. I had rather take my chances of occasional judicial lynchings than hamstring the usual course of justice, though I admit it is a matter of degree." Hand to Frankfurter, November 26, 1923, Frankfurter MSS, Box 63.

The crime survey movement began with the Cleveland Survey, which was researched in 1921 and published in final form in 1922. Roscoe Pound and Felix Frankfurter directed the research team of criminal justice specialists. The Survey was initiated and funded by a community trust, the Cleveland Foundation, acting at the behest of the city bar association and several civic associations. These members of the Cleveland civic elite wanted the Survey to be a limited one, designed so that its conclusions could "form the basis of substantial legal and administrative reforms in Cleveland."[20]

Pound saw the Survey in a broader context. He recognized that as a pioneer effort in empirical research on the administration of justice, the Cleveland Survey would have an impact far beyond the city it studied. His aim in understaking the study was

> to survey the administration of justice as a whole and in all its relations, bringing out what lawyers must be made to realize, that the judicial part of the administration of justice is only one cog in a complicated mechanism, and endeavoring to show how the mechanism works as a whole, wherein the whole mechanism and each part may function badly, and what we may be able to do about it.[21]

---

[20] Raymond Moley to Pound, December 22, 1920, Pound MSS, Paige Box 22. Moley, then a political science professor at Western Reserve, was the Foundation director.

[21] Pound to Julia Lathrop, February 2, 1921, Pound MSS, Paige Box 22.

Reflecting that aim, the Survey's published report included not only the expected lengthy study of the criminal courts, but seven additional studies. The other studies covered police administration, prosecution, correctional and penal treatment, medical science and criminal justice, legal education in Cleveland, and newspapers and criminal justice.[22]

The Cleveland Survey was only the first of several crime surveys and crime commissions initiated during the 1920s. This crime study movement reached a high point in November 1927 with the convening in Washington of a conference sponsored by the privately organized and financed National Crime Commission. In the same year, in Boston, a Harvard group directed by Frankfurter was beginning its first full year of work on a crime survey designed along very different lines and according to a different set of assumptions. Both approaches to the crime problem--the National Commission and the Harvard Survey--owed much to the Cleveland Survey, but they drew different lessons from that Survey.

---

[22] Roscoe Pound and Felix Frankfurter, eds., Criminal Justice in Cleveland (Cleveland, 1922). For details on the researching and writing of the Survey see the correspondence in Frankfurter MSS, Box 130, Library of Congress.

The National Crime Commission, which began work in 1925, followed a strategy similar to that of the Cleveland Survey: sponsorship and publicity by a visible and politically influential body of elite reformers, and technical work by professional experts. However, considering the scale of its inquiry, the Commission's budgets for its various committees did not match the outlay of the Cleveland group. Therefore, instead of conducting its own research, the Commission focused on stimulating local agencies to undertake inquiries, with an eye to eventual comparative study of the results at the national level. In response to the Commission's prodding and local political pressures, a number of state and local crime commissions were established. The commissions, however, were not primarily research organizations. They were fact-finding bodies, charged with discovering weak spots--in criminal law, in procedural rules, and in the machinery of justice--and with proposing legislative and administrative remedies for those weak spots. They did not attempt to ask fundamental questions about crime causation or about the deterrent effect of existing penal institutions, questions which might have stimulated a rethinking of basic assumptions about crime and criminal justice.[23]

At Harvard, meanwhile, Pound and especially Frankfurter were drawing very different lessons from the Cleveland Survey and were designing an entirely different approach to crime study. The Harvard Survey of Crime and Criminal Justice in Boston was more expensive, ultimately costing nearly four times as much as the Cleveland study, and it lasted longer than the Cleveland Survey. The Harvard-Boston Survey, which began to operate in 1926, did not yield any published results until 1934, and much of its work never appeared in published form.

Like all other crime surveys, the Harvard-Boston Survey was not totally disinterested research. It did aim to have an impact. According to the Harvard diagnosis, there were two major deficiencies in the way crime was handled in America: inadequate professionalism

---

[23] Alfred Bettman, "Relation of Crime Surveys to the Administration of Justice," n.d., Frankfurter MSS, Box 141; Richard W. Child, "The Year's Fight Against Crime in the United States," Address to the National Crime Commission conference, November 1, 1927, Baker MSS, Box 172. In 1926, according to Child, there were only three state or local crime commissions. By late 1927 there were twenty-six. In addition, fifty organizations had become sufficiently interested in the question of crime reduction to send representatives to the conference. The most important of the local crime surveys and commissions, in addition to the Cleveland and Boston surveys,

in the administration of criminal justice, and inappropriate differentiation of the various functions involved in criminal justice. Unlike most other crime surveys and commissions during the 1920s, which focused on the problem of how to make the criminal justice system more efficient so that it would convict and sentence a greater proportion of the accused at a faster rate, the Harvard-Boston Survey adopted the viewpoint that there was not very much wrong with the work of police, prosecution, and trial courts in the apprehension, prosecution, and conviction of criminals. Where the system needed reform, in the view of Frankfurther and his staff, was in the way decisions were made about the treatment of criminals after conviction. In their view, a new profession of experts, grounded in the behavioral, social, and biological sciences, had to be created, so that the treatment of convicted criminals would proceed on a scientific basis, with the emphasis on individualizing treatment. The new professionals would administer

---

were in Chicago, Philadelphia, Cincinnati, Baltimore, Memphis, Charlotte, North Carolina, and Hartford, New Haven, and Bridgeport, Connecticut. The most important state surveys and commissions were in Missouri, Georgia, Rhode Island, California, Minnesota, Pennsylvania, Illinois, and New York.

treatment designed to protect society but tailored to the needs of individual offenders.[24] Therefore, despite Frankfurter's declarations to the contrary, the Harvard venture was based on a set of assumptions and preferences rather than on an uncommitted and value-free approach to the crime problem.

Outside academia, the local crime surveys and commissions gave way in the late 1920s to the National Commission on Law Observance and Enforcement. This commission, popularly known as the Wickersham Commission after chairman George W. Wickersham, was the most publicly visible of all the crime surveys and crime commissions in the decade. Yet it was not typical and did not fit into the established pattern. The Wickersham Commission was charged with a comprehensive investigation of criminal enforcement in America, but its actual raison d'être was to defuse the politically thorny question of prohibition enforcement by farming it out to experts. The Commission, which was formed in 1929 and completed its work in 1931, eventually prepared fourteen reports. Most of the reports were on staple crime commission

---

[24] Frankfurter memorandum to members of the Survey, "Notes on General Report," May 27, 1930, Frankfurter MSS, Box 140; "Memorandum Harvard Law School Boston Crime Survey," n.d., ibid., Box 141.

topics. They were relatively noncontroversial, broke little new ground, and--like the Harvard-based criminal justice professionalization movement--were not widely heeded. Two reports were exceptions: the special report on law enforcement abuses in the Tom Mooney case in California, and the prohibition report. The Mooney report was suppressed by the Commission before publication, although it was published under private auspices in 1932. The prohibition report, which was published, aroused considerable publicity, even though the Commission had labored mightily to avoid an extreme statement. A majority of the Commission believed prohibition had become unenforceable by 1931. However, the final report was written in a way that softened force of the majority's view, as a concession to Wickersham, who was in the minority.[25]

The public controversy concerning the Wickersham Commission's work provided an ironic conclusion to the series of crime surveys and commissions, which the bar

---

[25] Wickersham to Pound, March 9, 1931, Pound MSS, Paige Box 24. The Commission affirmed its belief in the good purposes of the Eighteenth Amendment, especially the suppression of the saloon.

elite had hoped would reduce public criticism of the legal profession and the administration of justice and remove decision-making about the profession and the administration of justice from the public arena.

****

Between 1890 and 1930 the legal profession, like the rest of American society, experienced a major transformation. Three institutions played a central role in the bar's transformation: the large law firm, the law school, and the bar association. In 1890 many leading lawyers practiced in small firms, and a firm with five partners was considered large. By 1930 firms with ten, fifteen, or more partners were common, and professional status had become clearly identified with practice in such firms. In 1890 young men or (rarely) women preparing for the bar were as likely to get their training in a law office as in a law school. If they did attend a law school, they were, with a few exceptions, taught by part-time instructors using the lecture and textbook method. By 1930 the overwhelming majority of bar admittees had attended law school, very often a school staffed by full-time professors who used the case method. In 1890 bar associations resembled selective social clubs fully as much as they resembled professional associations. By 1930 many states had established compulsory state bar associations, and in all states and localities bar associations were engaged in a wide range of activities concerning legal education, the administration of justice, and professional self-regulation.

By all outward appearances, the legal profession between 1890 and 1930 had joined the organizational society. But it would be misleading to conclude that the history of the legal profession during these years can be summed up merely by a recounting of the structural development of large firms, law schools, and bar associations. Instead, a combination of ideological and social structural analysis is needed to tell the bar's story. The ideological dimension is crucial because many leading lawyers had a deeply ambivalent attitude toward the emerging organizational society and even the organizational changes in the bar itself. This ambivalence stemmed from the legal elite's reluctance to surrender its traditional ideas about social control and professionalism. These conceptions were rooted in the social realities of a more individualistic age, when the practice of law was one of only three learned professions.

Because of their ambivalence, the organizational activities of elite lawyers were more modest than the model of professional activity suggested by the organizational synthesis would have predicted. Bar associations failed to enroll a majority of lawyers and were only able to claim sporadic successes in lobbying efforts on behalf of higher education standards, reforms in the administration of justice, or greater professional self-regulation. Large law firms grew at a slower pace than did their corporate clients. Part of this slower growth is traceable to a deliberate unwillingness on the part of successful elite lawyers to practice within a large or quasi-bureaucratic firm. The bar elite observed the switch in legal training from law office to law school, but did not play an active role in promoting it. Within the law school world, those schools which most strongly emphasized technical knowledge were able to create a cohesive sense of self-identity and were able to establish themselves as a national elite; but they were not able to impose their conception of legal education on non-elite schools, in sharp contrast to trends in medical education.

The failure of the legal profession to conform fully to the organizational synthesis can be explained partly by the special characteristics of the profession: it was not, strictly speaking, a new middle-class profession. However, few professions do fully conform to the organizational synthesis' model of professionalism, and for reasons quite similar to the law's failure to fully conform. These reasons center on peculiarities of the work situation, which impede the free exercise of professional consciousness, and peculiarities of the profession's cultural self-definition.

A close analysis of elite lawyers' and law professors' work situations, organizational affiliations, and professional ideologies during the 1890-1930 period reveals the complex relationships among work situation, ideology, and associational activity, and demonstrates how the elite segments of the legal profession accommodated themselves to the organizational society. A combination of developments during the 1890s set the stage for the next forty years. A handful of firms, mainly but not exclusively in New York City, began to specialize in corporation law. This heightened identification with big business strongly influenced the elite's response to the conservative crisis of the 1890s. However, the bar elite's response to labor unrest, increasing legislative activism, and the Populist and Bryanite insurgencies was informed as much by a professional as by a commercial consciousness. Certain elite lawyers prepared the briefs which helped Supreme Court justices to discover such doctrines as substantive due process. Other elite lawyers participated in political reform movements designed, like the new judicial decisions, to resolve the conservative crisis favorably for the elite. Some of these elite lawyers joined with others during the same decade to infuse a new spirit of professional activism into bar associations, which had until then been primarily social clubs. At the same time, during the 1890s, profound changes. were occurring in legal training as young men seeking to enter law flocked into law schools. As law schools prospered, a small nucleus of full-time law professors emerged, many of them committed to the case method of instruction.

During the 1895-1915 period, these two groups--the elite practitioners and the elite professors--developed distinctive ideologies to interpret for themselves their changing professional roles. The bar elite came to recognize that society was coming to be composed of functioning groups rather than of atomistic individuals and that the social control function of old values and of the law itself was losing some of its efficacy. Of particular concern to the elite was what they called the menace of "over-legislation," which seemed especially threatening because it represented an erosion of the power of the judiciary. The emergence of the legislature to replace the judiciary as the growing point of the law was seen by the elite as a sign of the increasing role an uninformed public was coming to play in resolving questions previously left in the hands of lawyers. Although elite lawyers railed at these developments, they understood that the developments could not be completely reversed, given that so many of the new trends were closely associated with broad social and cultural changes resulting from the emergence of the new middle class.

Within the legal profession itself, the new middle class world-view was best represented by the elite law professors. They believed they were living in an age which required that the common law be modernized, systematized, and made more uniform nationally. Furthermore, they believed they were in a unique position to perform the task. They were aware, however, that they lacked influence; therefore, they sought by a number of activities during the 1895-1915 period to increase their influence, especially their influence on the practitioner elite.

In the long-run, after 1915, the professors' efforts to extend their influence bore fruit. But, in the short-run, they ran into resistance from members of the bar elite who perceived the intellectual affinity between the professors' ideas and the ideas of progressive reformers who not only proposed social, economic, and political legislation which the bar's leaders were suspicious of, but who endorsed such efforts as the judicial recall movement.

When the progressive movement declined as a force in American politics, elite lawyers were able to recognize that they and the law professors shared two important aims: reducing public scrutiny and criticism of the profession and the administration of justice, and removing decision-making about the profession and the administration of justice from the public arena. At the same time, the practitioners were beginning to appreciate more than ever before the desirability of the professors' long-time aim of rationalizing and systematizing the substantive law, the administration of justice, and the standards of the profession. That their own law practices were becoming more and more rationalized and systematized no doubt sensitized them to the issue. As a consequence, in the 1920s professors and practitioners cooperated as never before. On the other hand, the cooperation was not whole-hearted. The two groups worked together best in ventures which could be considered strictly professional. The American Law Institute was the best example of this. There was less cooperation, although it was still significant, in the movements for court reorganization, the integrated bar, higher bar admission standards, as well as in crime surveys and commissions.

By 1930 the structure and the ideology of the legal profession had been transformed from what they had been forty years before. To a certain extent, the structural transformation followed patterns set by the emerging organizational society. But leading lawyers never entirely committed themselves to the organizational society, preferring at first to keep alive historic conceptions of the law and of their professional role, and then learning, partially under the tutelage of the professors and legal progressives, that modernization of the law and of their role was not necessarily at variance with their conservative purposes.

BIBLIOGRAPHY

I. Primary Sources

        A. Manuscript Collections

Baker, Newton D. Library of Congress.

Bonaparte, Charles J. Library of Congress.

Chafee, Zechariah, Jr. Harvard Law School Library.

Frankfurter, Felix. Library of Congress.

Garfield, James R. Library of Congress.

Jessup, Philip C. Library of Congress.

Keener, William A. Columbia University Libraries.

Knox, Philander C. Library of Congress.

Parker, Alton B. Library of Congress.

Pound, Roscoe. Harvard Law School Library.

Root, Elihu. Library of Congress.

Seligman, E. R. A. Columbia University Libraries.

Stetson, Francis Lynde. Williams College Library.

Stone, Harlan F. Columbia University Libraries.

Thayer, Ezra R. Harvard Law School Library.

Thayer, James B. Harvard Law School Library.

B. Unpublished Oral Memoirs

Burlingham, Charles C. Columbia University, 1949.

Coudert, Frederic R. Columbia University, 1950.

Hand, Learned. Columbia University, 1957.

O'Brian, John Lord. Columbia University, 1952

Wardwell, Allen. Columbia University, 1952.

C. Legal Directory

Hubbell's Legal Directory. 1872, 1882, 1893, 1903, 1914, 1924.

D. Bar Association Addresses

Abbott, Austin. "Existing Questions of Legal Education." American Bar Association, Reports 16 (1893), 371-389.

Baldwin, Simeon E. "The Study of Elementary Law, a Necessary Stage in Legal Education." Association of American Law Schools, Proceedings 3 (1903), 23-40.

Bates, Henry M. "Law Schools and Reform in Procedure." Illinois State Bar Association, Proceedings 38 (1914), 399-412.

_____. "The Strategic Position of the Law Teacher and the Law School." Association of American Law Schools, Proceedings 13 (1913), 29-46.

Brewer, David J. "A Better Education the Great Need of the Profession." American Bar Association, Reports 18 (1895), 441-456.

Brown, Rome G. "Muckraking the Constitution." State Bar Association of Indiana, Report 18 (1914), 180-210.

Cook, Walter W. "A Council on Legal Education." Association of American Law Schools, Proceedings 16 (1916), 103-132.

Cooley, Thomas M. "Presidential Address." American Bar Association, Reports 17 (1894), 181-243.

Corbin, Arthur L. "Democracy and Education for the Bar." Association of American Law Schools, Proceedings 19 (1921), 143-155.

Coudert, Frederic R. "The Crisis of Law and Professional Incompetency." American Bar Association, Reports 34 (1911), 677-688.

Dillon, John F. "Presidential Address." American Bar Association, Reports 15 (1892), 167-211.

Finch, Francis M. "Presidential Address." New York State Bar Association, Report 24 (1901), 45-61.

Gilmore, Eugene A. "The Relation of the University to Professional Instruction in Law." American Bar Association, Reports 29 (1906), pt. 2, 52-65.

Gregory, Charles Noble. "The Past and Present of the Association of American Law Schools." Association of American Law Schools, Proceedings 9 (1909), 40-49.

_____. "State of Legal Education in the World." American Bar Association, Reports 23 (1900), 459-474.

_____. "The Wages of Law Teachers." American Bar Association, Reports 20 (1897), 511-522.

Guthrie, William D. "Presidential Address." New York State Bar Association, Report 46 (1923), 169-189.

Judson, Harry Pratt. "Education Preparatory to a University Law School Course." Association of American Law Schools, Proceedings 9 (1909), 137-140.

Keener, William A. "The Inductive Method in Legal Education." American Bar Association, Reports 17 (1894), 473-490.

Kirchwey, George W. "The Education of the American Lawyer." American Bar Association, Reports 27 (1904), 518-531.

Lewis, William Draper. "Legal Education and the Failure of the Bar to Perform Its Public Duties." American Bar Association, Reports 29 (1906), pt. 2, 34-51.

Libby, Charles F. "Presidential Address." American Bar Association, Reports 33 (1910), 331-418.

Lillard, Thomas M. "The New Federal Anti-Trust Legislation." Bar Association of the State of Kansas, Annual Meeting 32 (1915), 81-90.

McClain, Emlin. "The Best Method of Using Cases in Teaching Law." American Bar Association, Reports 16 (1893), 401-409.

McKeehan, Charles L. "Educational Requirements for Admission to the Bar." Pennsylvania Bar Association, Report 28 (1922), 346-355.

Manderson, Charles F. "Presidential Address." American Bar Association, Reports 23 (1900), 179-250.

Meechem, Floyd R. "The Opportunities and Responsibilities of American Law Schools." American Bar Association, Reports 29 (1906), 174-186.

Montague, Gilbert H. "Present Tendencies in the Anti-Trust Laws." New York State Bar Association, Report 50 (1927), 311-337.

Oliphant, Herman. "A Return to Stare Decisis." Association of American Law Schools, Proceedings 25 (1927), 67-83.

Parker, Alton B. "The Congestion of Law." American Bar Association, Reports 29 (1906), 383-394.

_____. "Presidential Address." American Bar Association, Reports 30 (1907), 339-443.

Peck, George R. "Presidential Address." American Bar Association, Reports 29 (1906), 297-382.

Pound, Roscoe. "The Causes of Popular Dissatisfaction with the Administration of Justice." American Bar Association, Reports 29 (1906), 395-417.

──────. "Enforcement of Law." Illinois State Bar Association, Proceedings 32 (1908), pt. 2, 81-100.

──────. "Taught Law." Association of American Law Schools, Proceedings 12 (1912), 55-76.

Rawle, Francis. "Presidential Address." American Bar Association, Reports 26 (1903), 261-340.

Richards, Harry S. "A Survey of the Progress in Legal Education." Association of American Law Schools, Proceedings 15 (1915), 60-76.

Rodenbeck, Adolph J. "The Reform of the Procedure in the Courts of the State of New York." New York State Bar Association, Report 34 (1911), 354-466.

Root, Elihu. "Reform of Procedure." New York State Bar Association, Report 34 (1911), 87-101.

Sterne, Simon. "Defective and Slipshod Legislation." American Bar Association, Reports 7 (1884), 275-301.

Stone, Harlan F. "Address of the President." Association of American Law Schools, Proceedings 17 (1919), 95-108.

Storey, Moorfield. "The American Legislature." American Bar Association, Reports 17 (1894), 245-272.

Sunderland, Edson R. "Teaching Practice." Association of American Law Schools, Proceedings 13 (1913), 49-62.

Taft, Henry W. "Some Responsibilities of the American Lawyer." New York State Bar Association, Report 43 (1920), 167-193.

Taft, William Howard. "The Administration of Justice--Its Speeding and Cheapening." Virginia State Bar Association, Report 20 (1908), 233-244.

Thayer, James Bradley. "Presidential Address." Section of Legal Education, American Bar Association, Reports 18 (1895), 409-428.

Troup, James O. "Presidential Address." Ohio State Bar Association, Proceedings 26 (1905), 73-99.

Tucker, John Randolph. "Presidential Address." American Bar Association, Reports 16 (1893), 159-211.

Vance, William R. "The Ultimate Function of the Teacher of Law." Association of American Law Schools, Proceedings 11 (1911), 28-43.

Warner, Joseph B. "The Responsiblities of the Lawyer." American Bar Association, Reports 19 (1896), 319-342.

Wetmore, Edmund. "Presidential Address." American Bar Association, Reports 24 (1901), 203-240.

Wickersham, George W. "Government by Administrative Commission, A Democratic Paradox." Pennsylvania Bar Association, Report 20 (1914), 263-294.

Wickser, Philip J. "Law Schools and the Law." Association of American Law Schools, Proceedings 28 (1930), 82-93.

Wigmore, John H., and Crossley, Frederic B. "A Statistical Comparison of College and High School Education as a Preparation for Legal Scholarship." Association of American Law Schools, Proceedings 9 (1909), 112-136.

E. Books and Articles

Abbott, Everett V., and Boston, Charles A. "The Judiciary and the Administration of Law." American Law Review 45 (July-August 1911), 481-512.

Ames, James Barr. Lectures on Legal History and Miscellaneous Legal Essays. Cambridge, Mass., 1913.

Baldwin, Simeon E. "Education for the Bar in the United States." *American Political Science Review* 9 (August 1915), 437-448.

_____. "The Study of Elementary Law, The Proper Beginnings of a Legal Education." *Yale Law Journal* 13 (October 1903), 1-15.

_____. "Teaching Law by Cases." *Harvard Law Review* 14 (December 1900), 258-261.

Barrett, Alexander G. "The Federal Trade Commission." *Central Law Journal* 81 (September 3, 1915), 166-171; (September 10, 1915), 183-189; (September 17, 1915), 201-207.

Bates, Henry M. "Defects in Our Legal System." *Michigan Law Review* 12 (January 1914), 167-184.

Bates, George M. "Negotiable Instruments Act in Michigan Legislature." *American Law Review* 37 (November-December 1903), 876-879.

Bausman, Frederick. "Election of Federal Judges." *American Law Review* 37 (November-December 1903), 886-891.

Berle, A. A., Jr. "The Expansion of American Administrative Law." *Harvard Law Review* 30 (March 1917), 430-448.

Brandeis, Louis D. *Letters of Louis D. Brandeis; Urban Reformer, 1870-1907.* Edited by Melvin I. Urofsky and David W. Levy. Albany, N.Y., 1971.

Brewer, David J. "Judiciary Immune to Corporation Influence." *Albany Law Journal* 66 (November 1904), 349-350.

Bryce, James. *American Commonwealth.* 2 vols. New York, 1910.

Chafee, Zechariah, Jr. "Socializing Legal Education." *The New Republic.* April 14, 1926, pp. 211-213.

Chicago Bar Association. *Summary of Activities*. Chicago, 1965.

Clark, Walter. "The Election of the Federal Judges by the People." *Albany Law Journal* 67 (August 1905), 235-237.

_____. "Law and Human Progress." *American Law Review* 37 (July-August 1903), 512-529.

Cohen, Julius Henry. *The Law: Business or Profession?* New York, 1916.

Dimmitt, Harrison S. [Downing, William Maybree]. "Life in the United States: New York Lawyer." *Scribners*, January 1932, pp. 23-27.

Fleischmann, Simon. "The Influence of the Bar in the Selection of Judges throughout the United States." *American Law Review* 29 (May-June 1905), 348-362.

Flexner, Abraham. *Medical Education in the United States and Canada*. New York, 1910.

Fowler, Robert L. "The Future of the Common Law." *Columbia Law Review* 13 (November 1913), 595-611.

_____. "The New Philosophies of Law." *Harvard Law Review* 27 (June 1914), 718-731.

Frankfurter, Felix and Pound, Roscoe. *Criminal Justice in Cleveland*. Cleveland, 1922.

Freund, Ernst. "Government and Law in America." *American Law Review* 34 (January-February 1900), 16-27.

Gallagher, Michael F. "The Federal Trade Commission." *Illinois Law Review* 10 (May 1915), 31-42.

Harley, Herbert. "Organizing the Bar for Public Service." *Journal of American Judicature Society* 8 (October 1924), 72-81.

Hicks, Frederick C., ed. *Arguments and Addresses of Joseph Hodges Choate*. St. Paul, 1926.

Hughes, Charles Evans. *The Autobiographical Notes of Charles Evans Hughes.* Edited by David J. Danelski and Joseph S. Tulchin. Cambridge, Mass., 1973.

Kales, Albert. "Methods of Selecting Judges." *Central Law Journal* 85 (December 14, 1917), 425-429.

Kerr, William D. "The Trade Commission and the Courts." *Illinois Law Review* 9 (December 1914), 338-344.

O'Neal, Emmet. "Reorganization of the Judicial Administration of Justice." *Central Law Journal* 86 (June 7, 1918), 406-415.

Phillips, Harlan B. *Felix Frankfurter Reminisces.* New York, 1960.

Pound, Roscoe. "Bibliography of Procedural Reform Including Organization of Courts." *Illinois Law Review* 11 (February 1917), 455-463.

Redlich, Josef. *The Common Law and the Case Method in American University Law Schools.* New York, 1914.

Root, Elihu. *Addresses on Government and Citizenship.* Edited by Robert Bacon and James Brown Scott. Cambridge, Mass., 1916.

Root, Elihu. "Judicial Decisions and Public Feeling." *Case and Comment* 18 (April 1912), 666-671.

_____. *Men and Policies; Addresses.* Cambridge, Mass., 1925.

Sherman, Charles P. *Academic Adventures.* New Haven, Conn., 1944.

Smith, Reginald Heber. *Justice and the Poor.* New York, 1919.

Stetson, Francis Lynde et al. *Some Legal Phases of Corporate Financing, Reorganization and Regulation.* New York, 1917.

Stone, Harlan Fiske. "Dr. Redlich on the Case Method in American University Law Schools." *Columbia University Quarterly* 17 (June 1915), 262-273.

_____. Law and Its Administration. New York, 1915.

_____. "The Public Influence of the Bar." Harvard Law Review 48 (November 1934), 1-14.

Sutherland, George. "Private Rights and Government Control." Central Law Journal 85 (September 7, 1917), 169-172.

Taft, Henry W. A Century and a Half at the New York Bar. New York, 1938.

Taft, William Howard. Ethics in Service. New Haven, Conn., 1915.

Untermeyer, Samuel. "What Every Present-Day Lawyer Should Know." American Association of Political and Social Science, Annals 167 (May 1933), 173-176.

Watkins, Edgar. "Courts versus Commissions." Central Law Journal 94 (April 28, 1922), 297-302.

Wigmore, John H. "National Crime Commission: What Will It Achieve." Journal of Criminal Law and Criminology 16 (November 1925), 312-315.

Williams, Wayne C. "The War and the State." Case and Comment 24 (March 1918), 771-774.

Williston, Samuel. Life and Law. Boston, 1941.

II. Secondary Sources

    A. Unpublished Dissertations, Theses, and Papers

Flocks, Sally. "Status Revolution and Professionalization: The Case of Simeon E. Baldwin." Seminar paper, Yale University, 1974.

German, James C., Jr. "Taft's Attorney General: George W. Wickersham." Ph.D. dissertation, New York University, 1969.

Gilb, Corinne L. "Self-Governing Professions and the Public Welfare; A Case Study of the California State Bar." Ph.D. dissertation, Radcliffe, 1956.

Hammack, David C. "The Centralization of New York City's Public School System, 1896: A Social Analysis of a Decision." M.A. thesis, Columbia University, 1969.

Johnson, David R. "Crime Fighting Reform in Chicago, An Analysis of its Leadership, 1919-1927." M. A. thesis, University of Chicago, 1966.

Katz, Joseph. "The American Legal Profession, 1890-1915." M.A. thesis, Columbia University, 1953.

Prewitt, Audra L. "American Lawyers and Social Ferment: Prelude to Progressivism, 1870-1900." Ph.D. dissertation, Northwestern University, 1973.

_____. "Bar vs. Bench: New Fears in an Old Relationship." Paper presented to a conference at the University of Texas, Arlington, n.d. (Mimeographed.)

Skolnik, Richard S. "The Crystallization of Reform in New York City, 1890-1917." Ph.D. dissertation, Yale University, 1964.

Sommer, Margaret F. "The Ohio State Bar Association: The First Generation, 1880-1912." Ph.D. dissertation, Ohio State University, 1972.

Steidle, Barbara C. "Conservative Progressives: A Study of the Attitudes and Role of the Bar and Bench, 1905-1912." Ph.D. dissertation, Rutgers University, 1969.

B. Books and Articles

1. Legal Biography

Barnard, Harry. *The Forging of an American Jew: the Life and Times of Judge Julian W. Mack*. New York, 1974.

Clark, Herbert W. "Henry Moore Bates." *Michigan Law Review* 47 (June 1949), 1049-1064.

Dean, Arthur H. *William Nelson Cromwell, 1854-1948; An American Pioneer in Corporation, Comparative and International Law*. New York, 1957.

Earle, Walter K. *Mr. Shearman and Mr. Sterling and How They Grew*. New Haven, 1963.

"Ernst Freund--Pioneer of Administrative Law." *University of Chicago Law Review* 29 (Summer 1962), 755-781.

Garver, John A. *John William Sterling*. New Haven, 1929.

Harbaugh, William. *Lawyer's Lawyer; The Life of John W. Davis*. New York, 1973.

Hixson, William B., Jr. *Moorfield Storey and the Abolitionist Tradition*. New York, 1972.

Howe, Mark A. DeWolfe. *Portrait of an Independent: Moorfield Storey, 1845-1929*. Boston, 1932.

Jackson, Frederick Herbert. *Simeon Eben Baldwin--Lawyer, Social Scientist, Statesman*. New York, 1955.

Jessup, Philip C. *Elihu Root*. 2 vols. New York, 1938.

Johnson, Arthur M. *Winthrop W. Aldrich: Lawyer, Banker, Diplomat*. Boston, 1968.

Keller, Morton. *In Defense of Yesterday: James M. Beck and the Politics of Conservatism, 1861-1936*. New York, 1958.

Koegel, Otto E. *Walter S. Carter; Collector of Young Masters; or, The Progenitor of Many Law Firms*. New York, 1953.

Kraines, Oscar. *The World and Ideas of Ernst Freund: The Search for General Principles of Legislation and Administrative Law.* University, Ala., 1974.

Levy, David W. "The Lawyer as Judge: Brandeis' View of the Legal Profession." *Oklahoma Law Review* 22 (November 1969), 374-395.

Lewis, William Draper, ed. *Great American Lawyers.* 8 vols. Philadelphia, 1907-1909.

Martin, Edward Sandford. *Life of Joseph Hodges Choate.* 2 vols. New York, 1921.

Mason, Alpheus T. *Brandeis, A Free Man's Life.* New York, 1956.

──────. *Harlan Fiske Stone: Pillar of the Law.* New York, 1957.

Morison, Elting E. *Turmoil and Tradition; A Study of the Life and Times of Henry L. Stimson.* Boston, 1960.

Pound, Roscoe. "Henry Moore Bates: 1869-1949." *Michigan Law Review* 47 (June 1949), 1057-1064.

Pringle, Henry. *The Life and Times of William Howard Taft.* 2 vols. New York, 1939.

Rogers, James Grafton. *American Bar Leaders: Biographies of the Presidents of the American Bar Association, 1878-1928.* Chicago, 1952.

Sayre, Paul Lombard. *The Life of Roscoe Pound.* Iowa City, 1948.

Urofsky, Melvin I. *A Mind of One Piece, Louis D. Brandeis and American Reform.* New York, 1971.

Wigdor, David. *Roscoe Pound: Philosopher of Law.* Westport, Conn., 1974.

Winkelman, Barnie F. *John G. Johnson.* Philadelphia, 1942.

2. Law and Legal Profession

Auerbach, Jerold S. and Bardach, Eugene. "Born to an Era of Insecurity: Career Patterns of Law Review Editors, 1918-1941." American Journal of Legal History 18 (January 1973), 3-26.

_____. "Enmity and Amity: Law Teachers and Practitioners, 1900-1922." Prospectives in American History 5 (1971), 551-601.

_____. Unequal Justice; Lawyers and Social Changes in Modern America. New York, 1976.

Austin, Edwin C. "Some Comments on Large Law Firms." The Practical Lawyer 3 (April 1957), 8-16.

Beth, Loren P. The Development of the American Constitution, 1877-1917. New York, 1971.

Bloomfield, Maxwell. "Lawyers and Public Criticism: Challenge and Response in Nineteenth-Century America." American Journal of Legal History 15 (October 1971), 269-277.

Brockman, Norbert C. "The History of the American Bar Association: A Bibliographical Essay." American Journal of Legal History 6 (July 1962), 269-285.

_____. "The National Bar Association, 1888-1893: The Failure of Early Bar Federation." American Journal of Legal History 10 (April 1966), 122-127.

Brown, Elizabeth G. Legal Education at Michigan, 1859-1959. Ann Arbor, 1959.

Calhoun, Daniel H. Professional Lives in America: Structure and Aspirations, 1750-1850. Cambridge, Mass., 1965.

Carlin, Jerome. Lawyer's Ethics: A Survey of the New York City Bar. New York, 1966.

_____. Lawyers on Their Own: A Study of Individual Practitioners in Chicago. New Brunswick, N.J., 1962.

Clark, Charles E. and Douglas, William O. "Law and Legal Institutions." In *Recent Social Trends in the United States; Report of the President's Research Committee on Social Trends*, pp. 1430-1488. New York, 1933.

Columbia University Foundation for Research in Legal History. *A History of the School of Law: Columbia University*. Edited by Julius Goebel. New York 1955.

Currie, Brainerd. "The Materials of Law Study." *Journal of Legal Education* 3 (Spring 1951), 331-383; 8 (1955), 1-78.

Delany, William and Alan H. Finegold. "Wall Street Lawyer in the Provinces." *Administrative Science Quarterly* 15 (June 1970), 191-201.

Donnell, John D. *The Corporate Counsel: A Role Study*. Bloomington, Ind., 1970.

Dooley, D. A., ed. *Index to State Bar Association Reports and Proceedings Including Also American Bar Association, Association of the Bar of the City of New York, Canadian Bar Association, New York County Lawyers' Association*. New York, 1942.

Eulau, Heinz and Sprague, John D. *Lawyers and Politics*. Indianapolis, 1964.

Friedman, Lawrence M. *Contract Law in America: A Social and Economic Case Study*. Madison, Wisc., 1965.

_____. *A History of American Law*. New York, 1973.

Geis, Gilbert. "Sociology and Sociological Jurisprudence: Admixture of Lore and Law." *Kentucky Law Journal* 52 (Winter 1964), 267-293.

Gordon, Robert A. *Business Leadership in the Large Corporation*. Washington, 1945.

Goulden, Joseph C. *The Superlawyers; The Small and Powerful World of the Great Washington Law Firms*. New York, 1972.

Haller, Mark H. "Urban Crime and Criminal Justice: The Chicago Case." *Journal of American History* 57 (December 1970), 619-635.

Handler, Joel. *The Lawyer and His Community*. Madison, Wisc., 1967.

Hansen, Millard W. "The Early History of the College of Law, State University of Iowa, 1865-1884." *Iowa Law Review* 30 (November 1944), 31-67.

Harvard University Law School. *Centennial History of the Harvard Law School, 1817-1917*. Cambridge, Mass., 1916.

Hazard, Geoffrey, C. ed. *Law in a Changing America*. Englewood Cliffs, N.J., 1968.

Hicks, Frederick C. *Materials and Methods of Legal Research*. Rochester, 1942.

_____. *Yale Law School: 1869-1894*. New Haven, 1937.

_____. *Yale Law School: 1895-1915*. New Haven, 1938.

Horwitz, Morton J. "The Conservative Tradition in the Writing of American Legal History." *American Journal of Legal History* 17 (July 1973), 275-294.

Hurst, James Willard. *The Growth of American Law: The Law Makers*. Boston, 1950.

_____. *Law and the Conditions of Freedom in the Nineteenth Century United States*. Madison, Wisc., 1956.

_____. "The Legal Profession." *Wisconsin Law Review*. Fall 1966, pp. 969-978.

_____. *The Legitimacy of the Business Corporation in the Law of the United States, 1780-1970*. Charlottesville, Va., 1970.

Johnson, William R. "Educational and Professional Life Styles: Law and Medicine in the Nineteenth Century." *History of Education Quarterly* 14 (Summer 1974), 185-208.

Kogan, Herman. *The First Century: The Chicago Bar Association, 1874-1974*. Chicago, 1974.

Ladinsky, Jack. "Careers of Lawyers, Law Practice, and Legal Institutions." *American Sociological Review* 28 (February 1961), 47-54.

Levy, Beryl H. *Corporation Lawyer--Saint or Sinner? The New Role of the Lawyer in Modern Society*. New York, 1961.

Martin, George W. *Causes and Conflicts: The Centennial History of the Association of the Bar of the City of New York, 1870-1970*. Boston, 1970.

Miller, William. "American Lawyers in Business and Politics." *Yale Law Journal* 60 (January 1951), 66-76.

Nash, Gary B. "The Philadelphia Bench and Bar, 1800-1861." *Comparative Studies in Society and History* 7 (January 1965), 203-220.

Paul, Arnold M. *Conservative Crisis and the Rule of Law*. Ithaca, N.Y., 1960.

Peltason, Jack W. *The Missouri Plan for the Selection of Judges*. Columbia, Mo., 1945.

Pound, Roscoe. *The Lawyer from Antiquity to Modern Times*. St. Paul, 1953.

Purcell, Edward A. Jr. "American Jurisprudence Between the Wars: Legal Realism and the Crisis of Democratic Theory." *American Historical Review* 75 (December 1969), 424-446.

Radin, Max. "The Achievements of the American Bar Association: A Sixty Year Record." *American Bar Association Journal* 25 (November 1939), 903-910; (December 1939), 1007-1013); 26 (January 1940), 19-26; (February 1940), 135-141; (March 1940), 227-230; (April 1940), 318-321.

Rahl, James A. and Schwerin, Kurt. "Northwestern University School of Law: A Short History." *Northwestern University Law Review* 55 (May-June 1960), 131-215.

Reed, Alfred Z. *Training for the Public Profession of the Law: Historical Development and Principal Contemporary Problems of Legal Education in the United States with Some Account of Conditions in England and Canada.* New York, 1921.

Reichstein, Kenneth J. "Ambulance Chasing: A Case Study of Deviation and Control Within the Legal Profession." *Social Problems* 13 (Summer 1965), 3-17.

Riesman, David. "Toward an Anthropological Science of Law and the Legal Profession." *American Journal of Sociology* 57 (September 1951), 121-135.

Rogers, James Grafton. "History of the American Bar Association." *American Bar Association Journal* 39 (August 1953), 659-666.

Rumble, Wilfrid E., Jr. *American Legal Realism; Skepticism, Reform, and the Judicial Process.* Ithaca, N.Y., 1968.

Rutherford, M. Louise. *The Influence of the American Bar Association on Public Opinion and Legislation.* Philadelphia, 1937.

Scheiber, Harry N. "At the Borderland of Law and Economic History: The Contributions of Willard Hurst." *American Historical Review* 85 (February, 1970), 744-756.

Schlesinger, Joseph A. "Lawyers and American Politics: A Clarified View." *Midwestern Journal of Political Science* 1 (May 1957), 26-39.

Schnader, William A. "The Uniform Commercial Code." *Harvard Review* 3 (Fall-Winter 1965), 48-62.

Siddall, Roger Beard. *A Survey of Large Law Firms in the United States.* New York, 1955.

Smigel, Erwin O. "The Impact of Recruitment on the Organization of the Large Law Firm." *American Sociological Review* 25 (February 1960), 56-66.

_____. *The Wall Street Lawyer.* New York, 1964.

Stevens, Robert. "Two Cheers for 1870: The American Law School." *Perspectives in American History* 5 (1971), 405-548.

Stolz, Preble. "Clinical Experience in American Legal Education: Why Has It Failed?" In *Clinical Education and the Law School of the Future*, pp. 54-76. Edited by Edward W. Kitch. Chicago, 1970.

_____. "Training for the Public Profession of the Law (1921): A Contemporary Review." In *New Directions in Legal Education*, pp. 227-257. By Herbert L. Packer and Thomas Ehrlich. New York, 1972.

Sunderland, Edson R. *History of American Bar Association and Its Work.* n.p. 1953.

Sutherland, Arthur E. *The Law at Harvard: A History of Ideas and Men, 1817-1967.* Cambridge, Mass., 1967.

Swaine, Robert T. *The Cravath Firm.* 3 vols. New York, 1946-1948.

_____. "Impact of Big Business on the Profession: An Answer to Critics of the Modern Bar." *American Bar Association Journal* 35 (February 1949), 89-92, 168-171.

Tinnelly, Joseph T. *Part-Time Legal Education: A Study of the Problems of Evening Law Schools.* Brooklyn, 1957.

Tompkins, L. J. *New York University Law School, Past and Present.* New York, 1904.

Twining, William. *Karl Llewellyn and the Realist Movement.* London, 1973.

_____. "Pericles and the Plumber." *Law Quarterly Review* 83 (July 1967), 396-426.

Twiss, Benjamin R. *Lawyers and the Constitution.* Princeton, 1942.

Warren, Charles. *A History of the American Bar*. Boston, 1911.

──────. *History of the Harvard Law School*. 2 vols. New York, 1908.

Watson, Richard A. and Downing, Rondal G. *The Politics of the Bench and the Bar; Judicial Selection Under the Missouri Nonpartisan Court Plan*. New York, 1969.

Wells, Richard S. "The Legal Profession and Politics." *Midwestern Journal of Politics* 8 (May 1964), 166-190.

Wigmore, John H. "Roscoe Pound's St. Paul Address of 1906: The Spark that Kindled the White Flame of Progress." *Journal of American Judicature Society* 20 (February 1937), 176-178.

3. The Professions (Other than Law)

Bonner, Thomas Neville. *American Doctors and German Universities; A Chapter in International Intellectual Relations 1870-1914*. Lincoln, Neb., 1963.

Burrow, James G. *AMA: Voice of American Medicine*. Baltimore, 1963.

Calvert, Monte A. *The Mechanical Engineer in America 1830-1910: Professional Cultures in Conflict*. Baltimore, 1967.

Edwards, Alba M. *Comparative Occupation Statistics for the United States, 1870 to 1940*. Washington, 1943.

Friedson, Eliot, ed. "Professions in Contemporary Society." *American Behavioral Scientist* 14 (March-April 1971), entire issue.

Gilb, Corinne L. *Hidden Hierarchies: The Professions and Government*. New York, 1966.

Glaser, William A. "Doctors and Politics." *American Journal of Sociology* 66 (November 1960), 230-245.

Goldner, F. H. and Ritti, R. R. "Professionalization as Career Immobility." *American Journal of Sociology* 72 (March 1967), 489-502.

Goode, William J. *Explorations in Social Theory*. New York, 1973.

Gouldner, Alvin W. "Cosmopolitans and Locals: Toward An Analysis of Latent Social Roles." *Administrative Science Quarterly* 2 (December 1957), 281-306; (March 1958), 444-480.

Hall, Richard H. "Professionalization and Bureaucratization." *American Sociological Review* 33 (February 1968), 92-104.

Israel, Jerry, ed. *Building the Organizational Society, Essays on Associational Activities in Modern America*. New York, 1972.

Karl, Barry Dean. "The Power of Intellect and the Politics of Ideas." *Daedalus* 97 (Summer 1968), 1002-1035.

Kett, Joseph. *The Formation of the Medical Profession: The Role of Institutions, 1780-1860*. New Haven, 1968.

Layton, Edwin T. *The Revolt of the Engineers; Social Responsibility and the American Engineering Profession*. Cleveland, 1971.

Lieberman, Jethro Keller. *The Tyranny of the Experts; How Professionals Are Closing the Open Society*. New York, 1970.

Markowitz, Gerald E. and Rosner, David Karl. "Doctors in Crisis: A Study of the Use of Medical Education Reform to Establish Modern Professional Elitism in Medicine." *American Quarterly* 25 (May 1973), 82-107.

Mills, C. Wright. *White Collar*. New York, 1951.

Montagna, Paul D. "Professionalization and Bureaucratization in Large Professional Organizations." *American Journal of Sociology* 74 (September 1968), 138-145.

Moore, Wilbert E. *The Professions: Roles and Rules*. New York, 1970.

Rueschmeyer, Dietrich. "Doctors and Lawyers: A Comment on the Theory of the Professions." *Canadian Review of Sociology and Anthropology* 1 (February 1964), 17-30.

Shryock, Richard H. *Medical Licensing in America, 1650-1965*. Baltimore, 1967.

Stevens, Rosemary. *American Medicine and the Public Interest*. New Haven, 1971.

Vollmer, Howard M. and Mills, Donald L., eds. *Professionalization*. Englewood Cliffs, N.J., 1966.

Wilensky, Harold L. "The Professionalization of Everyone?" *American Journal of Sociology* 70 (September 1964), 137-158.

4. General Works

Baltzell, E. Digby. *Philadelphia Gentlemen; The Making of a National Upper Class*. Glencoe, Ill., 1958.

Bendix, Reinhard. "Tradition and Modernity Reconsidered." *Comparative Studies in Society and History* 9 (April 1967), 292-346.

Blodgett, Geoffrey. *The Gentle Reformers: Massachusetts Democrats in the Cleveland Era*. Cambridge, Mass., 1966.

Buck, Paul., ed. *Social Sciences at Harvard, 1860-1920: From Inculcation to the Open Mind*. Cambridge, Mass., 1965.

Chandler, Alfred Dupont. Strategy and Structure: Chapters in the History of the Industrial Enterprise. Cambridge, Mass., 1962.

Curti, Merle and Carstensen, Vernon. The University of Wisconsin. 2 vols. Madison, Wisc., 1949.

Davis, G. Cullom. "Transformation of the Federal Trade Commission, 1914-1929." Mississippi Valley Historical Review 49 (December 1962), 437-455.

Eisenstadt, S. N. "Studies of Modernization and Sociological Theory." History and Theory 13 (1974), 225-252.

Fox, Bonnie R. "The Philadelphia Progressives: A Test of the Hofstadter-Hays Theses." Pennsylvania History 34 (October 1967), 372-394.

Galambos, Louis. "The Emerging Organizational Synthesis in Modern American History." Business History Review 44 (Autumn 1970), 279-290.

_____. "Parsonian Sociology and Post-Progressive History." Social Science Quarterly 50 (June 1969), 25-45.

Gersman, Elinor M. "Progressive Reform of the St. Louis School Board, 1897." History of Education Quarterly 10 (Spring 1970), 3-21.

Graham, Otis L. The Great Campaigns: Reform and War in America, 1900-1928. Englewood Cliffs, N.J., 1971.

Griffen, Clyde. "The Progressive Ethos." In Development of an American Culture, pp. 120-149. Edited by Stanley Cohen and Lorman Ratner. Englewood Cliffs, N.J., 1970.

Hawkins, Hugh. Between Harvard and America; The Educational Leadership of Charles W. Eliot. New York, 1972.

Hays, Samuel P. "Political Parties and the Community-Society Continuum." In The American Party Systems, pp. 152-181. Edited by Walter D. Burnham and William N. Chambers. New York, 1967.

_____. "The Politics of Reform in Municipal Government in the Progressive Era." Pacific Northwest Quarterly 55 (October 1964), 157-169.

_____. "The 'Shame of the Cities' Revisited: The Case of Pittsburgh." In The Muckrakers and American Society, pp. 75-81. Edited by Herbert Shapiro. Boston, 1968.

_____. "The Social Analysis of American Political History, 1880-1920." Political Science Quarterly 80 (September 1965), 373-394.

_____. "A Systematic Social History." In American History: Retrospect and Prospect, pp. 315-366. Edited by George A. Billias and Gerald N. Grob. New York, 1971.

Higham, John. "Hanging Together: Divergent Unities in American History." Journal of American History 61 (June 1974) 5-28.

Hofstadter, Richard and Hardy, C. Dewitt. The Development and Scope of Higher Education in the United States. New York, 1952.

Hofstadter, Richard and Metzger, Walter P. Development of Academic Freedom in the United States. New York, 1955.

Issel, William H. "Modernization in Philadelphia School Reform, 1882-1905." Pennsylvania Magazine of History and Biography 94 (July 1970), 358-383.

Kennedy, David M. "Overview: The Progressive Era." The Historian 37 (May 1975), 453-468.

Kolko, Gabriel. The Triumph of Conservatism. New York, 1963.

Marcus, Robert D. Grand Old Party; Political Structure in the Gilded Age 1880-1896. New York, 1971.

Pease, Otis. "Urban Reformers in the Progressive Era: A Reassessment." Pacific Northwest Quarterly 62 (April 1971), 49-58.

Peel, J. D. Y. "Cultural Factors in the Contemporary Theory of Development." Archives europeenes de sociologie 14 (1973), 283-303.

Rothman, David J. Politics and Power; The United States Senate 1869-1901. Cambridge, Mass., 1966.

Schneider, Louis. "On Frontiers of Sociology and History: Observations on Evolutionary Development and Unanticipated Consequences." Social Science Quarterly 50 (June 1969), 6-24.

Shiner, L. E. "Tradition/Modernity: An Ideal Type Gone Astray." Comparative Studies in Society and History 18 (April 1975), 245-252.

Storr, Richard J. Harper's University. Chicago, 1966.

Tipps, Dean C. "Modernization Theory and the Comparative Study of Societies: A Critical Perspective." Comparative Studies in Society and History 15 (March 1973), 199-225.

Tyack, David B. The One Best System; A History of American Urban Education. Cambridge, Mass., 1974.

Weinstein, James. The Corporate Ideal in the Liberal State: 1900-1918. Boston, 1968.

Wiebe, Robert. "The Progressive Years, 1900-1917." In The Reinterpretation of American History and Culture, pp. 425-442. Edited by William H. Cartwright and Richard L. Watson. Washington, 1973.

_____. The Search for Order 1877-1920. New York, 1967.

Wilensky, Norman. Conservatives in the Progressive Era: The Taft Republicans of 1912. Gainesville, Fla., 1965.

Williams, William Appleman. The Contours of American History. Cleveland, 1961.